The Unsustainable Costs
of Partial Deregulation

The Unsustainable Costs
of Partial Deregulation

Paul W. MacAvoy

Yale University Press

New Haven & London

Set in Adobe Garamond and Stone Sans types by The Composing Room of Michigan, Inc. Printed in the United States of America.

Library of Congress Cataloging-in-Publication Data

MacAvoy, Paul W.
  The unsustainable costs of partial deregulation / Paul W. MacAvoy.
      p. cm.
  Includes bibliographical references and index.
  ISBN 978-0-300-12128-5 (cloth : alk. paper)
  1. Public utilities—Deregulation—United States. I. Title.
  HD2766.M33 2007
  338.4'33636—dc22

                                        2007001335

A catalogue record for this book is available from the British Library.

The paper in this book meets the guidelines for permanence and durability of the Committee on Production Guidelines for Book Longevity of the Council on Library Resources.

10 9 8 7 6 5 4 3 2 1

Contents

List of Figures, vii

List of Tables, ix

Preface, xi

1 Introduction to Network Technology and Market Structure, 1

2 The Regulation of Networks, 13

3 Electric and Gas Network Performance and Partial Deregulation, 36

4 The Strategic Response of Pacific Gas and Electric Corporation
   to Partial Deregulation during the California Power Crisis, 69

5 The Long Distance Telephone Networks and Partial
   Deregulation, 94

6 The Singular Result of Partial Deregulation and What Can
   Be Done, 129

Notes, 147

Bibliography, 165

Index, 173

Figures

1 The simple network, 4

2 Transmission grid and major demand centers in the West, 5

3 Interstate pipeline profit margins by region (selected companies), 41

4 Bidweek basis differential between the Henry and Dominion hubs, 42

5 Bidweek basis differential between NGPL Midcontinent and Chicago City Gate, 43

6 Bidweek basis differential between Rocky Mountains CIG and Chicago City Gate, 44

7 Bidweek basis differential between El Paso Permian (Waha, Texas) and southern California border, 44

8 Transco monthly transmission volume and basis from Henry Hub, 49

9 NGPL monthly transmission volume and basis to Chicago City Gate from Waha and NGPL Midcontinent, 49

10 El Paso Natural Gas monthly transmission volume and basis to southern California border, 50

11 Economic value added (EVA) for selected pipeline companies by region, 51

12 6:00 p.m. basis differential between ERCOT West and Houston (base), 60

13 6:00 p.m. basis differential between CAISO zones NP15 and SP15 (base), 61

14 8:00 p.m. basis differential between Connecticut and Maine (base), 63

15 8:00 p.m. basis differential between New York City and the west zone, 64

16 8:00 p.m. basis differential between PJM and PPL (base), 64

17 Economic value added (EVA) for electric power companies by region, 67

18 California power exchange day-ahead prices (April 1998 to May 2001), 86

19 Unbundled network element full platform (UNE-P) versus marginal costs of network services, 127

20 "Basis" spikes and lost consumers surplus, 132

21 A hypothetical basis spike in broadband services, 136

Tables

1 Eastern region: HHI of interstate pipeline capacity, 38

2 Midwestern region: HHI of interstate pipeline capacity, 39

3 Western region: HHI of interstate pipeline capacity, 39

4 Estimated conjectural variation coefficients, 45

5 Utilization of interstate pipeline capacity by region, 48

6 Economic value added by pipelines in the three regional markets, 51

7 Selected electric generating capacity owned by utilities and others, 57

8 Price-cost margins for electricity distribution systems, 58

9 Estimated conjectural variation coefficients for network service providers, 65

10 Divestiture of utility generation assets, 79

11 Annual dividends paid by PG&E Utility to PG&E Corporation, 83

12 PG&E utility income statement, 84

13 Shares of toll service revenues, 1990–2004, 101

14 Interstate standard message toll service price, 104

15 Interstate discount message toll service price, 104

16 Interstate traffic-sensitive access charge, 105

17 The price-cost margin for standard message toll service, 1990–2004, 106

18 The price-cost margin for discount message toll service, 1990–2004, 107

19 Average revenue per minute for all switched toll services, 108

20 Average revenue per minute–cost margins for long distance carrier revenues, 109

21 Earnings margins on revenues, 110

22 Estimates of long distance service price elasticities, 111

23 Estimated conjectural variation coefficients for the three incumbent long distance service providers, 112

24 Estimated long distance conjectural variation coefficients for all long distance carriers based on average revenue per minute, 113

25 Conceptual changes in price-cost margins, 116

26 Relative performance of indices of common shares, 1996–2004, 117

27 Annual toll service revenues, 119

28 Interexchange carrier EBITDA, 1994–2003, 120

29 Interexchange carrier economic value added, 121

30 Average conjectural variation coefficients before and during Universal Service Fund charge recovery, 124

31 Lost consumer surplus from gas price spikes, 1990–2003, 133

32 Lost consumer surplus from electricity price spikes, 2002–04, 134

Preface

During the past thirty years the public utilities in electricity and gas distribution and in telephone services have been in the process of transforming corporate and thus market structures, with adverse consequences for their performance in the delivery of services. The new structures were single-service oriented, wrought in the crucible of intense political heat under the guise of regulatory reform, which they were not. They came to the fore just as it became possible to deliver services more efficiently in networks designed to provide larger and more complex bundles of services. This change in the direction of regulatory reform, to increase the number of firms delivering service, conflicted with economic and technological forces to reduce the number of firms to provide new and better services. The public plans and programs that were supposed to be the means of expanding service quality and volume in open competitive markets instead stalled, in partial deregulation, with the regulatory agencies focused more than ever on details in price regulation that caused network system breakdowns, stagnant investment, and corporate bankruptcy.

This pattern of partial deregulation has been recognized in specific industry studies and in economic testimony before the relevant state and national regulatory agencies. The results in telecommunications, for example, have been delineated by Roger Noll:

> The Telecommunications Act of 1996 . . . illustrates the mixed and ever dubious progress in recent regulatory policies. That legislation deregulates cable television, gives the Federal Communications Commission power to overturn anticompetitive state regulations and to decide not to regulate if it deems a market sufficiently competitive. But the legislation also created a multi-layered, complex regulatory process not only for introducing competition, but also for using regulation to protect against the largely illusory myth that technological progress and competition somehow threaten the ubiquitous provision of telephone connections to virtually everyone.[1]

Reform in gas transmission markets has been focused on what happens when line capacity cannot carry volumes now required during peak winter demand periods. As described in a white paper by Energy and Environmental Analysis, Inc., "approximately $19 billion of investment will be needed for replacement of current pipeline to maintain existing capacity . . . [and] nearly $62 billion will be needed for new pipeline and storage projects . . . extended periods of high gas prices and increases in price volatility have been a direct result of the lack of development of [these projects]."[2] Price volatility has greatly increased in recent winters: "in the winter heating seasons of 2000–01 and 2002–03 gas prices spiked to levels that had previously seemed unimaginable."[3] Prices in gas transmission service markets have been substantially but not completely deregulated "in order to reduce or eliminate the risk that there will be delays in the development of natural gas infrastructure"; even so, the regulatory agency at the federal level "[has to consider] actions that attract capital to pipeline and storage projects."[4]

Partial deregulation in electricity started with requiring the separation of power generation, transmission, and distribution. Such complete separation, however, has been achieved for only a limited number of utilities; many more have stopped short, with partial sales of their power plants and leasing but not sale of grid systems to an independent regional transmission organization. The extent of restructuring has been significantly limited by the blowout in California in 2000–01 of that state's plan by unprecedented price spikes in wholesale power and transmission markets and rolling blackouts in the northern part of the state. Blackouts in the Midwest and Northeast the next year focused attention on the lack of reliable capacity in transmission systems. That is, "existing long distance transmission infrastructure is insufficient to support the changes that have come about in the industry since deregulation of the early 1990s."[5] The solution has been to establish the partial deregulatory status quo, "while FERC [the Federal Energy Regulatory Commission] intends . . . to encourage competition and healthy markets . . . its approach creates ordered competition not a competitive order that will enable industry to benefit from innovations in technology, organizations and institutions."[6]

The outlook for power transmission under partial deregulation may be worse than what one expects to follow from "ordered competition." According to Roger Gray of Energy Pulse, "the real long term tragedies of the failed California Experiment are two fold. First, we have yet to fully understand how public policy could have failed so badly . . . second, we must not fall back on the 20th century utility model because we perceive it to be safe. This will effectively end progress and innovation in the utility sector."[7]

One is struck by the similarities in these appraisals of the condition of the three industries, and of the roles the regulatory agencies played in managing deregulation in patterns that caused their current lack of capacity and quality service.

In the two transmission grids subject to FERC controls, electricity and gas, deregulation stopped at the focused control of prices at critical links or nodes in delivery networks controlled by one or few service providers. Because of the presence of few service providers, and the inference that they would ratchet up prices during peak demand periods, the response has been to impose caps on price increases. But that solution failed to generate profit returns that would make it possible to expand capacity or increase the number of providers. Price controls in "managed" partial decontrol centered on the bottleneck, setting limits that had prevented the elimination of the bottleneck.

The results were similar because they were motivated by a singular pick-and-choose decision process. As indicated by Michael Boskin, chairman of President G. H. W. Bush's Council of Economic Advisers, "the government ought to deregulate where competition or its prospect is likely."[8] But the prospect of completely deregulating market structures where there are large numbers of suppliers of approximately uniform services has not been realized because these industry networks have been driven by technologies that limit the number of service providers. Only one link is needed for efficient service to a market with numerous subscribers, or only one node is needed to provide switching at the lowest cost across hundreds of links. Although this condition was not universal, given the fact that many duplicate links or nodes had costs close to zero, it still had to result in a short list of network carriers destined for removal of controls.

Those levels of industry so selected have been integrated into the still regulated layers where regulation focused on the control of bottlenecks and set prices for those network services provided by only one to three corporations.

This study in partial deregulation searches out the common elements of the effect the focus on bottlenecks has had on the performance of the major corporations in the electricity, gas, and telecom industries, given the relationship between network technologies and market structure, and the way in which regulation cuts into investment in infrastructure. We find the sustaining presence of one to three providers in most markets for each industry, particularly at the retail level, where the incumbent utility remains dominant. The incumbents subject to reform in wholesale gas and telecom transmission became subject in their markets to forced entry of independents; those in power transmission were bundled together to form a single entity in a wholesale service transmission market. We also find that this structural reordering in the three packages of services has not substantially changed the extent of control of supply—market power—in the past fifteen years.

The limited number of providers in service delivery has led us to focus on their interactions of price and service offering. The few carriers in theory, in a world of no regulation, would be able to determine levels of prices and profits. The economic theory of pricing in oligopoly, when there are two or more overlapping networks, contains illuminating insights into how prices exceed competitive levels, or interact with regulatory caps, to generate earnings that sustain growth in capacity and service quality. Within the partially deregulated framework, we find a general tendency of the interaction to be to drive prices down, toward but not reaching competitive levels (i.e., of prices equal to marginal costs). Our investigations led to findings that on basic services in all three industries, prices were not at marginal cost or "competitive" levels but were low enough to fall short of average total costs, that is, to prevent any one carrier from generating cash flow sufficient to recover its previous investment outlays inclusive of the cost of equity capital. There have been a few significant exceptions, where the regulatory agency allowed the oligopoly to attain price levels higher for political purposes. But no major network system has been allowed to generate cash flow sufficient to prevent price spikes brought on by shortages of capacity. And during capacity shortages in California, price caps imposed on retail power were at levels one-half of wholesale prices realized in the partially deregulated auction market.

In each industry the major supply companies have set price-cost margins constrained by regulatory price caps of one type or another, but such caps in the context of generic strategies have resulted in a broad, more or less uniform type of oligopoly behavior. The caps focused on operations at bottlenecks. These were capacity-constrained single-supplier links in pipelines or wirelines that, when there were excess demands for space, tended to produce sharp increases in product prices at exit points, that is, "spikes" in prices of the limited amount of product delivered at the exit node. Across all three industries, the deregulation mantra had been "prevent the consumer from experiencing price increases." The result of caps then was constraints in link prices for service during peak demand periods, leading paradoxically to shortages that were relieved by broker-dealer commodity price increases.

All of this is unraveled in this book in a narrative that takes place at two levels. First, we address the interaction of network market structure and partial deregulation on pricing as practiced by FERC and the Federal Communications Commission (FCC). Chapters 1 and 2 introduce common elements of networks in electricity and gas transmission and telephone services, as well as common elements of transportation "partial" regulation, in which the agency determines pricing caps targeted against high-priced services when there are two or three service providers.

To deal with unique aspects of performance in each of these industries, the narrative's second level describes results that differ not in nature but in their extent. Chapter 3 describes specific pricing and service offerings of the gas and electric industries and associates them with attributes of deregulation in those industries. The "regulatory reform" process took place there on the basis of congressional or agency initiatives at different times from 1980 to 2002. But these initiatives all involved separating local production of whatever was transported from transmission by the network carrier (where previously the carrier owned what was delivered). The reform process had two goals: that product markets at points of origin would be deregulated, since divestiture would generate numerous suppliers, and that markets for final delivery services would be released from price controls only after the entry of (again) numerous independent retailers. The transmission grid could not be broken into independent entities that would be competitive enough for the elimination of price controls. This partial deregulation, after the fact, involved price controls at the retail level and transmission services at the wholesale level. The consequence of continuing controls in electricity and gas transmission included frequent excess demands on link capacity, which worked through the network to create price spikes for the product at terminal nodes. Chapter 4 describes the extreme case of the performance of Pacific Gas and Electric Corporation, which was driven into bankruptcy when deregulated wholesale markets realized prices higher than those capped at retail for power delivered over a patched-together statewide grid that was also functioning under price caps.

Chapter 5 analyzes the performance of incumbent local and long distance telephone networks that provide the predominant service in "mass" and "business" wireline service markets. The price cap policies of the FCC, for local access services provided to long distance carriers, when combined with the strategies of three dominant long distance carriers resulted in a pattern of corporate behavior that rendered the local exchange carriers unwilling to invest in broadband technologies for rapid access to the Internet. Here the FCC was totally involved in every aspect of network element pricing for each of the four regional local service providers providing access to long distance.

From the middle 1980s, when settlement of the federal antitrust case against AT&T resulted in separating local retail from national long distance service provision, the long distance company price-cost margins were sustained in the range of 50 to 70 percent, while returns on capital were still at levels below those necessary to sustain and recover wireline network investments. There was an important exception. The long distance carriers took the opportunity provided by the FCC to set higher price-cost margins to generate cash flow for a Universal Service Fund required by regulation. This was in keeping with the FCC facilitating entry by independents to reduce prices while still taking the opportunity to assist in raising prices where there was not sufficient cash flow to fund a federal program. But there were constraints both on the capacity expansion of advanced technology networks and on returns to investors. Chapter 6 considers the implications of capacity constraints in the form of price spikes in these industries in terms of whether they call for "reform" by undertaking to restore regulation ("retro-regulation") or to complete deregulation to the limit as an endgame.

The readers, critics or enthusiasts, of various drafts of this work have been more than helpful in reaching this point. George Borts (Brown University) provided an elegant and highly relevant version of oligopoly (conjectural variation) theory; Richard Lee Schmalensee (MIT) corrected my estimates of conjectural variations in Chapter 5; and Larry Darby (Darby Associates), Thomas Hazlett (George Mason University), Gregory Sidak (Georgetown Law School), and Dennis Weisman (Kansas State University) went over the chapter on telecommunications as if my intent should be that each word should be correct. Jean Rosenthal (Yale Senior Olin Fellow) checked and measured the gas and electricity chapter with colleagues in the regulatory agencies and the corporations. The Yale Olin Fellows, all second-year MBA candidates, crunched numbers for the charts and tables on HHI, price spikes, EVA, and the Lerner Index; they included R. Wonodi, A. LeCuyer, C. McCune, and S. Hassell (electricity), G. Ageshin and C. Reyes (natural gas), and A. McGowen, G. Sypeck, and A. Vohra (telecommunications). They will never forget EVA. My gratitude to all for the care and consideration they provided.

This book has been an "endgame" itself, since it is the last project at the Yale School of Management funded by the John Olin Foundation. The Yale Olin projects have consisted of more than two dozen working papers, subsequent journal articles, and four books published by the MIT Press, Yale University Press, Princeton University Press, and Stanford Business Books. The work for these publications centered on understanding the relationships of corporations to complex and interventionist government regulation at the state and national levels. The funding over twelve years, 1992–2004, by this foundation exceeded $1 million. For those involved, the gains in learning and experience from such cooperative analytical work in my estimation greatly exceeded the "dollar worth."

The Olin Foundation has now departed, having spent its endowment and closed its doors, according to the wisdom of its founder. It will be missed, not only by those involved in research on regulation at Yale but also by those who enjoyed the foundation's support of research in law and economics in universities across the country. I am grateful for the assistance of Senior Olin Fellow Jean Rosenthal on this work as well as on previous Olin projects, and of the Olin Fellows who worked so diligently and imaginatively with me; and I dedicate this, the last in my line, to the late William E. Simon, president, and James Pierson, executive director, of the Olin Foundation.

**The Unsustainable Costs
of Partial Deregulation**

Chapter 1 Introduction to Network Technology and Market Structure

In electricity, natural gas, and telecommunications markets, the configuration for the delivery of services, whether in terms of shares of sales, revenues, or product, is determined by network technologies. In each of these industries, a product is received at a network's nodes and transported on links to hub switches, where it is directed to other links to the retailer or consumer. The business consists of the service functions of collection, transmission, and distribution, which are neither necessarily integrated backward into making the product nor forward into retail delivery of that product to the consumer. Although the language varies depending on the industry, *collection* occurs in each case, whether in taking electricity from the generating plant or withdrawing natural gas from the ground or from a liquefied natural gas facility, or receiving a phone call on a local exchange system. Similarly, in each case *delivery* to the final consumer begins at local exchange facilities and ends at a lamp or kitchen stove or telephone. Between these endpoints, networks gather individually generated signals or molecules of energy at a node, and switch and/or transmit them by links to a final node for delivery to an individual or organization for final disposition.

One can describe this system of nodes and links as servicing electricity, gas, and telephone call delivery. The configuration of each network is of course different—the links of gas pipelines are high-pressure tubes of thirty-six inches or more in diameter; those of power transmission systems are insulated wires of less than six inches; and those of telephone long distance systems are optical fibers with diameters that are a fraction of an inch. Even so, there is also important uniformity. The technologies have all improved over time, with recent advances connecting larger numbers of providers and users, reducing link lengths, or even eliminating physical links altogether, while still providing connection services in physical hubs. The newer links or pipes of one sort or another deliver throughput at an exponentially higher rate per unit space. In general, the greater the volumetric throughput, the lower the unit costs of providing service, given that capital costs of tubes are linear with respect to surface area, but throughput is exponential with respect to interior volume. There are also throughput cost reductions in switching, but these are not generic, although they have been significant in scale as a result of the application of digital technologies.

Of course, gains from scale are limited to some extent in each of the three industries. There is not just one single gas transmission line between the largest area of gas reserves (in East Texas and Louisiana) and the largest concentration of consumers (in the Northeast seaboard) because there is no extant technology for a single pipe with a diameter large enough to contain all the required throughput. A single hub-spoke system for delivering all the electric power demanded at major population centers in northern California is technically feasible but not economically the most efficient, given that redundancy can be useful for responses to forced outages; and the legacy multiple systems operate now with short-run variable costs that are less than the long-run marginal cost of a single system. Thus there has been a case in larger markets for two or three independent networks transmitting to the city gate. In telephone communications, the limits on a single node/hub long distance system in the entire country have been due to regulation, not to throughput volume; new technology has replaced links with "wireless" and nodes with "switchless" alternatives. The result has been that unless variable costs of incumbents have been close to zero then smaller independent systems have become more efficient. Neither an incumbent nor an entrant in long distance/local exchange service markets in the past decade has established a system capable of carrying all the traffic; here, particularly with long distance service providers, economies of scale have not been determinative so that three or four overlapping service providers have continued to provide service to the city gate.

Service on all these networks takes place in real time. The ability to store electricity is extremely limited. Natural gas is delivered almost immediately at the wholesale node as retail distribution service providers call for it in their pipes, with a quarter of delivery volumes from underground storage near delivery nodes and the rest from "line pack" in long distance pipes. Individual callers do not wait for a connection in a telephone network, except on rare occasions when there is no dial tone because the system is fully occupied. Data transmission can be postponed for brief periods, but messages and data that support personal and business decisions cannot be stored. In all three industries, for the most important services—those most in demand—the consumer does not turn to extensive standby inventory when service is denied. These market structural conditions establish competitiveness of service provisions that are different from those in other service industries.

THE SIMPLE ARGUMENT FOR CONCENTRATED MARKET STRUCTURE

The conditions make the case for a limited number of individual company systems, specifically relative to market size. The argument is that there are limited links, and newer technologies that characteristically allow additional links to connect to a single hub without commensurate increases in hub capital investment in switching. Also, costs do not increase proportionate to higher quality of service—when continuity of service is the relevant measure of quality, larger size provides increases in redundancy, lessening the frequency of (unexpected) outage. Compare a dual-service network of the simplest sort, with hub A linked to delivery nodes B and C to a larger network with an added link from B to C (see Figure 1). As an alternative, imagine that an independent network owns the switch at B and link to C. If a break in link AB shuts down service from A to B, the larger single or joint network can restore service by switching the signal through AC to CB. But the joint system including an independent BC network would do the same by encountering transaction costs.

As another example, an electricity transmission system connecting many more sources of available generation would access more alternative sources should any one facility fail. Then, in many but not all instances, in a system with more product sources, only interruptions of numerous plants large rela-

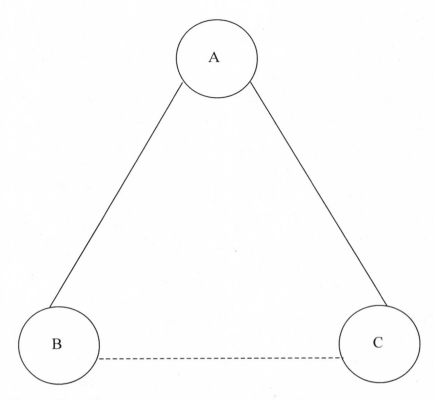

Figure 1. The simple network

tive to the size of the market would lead to a break in real-time service. That condition most likely has come to affect decisions that now reduce scale in electricity, gas, and telecommunications transmission services.

The transmission grid of the western states illustrates the scale and geographic spread of current separate networks in electricity. The head end in generation sends the electricity, often at remote facilities, to be distributed to multiple hubs, where it is purchased at wholesale and switched at retail to households and industries by a retailer (see Figure 2). Within California, for example, the transmission capacity, consisting of two or three high-voltage systems of power lines, provides link capacity traded off for more product from entry nodes of more adjacent generating plants. As the market expands, with more subscribers at any node, higher capacity lines are added, necessarily increasing the potential for more transmission in the incumbent networks when linkage goes out of service.

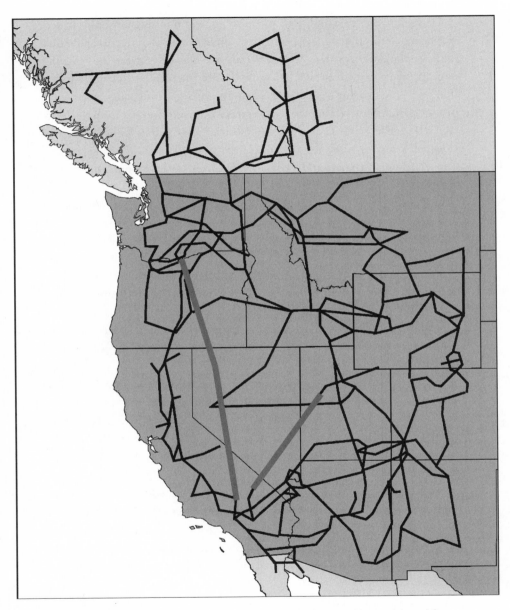

Figure 2. Transmission grid and major demand centers in the West (*Source:* Adapted from Carl R. Danner and Bruce M. McConihe, "The Western Transmission Grid: The Urgent Call for Investment," prepared for Edison Electric Institute, San Francisco, California, and Washington, D.C., 2001.)

These hypothetical conditions in electric power transmission result in service being concentrated in at most two or three networks at the receiving hub for large population centers. If there is only one network serving the receiving node in a retail market, there are two and possibly three independent transmission grids, each having separate sets of nodes and links integrated by switches into a regional network that transports power from locations far from the nearest retail receiver node. Pacific Gas and Electric Corporation, for example, provides retail service based on power received from Oregon, Washington, and Canada through separate grids, not all of which are owned by one supplier (see Figure 2).

In addition, this retailer takes hydropower from Oregon and Washington from one network, fossil- and nuclear-generated power from Arizona from a second network, and natural-gas–fired, nuclear, and hydroelectric power from a third network linked to northern and southern California. All these major generating sources, along with multiple smaller sources, are connected by transmission links owned by the three large retail distribution companies but operated by the California Independent System Operator (CAISO) connecting plants throughout the state. These overlapping link systems reduce concentration in power generation to the extent that plants of multiple owners offer alternative power supplies.

In gas transmission networks, there are three major subnational markets. Within each, three to five independent pipelines provide service over links from source gas fields in the Southwest, the Rocky Mountains, and Canada to the highly populated areas of the north and west. In the Northeast there are the equivalent of five equal-sized pipeline gas supply sources in the major population centers, while less populated states in northern New England have from one to less than two equal-sized service suppliers. In the Midwest, the largest population states have four or five equal-sized pipelines providing service while less populated states, such as Wisconsin, have between two and three equivalent-sized pipelines. California has the equivalent of three to four equal-sized suppliers, but there are only one or two in the other states of the West and Northwest.[1]

In long distance telecommunications, there are fewer than a half-dozen independent networks in what are two national markets, for "mass" residential service and "business" service. The telecommunications markets differ from those in electricity and gas in that the largest service provider, AT&T, was losing share, initially in the 1980s and early 1990s, to the second and third largest providers and losing even more share to smaller, more specialized entrants in the late 1990s and early 2000s. The first incumbent, AT&T, had a message-minute share of 79 percent in 1987, for the two markets together, following federal court implementation of an antitrust divestiture decree beginning in 1984. That share declined over fifteen years, to 35 percent in 2002. The share of the second largest service supplier, MCI WorldCom, increased from 9 percent in 1987 to 25 percent in 1998, then fell to 22 percent in 2002. Sprint, the third largest, at 6 percent in 1987, stabilized between 9 and 10 percent in 2002. These three incumbents in the 1990s collectively lost share to regional or specialized entrants on the fringes of the national mass and business markets—to regional wholesalers seeking to provide transport by leasing links from AT&T, MCI, and Sprint and to extend wholesale service in private lines of large industrial users. Thus, a rough approximation of market-wide concentration would have the largest service supplier provide twice the share of the second, and the same for the second and third, but together constituting more than 80 percent of service volume, with a fringe of complementary smaller firms.

Despite individual differences, then, the characteristic market structure in these industries has been that of "fewness," an attribute requiring each supplier to take account of the effect of the terms and conditions of others on its demands for service. The conduct of the limited number of providers has to be necessarily interactive: the service demands of any one carrier determined by offerings of others. Given that the entry and exit of large-scale network-level capacity has been limited and the major service providers have not changed, the interaction patterns in demand have become repetitive. The first power grid or gas pipeline or long distance telecommunications carrier has remained the largest. It has interconnected with the second and third largest service providers and has contested new entrants that were to offer limited service at the margin. These incumbents have been only semi-independent of each other, by and large, with repetitive demands and interconnection, so that they each adjust the same pricing strategies to the prices and conditions of service of the two or three other network suppliers.

THE CONDUCT OF NETWORK OPERATORS
IN CONCENTRATED MARKET STRUCTURES

These network structures with a limited number of large suppliers fit the economic theory classification of *oligopoly* firms and markets. Without trepidation we proceed to compare the descriptive propositions in oligopoly theory as to price, costs, demand elasticities, and concentration of supply with the market behavior of companies operating the networks. Given the limited number of market participants, sellers have the potential to act with some knowledge of each other's conduct to set prices. Numerous oligopoly theories describe markets in which the conduct or strategies of one supplier are affected by those of other large service suppliers. These specific theories describe resulting price levels, each based on the extent of collusion among the network operators. Here, we consider three of these theories centering on different price levels relative to costs.

In addition, we seek to describe the extent to which the regulatory process specific to partial deregulation has also affected the price and production decisions of the networks. This requires that we take two steps: (1) select the oligopoly models that best describe behavior, and (2) determine the extent to which the regulatory process distorts that behavior. The first step is to observe and analyze how the volume and pricing data compare with those expected from monopoly, and from oligopoly, for example, Cournot and Bertrand oligopoly model behavior. The next step is to assess whether the behavior of suppliers in the market deviates from "pure" model behavior because of, or in association with, the interventions of the relevant regulatory agencies. The principle of Occam's Razor applies, suggesting that the most fitting construct is the one that is simple and transparent, while describing observed patterns of behavior.

The behavioral indicator of central interest is the representative price-cost margin. If price is the instrument for generating revenues, and price-cost margin is the source of earnings from revenues, then interactive behavior of market participants that takes margin levels to the level of long-run marginal cost earns a rate of return on investment equal to that for alternative (risk-adjusted) investments. In this context, with three or fewer sources of network services, interactive behavior can generate price-cost margins that earn returns to sustain replacement and expansion of capacity. Fiber-optic or gas throughput capacity in relevant markets could be at levels that provide service expansions consistent with growth in service demands. The issue is whether price caps of federal and state commissions could push those margins to lower levels, cutting off growth of capacity.

To proceed, we construct an estimate of unit cost and an estimate of the price-cost margin to compare with one or the other levels descriptive of the various types of oligopoly. The price-cost margin so observed is constructed as a ratio of price, known as the *Lerner index,* equal to the difference between price (p) and marginal cost (mc), divided by price, or $[(p - mc) / p]$. The value of the Lerner index has a range of 0 to 1. For a market to be considered free of any manifestations of interactive behavior, the Lerner index has to equal 0.[2] When there are few firms, but a lack of coordination in pricing, this result is called a *Bertrand oligopoly*, in which prices recover only short-run marginal costs. Such behavior prevails in markets when price is the determinant of share, when products are close to identical, and when collective predetermination by implicit or explicit agreement on the price level is not achieved. That is, each firm's pricing is independent of that of other suppliers, ruled by discounting any positive margin until it is eliminated.

But when interactive strategy does prevail, the Lerner index does not always approach 0. It is possible for the few large service providers to achieve prices higher than marginal costs, through collective management of some type of agreement in what is called a *Cournot oligopoly*. Consider a scenario in which the large incumbents are able to assume that others will stay the same, whatever price they set. The determining condition for the resulting price level is then the concentration among providers in the market, as measured by the Herfindahl-Hirschman index (HHI) (the sum of the squares of market shares). The more concentrated the market, that is, the higher the value of the HHI, the more price will exceed marginal cost.[3] The argument is that individual restraint on increasing market share implies implicit but collective control to restrict supply, and that the extent of restriction is greater if there are fewer suppliers. The response pattern of each service provider, to choose not to respond to an expansion or restrictive initiative of another provider by changing its offering of service, works to restrict the aggregate level of service to Cournot oligopoly levels.

This is not a sufficient condition, however. As implied by Bertrand oligopoly, high concentration by itself does not imply a high price-cost margin. For example, a market may have such effective product substitutes that the product may be found to have a high elasticity of demand. (*Demand elasticity* measures the extent to which demand responds to a change in price by the coefficient *e*, equal to the ratio of the percentage change in quantity demanded to the percentage change in price.) In this case, greater buyer responsiveness to price increases will reduce the price-cost margin. The more extensive the practice of switching to other products in response to price increases and of going back in response to price decreases, the lower will be the expected value of the Lerner index in the context of Cournot strategic behavior.[4]

With the same level of concentration and price elasticity, the extent of direct interactions in a firm's decision making related to price or throughput levels determines whether it is functioning as a Bertrand or Cournot oligopoly. This conduct, or strategic behavior, of the service provider is the *conjectural varia-tion* (denoted by v), that is, the extent to which service levels of other providers change in response to a change.[5] When service providers increase or decrease capacity and available throughput together, v is positive, and price-cost margins exceed Cournot levels. When interactive responses are not present, v is 0 and the price-cost margin is characteristic of Cournot oligopoly. When responses are in the opposite direction, and v is negative, then margins are characteristic of a Bertrand oligopoly. If a provider takes a network out of service, others in the market are faced with two options: maintain their current levels of output ($v_i = 0$ for firm i) or cancel out the reduction by increasing output ($v < 0$). That range is from Cournot ($v = 0$) to Bertrand ($v < 0$) behavior, causing price-cost margins to range from an increase due to higher concentrations with Cournot to no change with Bertrand.

The relationship between market behavior and theory in this formulation is particularly amenable to testing with data available from public sources. From the two assumptions that the firm maximizes profits (marginal revenues equal marginal costs) and that demands are interactive (quantity demanded of firm 1 changes when that of firm 2 changes), then with market price p and quantity q, but firm price p_i and output q_i, market and firm marginal cost (or constant unit variable cost) c_i,

(1) $$p - c_i = q_i \cdot p\,(1 + v_i) \,/\, eq$$

is the first-order condition for the profit-maximizing firm production level.

For the representative enterprise, when rewritten as the Lerner index,[6]

(2) $$(p - c_i) \,/\, p = (q_i \,/\, q)\,(1 + v_i) \,/\, e$$

Here, when the left side of Equation 1 is multiplied and divided by q_i, then $(pq_i - c_i \,/\, q_i) \,/\, pq_i$ is an approximation of the firm's price-cost margin, and the right side is $q_i \,/\, q$, the firm's share of market output (or sales, if multiplied and divided by market price) multiplied by the firm's conjectural variation (the change in market output divided by the change in this firm's output, $[1 + v_i]$) all divided by the market elasticity of demand, e.

For the market as a whole, summing across firms,

(3) $$(pq - \Sigma c_i q_i) \,/\, pq = \text{HHI}\,(1 + v) \,/\, e$$

where the left side of Equation 3 is the market-wide price-cost margin and the right side is the HHI times the average conjectural variation divided by market elasticity.

The equation provides magnitudes of three determinants of the Lerner index: concentration measured by HHI, conjectural variation, v, and demand elasticities, e. These can be approximated for both firms and markets in the network industries for comparison with the behavior of few providers in Cournot or Bertrand oligopoly. More important, however, the left side of Equation 3 divided by the concentration measure and multiplied by the elasticity measure can be used to approximate $(1 + v)$ to trace changes over long periods in the interactive behavior of the networks. The index of market concentration may decline and the elasticity of demand may increase, leading to Lerner estimated margins that were lower in later years. If the Lerner index declines by more than would be consistent with these adjustments, then reductions in conjectural variation, from reduced interfirm cooperation, would be indicative of less Cournot-like behavior and more Bertrand-type behavior. Such a movement may have occurred when regulation was breaking down or partial deregulation was being established.[7]

It is important to note that Bertrand and Cournot oligopolies do not derive from overt collusion among few service providers. There is no overt collusion unless explicit interactions have been worked out between firms before prices are set and contracts made for delivery. But actions of one can cause repetitive reactions that have been construed as "tacit" collusion, as follows: "Tacit collusion occurs when firms are able to coordinate their behavior simply by observing and anticipating their rivals' pricing behavior. Because all firms recognize their mutual interdependence and the advantages of coordination, a firm might well anticipate that any increase in its price will be matched by its rivals. Firms will adopt a course of action—raise their price—in the knowledge that it is mutually beneficial if all firms adopt the same course of action."[8] To distinguish this from overt collusion, there is no "association of firms that explicitly agrees to coordinate its activities."[9] Such an organization has been described in my book *The Trunk-Line Railroad Cartels and Interstate Commerce Commission Before 1900*. Four railroads with networking from the upper Midwest to the East Coast developed a formal company to solve two interrelated problems: to reach agreement on transport prices and/or shares in a forthcoming traffic season, and to agree on the means to enforce the prices and shares in order to prevent discounting that would shift shares away from the agreement. Enforcement worked when those firms loyal to preset price levels were rewarded by compensation from organization funds while other railroads deviated from the preset levels, making deviant behavior unprofitable and therefore less likely.[10]

Central to this theory of conduct in oligopoly is that overt collusion leads to higher price-cost margins. Cournot non-collusion results in conjectural variation values near 0 (Cournot), whereas overt collusion seeks the best collective (or monopoly) price, that at the Lerner index $(p - mc) / p = -1 / e$ at the monopoly level.

With these specifications of price-cost margin levels associated with *types* of oligopoly conduct, we can compare margins estimated for network service providers in their operations over the past fifteen years for periods of complete regulation with those for periods of partial deregulation. Estimated price-cost margins then can imply changes in patterns of conjectural interplay due to changes in regulations. Changes in Lerner margins can be explained by those in HHI, v, and e and, of not least importance, changes in regulation working through these determinants.

There are of course numerous complexities in firm performance due to specific practices in the delivery of these three kinds of service. If the pattern is Cournot-like, then the largest incumbent has set its capacity, and capacity utilization parameters, so that prices in the ensuing bid period do not disturb market shares. Alternatively, for the Bertrand description to be a more likely fit for the oligopoly, prices have to determine shares directly, and a "one-shot" round of price setting is the set pattern.

It makes a great difference how oligopolists have performed in the context of specific regulations. Over the past fifteen years, the context for each of these industries included some aspects of phased deregulation, a magnitude change from public utility control of prices to partial decontrol, excluding only certain "high" prices. The timing of this process has varied in these three industries, and some services are almost completely free of regulatory price controls, while others are still subject to regulatory constraints.

Chapter 2 The Regulation
of Networks

The interaction between the oligopoly strategies of firms and the directives of regulatory agencies to determine prices and service offerings results in defining the "performance" of network service providers. Regulatory agency directives determine not only who the service provider is but also which customers are to receive service. This suggests that each of the three industries is subject to complex pricing rules, many of which are the result of using common methods of regulatory control on network companies.

These methods changed, as "phased deregulation" swept across gas transmission, electricity transmission, and telecommunications. Traditional utility regulation limited entry, to establish exclusivity in service provision for the first-comer network; required the network to own the product and deliver service under long-term contracts at wholesale or retail levels; and limited prices so that sales revenues covered all fixed and variable costs of service. The changes wrought in phased deregulation consist of (1) requiring the separation of the ownership of a product from the transmission of that product and then from retail distribution, (2) imposing new networks on those already established, in order to reduce concentration in service provision, and (3) replacing price level controls that are based on agency review of costs of service with generic price caps that would decline over time with growth in the economy and in industry productivity.

The regulatory changes fundamentally changed network company performance. Termed *reform,* or *phased deregulation,* they did not take place at the same time in each industry, and they also had unique attributes when they were imposed in electricity versus gas transmission. But they did have characteristics in common, which are reviewed in the context of each industry, beginning with the most comprehensive and specific of regulatory directives to deregulate, that in telecommunications.

TELECOMMUNICATIONS: FROM REGULATION
TO LITIGATION

Telecommunications public policy extends back to the late nineteenth century. When AT&T's patents for wireline telephone networks expired in 1893, its monopoly in local service was eroded by duplicative entry of other local carriers, resulting in extensive network overlay. By the beginning of the twentieth century, the nascent industry was marked by enough independent companies that together the entrants serviced more subscribers than AT&T. As the dominant firm, AT&T responded by centering its strategy on acquiring regional independent companies, thus reducing the number of service providers in local exchange markets. The increase in AT&T's share nationally attracted antitrust scrutiny, and to forestall proceedings under the Sherman Act that would have charged AT&T with monopolization, the company agreed to comply with controls by state regulatory agencies that set prices based on costs of service.

With advances in the technology of wireline systems, for which it was mainly responsible, AT&T succeeded in establishing a long distance network after connecting its local systems and thereby in providing an integrated local and long distance exchange service.[1] Further steps to consolidate the system were matched by the establishment in 1938 of a split between the regulatory authority and federal and state agencies, with the Federal Communications Commission (FCC) licensing long distance services and state agencies licensing local exchange services.

There have been conflicting justifications for this policy of merger approval (an antitrust action) given that price regulation was imposed (a "utility" state regulation action). The public interest justification was that telephone service was a "natural monopoly," so that mergers could result in cost savings from scale, and monopoly prices would be reduced by utility regulation. In contrast was another argument: "The formation of one 'monopolistic' telephone network came about not because of the free market or the so-called natural monopoly nature of telecommunications, but because of the opposite principle— government intrusions into the free market."[2] The intrusion was welcomed by AT&T, as the political cost it had to pay to be allowed to complete the mergers, which were the means by which higher price-cost margins could be achieved.[3] Whether because of efficiencies or monopoly creating mergers, the structural monopoly was firmly in place by the 1940s. Protected by regulatory licensing requirements that served as barriers to entry for other carriers, AT&T developed an integrated network that extended from production of equipment, to transport and switching of business and residential messages in an integrated local long distance network, to billing for services. It eventually received challenges to monopoly status, by independent carriers at one or the other stage, based on the rationale that market entrants would bring new technologies to the equipment and exchange markets that would reduce prices. The efficiency argument was central: entry would take place where the segments did not demonstrate economies of scale evident in local exchange. The FCC approved the entry of special service networks and did not limit these networks as they expanded into long distance switched services. AT&T responded by taking deep reductions in prices in those markets where entry was taking place; it also provided notably poor service in complying with requests for access from new entrant carriers seeking to originate and terminate calls on its network.

The Department of Justice filed antitrust proceedings against AT&T in 1974 based on charges that its strategies responsive to entrants constituted actions to sustain monopoly in violation of the Sherman Act. A settlement in that case in 1984 called the Modification of Final Judgment (MFJ), by the circuit court hearing the case, led to restructuring service in long distance markets. The MFJ required AT&T to submit to competitive entry in the long distance service market and to divest its local exchange companies, known collectively as the regional Bell operating companies (RBOCs). That left the incumbent AT&T with a long distance hub-and-spoke network side by side with other long distance carriers at switches that access and deliver messages originating and terminating in local exchange networks.

AT&T saw its long distance market share decrease from the inception of the new regulatory system, consisting of appeals to the circuit court with jurisdiction to implement the MFJ. New specific regulatory requirements of the court were imposed on AT&T to provide services, and of the FCC to file pricing and service tariffs, and to pay access charges for services received from local exchange carriers. As a result, two fully established independent carriers, MCI and Sprint, developed from the limited entry process. The access charges were 50 percent higher for AT&T than for other long distance carriers, and AT&T's tariffs proposed in FCC filings were available to the others before they went into effect.[4] AT&T's revenues increased only 11 percent in the six years after divestiture, while MCI's revenues increased 750 percent and Sprint's realized increases of 800 percent, to establish by 1999 a 41–24–10 market share split.

In practice, the regulation worked, through AT&T submitting long distance tariffs that the two independents inspected and adjusted to before they went into effect on AT&T.[5] This procedure resulted in collective price formation, with price levels subject only to an FCC finding that AT&T's price was not above the limit set for a "dominant" carrier (a price cap based on predivestiture levels of FCC-regulated prices).

This regulation of tariffs required under the MFJ was at odds with the deregulatory platform of the 1980s in Congress and the administration of President Ronald Reagan. It at least indirectly supported prices at levels between the utility cost-of-service level and those required for an "umbrella" for the two lesser entrants to sustain their new, smaller scale service offerings.

With the MFJ, the state-regulated local exchange RBOCs retained control of the links and nodes that provided end-user access to long distance service. The local exchange node providing access to the three long distance carriers then "becomes a bottleneck or essential facility for competitors."[6] The essential facility became the regulatory focus, with local exchange carriers seeking to enter the long distance market on terms for use of this node that levelized its price with that of AT&T. The MFJ court was subject to sustained carrier pressure for such advantages to open markets of the one for the other until the court process was in virtual collapse. Legislation was passed to take up the challenge, with the Telecommunications Act of 1996 (TA96) stating the intention of Congress to open local exchange to entry and then to open long distance to local exchange providers. The legislation's goal was to assure that any incumbent local carrier did not use the long distance switch to divert traffic when establishing its own long distance service and when any long distance carrier competed in local exchange. The separation of local and long distance was to be reversed, and both would be transformed into integrated carriers.

Just as fifty years of regulation of long distance prices had been a joint venture between companies and the federal regulatory agency, deregulation was to be achieved by company plus agency initiatives in the implementation of TA96. The telephone restructuring was to focus on increasing the number of service providers in both local and long distance service markets by establishing expansive rules on entry into both sets of markets. There is no question that TA96 was complicated as a result of requiring conditions for simultaneous cross-entry. The complications followed from not resolving conflicts between carriers seeking lower cost access in local exchange and those seeking high price-cost margins in long distance which resulted in implementation that was more regulatory than deregulatory. The FCC, without explicit congressional guidance but within statutory deadlines, worked out orders that regulated in extreme detail the procedures establishing entry.

We may never know whether, in drafting this legislation, Congress was being deliberately open-ended or was manifesting an inability to designate a process of deregulation that would result in competitive behavior. The purpose of TA96 was "to promote competition and reduce regulation," but the FCC could not achieve either of these goals in its first five years of implementation. Indeed, whether hamstrung by conflicting dictates or mistaken in its understanding of congressional intent, the FCC in its implementation managed to *suppress* competition and *increase* the scope of regulation.

Both Congress and the FCC acted as if they believed that competition in local exchange required "facilities-based entry"; that is, new entrants were to build their own wireline links and switching hubs, including interconnection with the incumbent Bell local exchange network. Congress saw the presence of a number of new facilities-based providers as tangible evidence that local exchange was becoming competitive; it had never specified how many new companies or networks were required before pricing in fact would become competitive—whether two, or perhaps ten, were sufficient—but it was dedicated to the proposition that more service providers from the ground up would be more competitive. The FCC also regarded facilities-based competition as the solution to the local bottleneck because it envisioned the new networks as providing multiple long distance access switches. There would be a "network of networks," each independent enough to offer the others access to the retail or wholesale subscriber. When that point was reached, the FCC could foresee substantial deregulation, including elimination of cost-of-service price control by the state agencies of the incumbent local exchange carriers.[7] That did not come about, in large part because of the FCC's requirements for prices to be charged by local exchange carriers for services to long distance carriers seeking to enter local exchange.

The mechanisms by which "competitive" local exchange carriers were to enter into local markets were set forth in Section 251 of the TA96—a set of rules on service resale, number portability, dialing parity, access to rights-of-way, and reciprocal compensation for use of interconnecting networks. This section also specified obligations for incumbent local exchange carriers to negotiate terms in connecting agreements in good faith, to provide interconnection to any requesting competitive local exchange carrier, to provide nondiscriminatory access to and cost-based rates for use of its unbundled network elements (UNEs), and to offer a package of services to competitive local exchange carriers functioning as retail resellers at prices equivalent to incumbent wholesale charges.[8]

These implementation rules shifted the direction of strategy for any local entry candidate. An entrant in the local exchange market could interconnect a full-facilities new network with an incumbent network utilizing, or putting in place, only certain elements, while leasing other elements from the incumbent network that it lacked. In the extreme, an entrant could lease the full package of incumbent links, hubs, and nodes making up a local network. These options were far removed from the facilities-based entry initially intended. Rather than leading to independents putting in facilities to bring about reduced concentration in service supply, they served to induce the entrant to use the existing capacity of incumbents. This made sense as a strategy for new firms, but did not increase local exchange competition. Any new network was duplicative, at least in part. Any new service would take place at prices the entrant set in conjunction with the lease costs of elements of the incumbent.

Section 251 of TA96 appeared to be a rational approach to achieving separate, if duplicative, entry in local exchange service markets. But the FCC interpreted Section 251 as if to give entrants a low-priced claim on the use of incumbent facilities. The commission required interconnection "at any feasible point," which it interpreted as a condition, not a location. In doing this, the commission gave entrants rights to demand a network element that an operating company was technically able to provide.[9] In applying the "necessary and impair" standard,[10] any network element of an operating company was to be made available that prevented entrants from being "impaired," that is, at a cost disadvantage. In effect, then, the FCC required the availability of all nodes, links, hubs, and software of incumbent networks and even went so far as to designate responsibility to the incumbent for combining the UNEs for the entrant. In interpreting Section 251(i), the "pick and choose" clause, the FCC gave entrants "the ability to choose among individual provisions contained in publicly-filed interconnection agreements." To any independent entrant, dependent packages of elements taken from the incumbent were more attractive than independent facilities.

The commission further required that the package of unbundled elements be priced by the incumbent so as to be "attractive" to the entrant. The FCC, in accordance with Section 252 of TA96, outlined procedures for negotiation, arbitration, and approval of bilateral agreements on the use of basic exchange elements and systems. Most significant was Section 252(d), which authorized pricing standards to be set by state regulatory agencies regarding the interconnection and use of UNEs.[11] Despite the act's intent that the FCC would set the standard but state agencies would regulate prices on elements, the FCC established a pricing method not ostensibly to "assist" states in accomplishing their requirements under Section 252(d) but for the states to replicate line by line. States, which were in theory able to decide to do otherwise, duplicated the FCC "guidelines" in practice. Congress stipulated different pricing methodologies for independents in accessing local exchange networks, depending on whether they were partially facilities-based or were full resellers.[12] The FCC, however, did not recognize this distinction in its implementation. After many months of convening, the commission determined that prices be set by state agencies to recover "total element long-run incremental cost" (TELRIC), the incremental costs of a future most efficient network, operating in a near, to not so near, future new technological configuration.

Defining the service-generating system in such a context required speculation about future technologies. Then TELRIC pricing was based on estimations not of marginal but of incremental costs incurred in a stipulated future network configuration still to be constructed and operated.[13] The argument for TELRIC was that it would be the floor of the future market price under competitive conditions. The counterclaim from incumbents was that although there would be a technologically advanced market sometime in the future, the pricing conditions in that market were not now relevant. Current prices should be based on the costs of offering this year's UNE services.[14] By choosing to go to speculative estimates of future costs, the TELRIC implementation process extended the scope of regulation. As Robert Crandall and Jerry Hausman suggest, it was "a major step backward from the recent tendency of state regulators and the FCC to abandon cost-based regulation."[15] This methodology moved even beyond a "cost-based" to a "cost-assumed" basis, which by its very nature had neither upper nor lower bounds.

But there was a reason for the FCC's approach based on the FCC's point of view as to what should be done. In any attempt to create a more dispersed market structure, or its appearance, in the form of more service providers, regulators offered to new entrants extensive use of incumbent capacity on terms designed to accelerate the entry of independent local carriers. In effect, TELRIC pricing created entry, substituting for capital outlays that would not otherwise take place.[16] But this FCC initiative broke new ground in deregulation policy in that it required the incumbent to justify its prices for the use of its capacity that were lower than its current costs of service. TELRIC took that step, or made that step possible, to enable more rapid entry into local exchange service markets.

And this would in turn be the basis for more rapid entry into long distance markets. TA96 required that for Section 271 certification of an RBOC to enter into a long distance market in its service territory, the RBOC first had to demonstrate that its local markets were open to competition. In addition, Section 271 requirements for certification to enter long distance markets included compliance with a fourteen-point "Competitive Checklist" which was to determine that the RBOCs would provide long distance services only in a separate entity, and that such long distance entry satisfied the "public interest."

According to TA96, the responsibility of the FCC in the Section 271 application process was that of enforcing the checklist. Meeting the fourteen requirements proved to be difficult. The FCC chair considered the requirements "modest conditions,"[17] but the results were to the contrary, given the FCC's denial of all of the 271 applications it received in the first few years after the act was passed. The first company to gain authorization was Bell Atlantic (Verizon) in New York State, four years after submitting its first application.[18] This broke down the barriers. In 2001, five years after passage of TA96, FCC proceedings involving checklist requirements led to approval of applications from nine local exchange carriers, and in 2002 to approval of thirty-five more applications. Local exchange firms had been kept out of interstate service markets for seven years after Congress had invoked standards for allowing incumbent Bell operating companies to go into long distance markets in their respective service regions. The local exchange companies could then, in 2003, provide alternate long distance service in markets in which AT&T, MCI, and Sprint had been an established oligopoly since 1984.

Approvals had been slow for several reasons. The act itself created incentives for long distance carriers to avoid qualifying the local exchange carriers to enter long distance markets by delaying their own required local service preentry. When an incumbent long distance carrier entered local markets, it created a new independent local entity on a very large scale, which then qualified the local carrier in its local markets as having met checklist requirements to enter long distance. In other words, the long distance carrier put its own markets at risk of entry by entering local exchange markets.[19]

This type of game-playing was not the intended action for complying with TA96. According to Congress, the Section 271 approval process was to facilitate consumer opportunity to have the choice of more than one company to provide both local and long distance services. However, in the implementation of Section 271, the FCC's process in effect gave long distance incumbents the decision rights as to whether any carrier could bring to market bundled local and long distance services. The predictable response of local incumbent carriers was then to adopt strategies that delayed their unbundling of network elements and their offer to others of access to switches to these elements. Local carriers in general paid fines rather than comply with timely and good service with the open-entry requirements of TA96.[20]

The FCC's interpretation of Section 251 and 252, its foray into pricing network elements, and its reviews of Section 271 submissions had consequences. They prolonged delays of entry into local and long distance markets. The decisions and orders of the commission's implementation process of these sections also led to protracted litigation. According to former FCC legal counsel, "the FCC might more effectively have encouraged the introduction of competition in the local markets had it taken an approach less antagonistic toward parties affected by its local competition rules and more defensible in light of the statute's provisions."[21] But challenges to the FCC's local competition rules began almost immediately after its "First Report and Order" to implement TA96 was published. The incumbent local exchange carriers, and state utility commissions, objected to TELRIC network element pricing in challenges so numerous that they had to be consolidated in the U.S. Court of Appeals for the Eighth Circuit (*Iowa Utilities Board v. FCC*). In 1997, this court vacated key sections of TELRIC methodology, rejected FCC jurisdiction in determining UNE pricing, and rejected the FCC's "necessary and impair" standards for determining whether certain network elements had to be put up for lease.

Although the court did not entirely vacate the "First Report," it gutted its principal provisions, requiring the commission to begin again in specifying the standards for certifying entry into local and long distance service markets. But despite this ruling, one month later, the FCC based its rejection of Ameritech's Section 271 application on that company's failure to adhere to TELRIC pricing, concluding that "for purposes of checklist compliance, prices for interconnection and UNEs must be based on TELRIC principles."[22]

In 1999, the Supreme Court, on appeal of the Iowa decision, rejected the appeals court approach to find that the FCC's rules governing unbundled elements were, with the exception to Rule 319, consistent with the act, and it supported FCC intervention into the state-by-state price regulation process. However, it vacated FCC Rule 319, the "necessary and impair" standards through which the FCC gave blanket access to entrants of all significant network elements. The Supreme Court did not reject TELRIC pricing but remanded to the Eighth Circuit the issue as to whether under "just and reasonable" standards, pricing conceptually could be based on forward-looking costs rather than historical costs. It also remanded the issue of the extent to which the bundle of network elements was required to be leased to entrants.

The race to the courthouse continued as a result of these issues on remand from the Supreme Court. The court of appeals vacated TELRIC on the grounds that it was based on a *hypothetical* network but upheld the FCC's methodology of forward-looking rather than historical costs. The FCC responded in November 1999 with its "Third Rule and Order" (UNE Remand Order), which addressed the "necessary and impair" standards of Section 251 by redefining "impair." The court of appeals disagreed with this action and in May 2002 remanded these rules and told the FCC to determine which UNEs must be offered on an unbundled basis (*USTA v. FCC*). For a third time, the FCC's "necessary and impair" standard was vacated, and there was no standard for determining which network elements incumbents were required to offer to local exchange entrants.

On August 21, 2003, the FCC responded to the appeals court, this time in its "Triennial Review Order," by taking the position that it had comprehensively reexamined the network element unbundling obligations to develop a definitive list of elements to be made available. Once again, the appeals court disagreed. In March 2004, the Court of Appeals for the District of Columbia granted the FCC sixty days to rewrite these rules because of the FCC's "failure, after eight years to develop lawful unbundling rules, and its apparent unwillingness to adhere to prior judicial rulings."[23]

The response from the FCC was divided. Chairman Michael Powell instructed his staff to begin writing the unbundled rules, while three of the commissioners (Kevin Martin, Michael Copps, and Jonathan Adelstein) issued a statement that they would seek a stay and would appeal the decision to the Supreme Court. Three months later, in June 2004, the FCC issued a two-line statement: "the Office of the Solicitor General has informed the Commission that it has decided not to appeal the D.C. Circuit decision vacating the Commission's local telephone unbundling rules." In August 2004, one year after the appeals court decision, the FCC issued a notice that it would solicit comments on "alternative unbundling rules" and was granting itself a stay by freezing all UNE lease charges in effect as of June 15, 2004—the deadline set by the D.C. circuit court—until it was able either to provide final rules or to accede to the publication of interim rules. Three days later the local exchange operating companies requested that the appeals court invalidate the notice because the FCC had exceeded its authority by seeking to prolong the court-ordered extension.

While the courts were so engaged, TELRIC pricing had been in operation long enough to show the effects on both local and long distance service providers. The incumbent long distance carriers seeking entry into local exchange had mostly abandoned programs to undertake capital investment in their local exchange facilities; instead, they had entered into leasing local network elements and/or a package of UNE services under contract with incumbent local exchange carriers. In effect, the price inducement schemes of the FCC were carried out by the state regulatory agencies to cause entrants to reduce investment in their own facilities;[24] and the local exchange incumbents in turn reduced their investment in upgrading and expanding facilities that would provide entrants with these services from leased equipment.

A forced regimen designed to create entrants into local exchange had done little more than cause entrants to put their nameplates on the existing hardware of incumbent carriers.[25] The entrants subsequently did not provide facilities-based service alternative to that of the local carrier, they did not address the local loop bottleneck, and, given the built-in disincentives for incumbent investment, did not add to local exchange capacity.

There were basic problems, not solutions, from TA96 as implemented by the FCC. The state-by-state requirement of TELRIC prices by the local exchange regulatory agencies produced a standoff. Because local entry by the long distance carriers based on leased network elements was sporadic, the RBOCs could not make the case for Section 271 authorization to enter long distance markets. Neither local nor long distance markets experienced substantial independent entry for five years after the passage of TA96.

These results in turn led to a standstill of long-term investment in new telecommunications technologies. The RBOCs did not see an investment opportunity in the expanding transmission of Internet messages for residence and small business subscribers when the new hardware would have to be leased at TELRIC prices as part of UNE service packages. Even though the FCC informally confirmed that broadband investments were off-limits for TELRIC pricing, substantial Internet transport investments awaited court decisions to come.

Finally, by 2002 the FCC had to face the fact that conditions for entry into local and long distance markets, based on the commission's implementation plans, were not consistent with the deregulatory intent of TA96. The FCC took another approach. In qualifying Bell Atlantic in New York State for long distance service, instead of adhering to the competitive checklist that required evidence of local entry by the large long distance carriers (which had not taken place), the commission accepted "virtual" entry, that is, the existence of the technical conditions for access in the nodes and links of the incumbent that made entry physically possible if a potential entrant were ever interested. Proof of virtual reality was expensive, requiring an audit of switch and link architecture throughout the state by a national accounting firm, but it made the case for entry as a regulatory matter. FCC approval in virtual time succeeded in that within two years Section 271 authorizations of the four subnational incumbent RBOCs into long distance markets were completed in all the states in their service regions. It remained to be determined in the second five years after TA96 whether Section 271 authorization of entry into long distance markets of one Bell operating company in each service region affected the strategies extant among the three large long distance carriers. Ten years after passage of TA96, the intent of the act to create competitive telecom markets had succeeded in putting at most one large entrant into local exchange and one large entrant in each of the RBOC regions into long distance.

ELECTRIC AND GAS TRANSMISSION:
REGULATION TO PARTIAL DEREGULATION

The federal government has played the central role in regulating transmission networks for electricity and gas since the early twentieth century. The first step in the federal regulation process was the establishment of the Federal Power Commission (FPC) in 1920, which brought together pricing controls in various federal hydroelectric facilities. But until 1928 the FPC existed primarily on paper with one employee, and other employees borrowed from its three supervising cabinet agencies (the war, interior, and agriculture departments).

By the late 1920s, sixteen holding companies were responsible for 75 percent of electric generation capacity in the country, each in a different geographical region, in which the retail distribution company with which a holding company was affiliated had a state franchise–based monopoly. Further regulatory organization—through the Public Utility Holding Company Act and the Federal Power Act in 1935—focused on this concentration in electric markets.[26]

The Federal Power Act declared that regulating prices (rates) of wholesale transactions of electric power in interstate commerce was to be undertaken "in the public interest."[27] But this was to become regulation of power transferred to a different owner-distributor at the city gate and did not extend to prices on wholesale transfers within the company, and most electricity was generated, transmitted, and distributed by the same (vertically integrated) local utility. Thus only limited transactions were subject to controls; any regulation of the integrated entities had to come from state agency controls of retail rates within individual states. By 1941, forty states had established the regulation of gas and electricity to residences at retail, and for some aspects of direct sales to industry at wholesale. That extended the reach of state regulation back to the costs of generation, transmission, and distribution.

The 1935 Federal Power Act also restructured the FPC as an independent five-member commission with responsibility for regulating wholesale interstate power prices and, through the Natural Gas Act of 1938, for regulating interstate sales of natural gas for resale to local gas distribution companies. The agency design followed that of the Interstate Commerce Commission, which had been established in 1887 to regulate railroad rates on transport services across state lines, by concentrating on case-by-case decision making as to whether the pricing tariff was "just and reasonable." This called for using estimates of total direct costs of service to set prices that would generate revenues not to exceed those costs in the future. In 1978, Congress reorganized this agency to establish the Federal Energy Regulatory Commission (FERC), as a branch of the new cabinet-level Department of Energy, after disastrous shortages of natural gas in the early 1970s brought on by FPC caps on prices of gas at the wellhead that were set too low to clear markets in which the requested pipelines were the principal purchasers.

Since the completion of its formative period, essentially ending in the 1980s, FERC has defined its mission as follows:

> [The agency] establishes just and reasonable rates for the transmission and sale of wholesale electric power in interstate commerce. It also regulates permanent interconnections of electric utilities and promotes the adequacy of interstate electric power service . . . its responsibilities today in wholesale electricity include: (1) Approval of rates for wholesale sales of electricity and transmission in interstate commerce for jurisdictional utilities, power pools, power exchanges and independent system operators; (2) Oversight of the issuance of certain stock and debt securities,

assumption of obligations and liabilities, and mergers; as well as review of officer and director positions held between officials at utility companies and certain firms with which they do business.[28]

Wholesale power distribution rates and gas pipeline service rates were to be based on the costs of construction and transmission in the link-node networks. FERC used the previous administrative process to determine that rates were "just and reasonable." For electricity, its rate setting was based on "test-period" (earlier recorded) estimates of operating expenses for transmission services, plus recovery of depreciation, interest expense, and a defined rate of return on equity investment in facilities that provided those services. This review of test-period statistics was set out in public proceedings, with the utility submitting the proposed tariff rate schedule and the supporting estimates of costs, which were then subject to challenge by counterestimates of FERC staff analysts and intervening power purchasers. After the review was complete, the commission approved a new tariff. Implementation was delayed until all parties had an opportunity to comment. If the process became extended, rates were put into effect subject to refund.

Federal regulation of natural gas transmission extended beyond that to include price control of gas at the wellhead that was being transported through the network. The Natural Gas Act of 1938 specified regulatory jurisdiction over prices in contracts for the "sale for resale" of interstate natural gas. A Supreme Court interpretation of "sale for resale" in 1954 extended controls to the retail distributors and also to the separate transaction for wellhead gas going into the pipeline at the producing fields. With state regulation of the retail distributors, this fully regulated each of three transactions from the wellhead in Texas to the retail burner tip in New York City.

The FPC undertook lengthy proceedings to establish prices for "merchant" service by the pipeline that included purchase of field gas and transport from the field to local utilities. Each pipeline had a different merchant service, as a result of its capital and operating cost profile and of its different wellhead purchase history. But the 1954 Supreme Court decision prevented the FPC from any longer accepting the wellhead prices paid by the pipeline as part of the merchant package. The commission faced the necessity of setting thousands of field contract prices one by one. Having to streamline proceedings, in order to regulate gas prices at all, it set in place a ceiling price for all wellhead gas in a basin region using averages of regional production costs rather than well-specific costs for any one contract. The overarching goal was to hold prices for volumes transported by the northern network to cost levels experienced in the past ten years, when costs of the discovery and development of new gas were increasing.

The Natural Gas Act set forth the responsibility for the regulation of natural gas generally as "in the public interest,"[29] and in 1955 the agency stated its view of how to act on this responsibility: "The Commission in administering the rate regulation provisions of the Gas Act has the primary obligation of prescribing rates that are just and reasonable to protect the interests of utility customers, while at the same time safeguarding the rights of investors to the end that new capital will be attracted to permit companies to carry out their functions in a manner conducive to orderly expansion necessary to meet consumer needs."[30] The trade-off in pricing implicit in this statement of intent was evident in the use of the phrase "while at the same time." The caps were set at the average historical cost; but as lower cost sources of gas supply were depleted, they had to be replaced by higher cost gas that required more investment at higher (risk incentive) rates of return. These responsibilities to seller versus those to buyer conflicted at key points, and the decision to favor the buyer left the buyer without sufficient supply. By the early 1970s it became apparent that the regional caps had reduced new gas reserves to levels insufficient to generate enough production to meet demands. As bid prices outside of interstate regulation (for example, sales within Texas) increased, gas under regulated interstate price caps decreased, shifting supplies out of interstate trade. In response, the FPC and then FERC in self-generated proceedings undertook a series of cap releases, by which prices of new gas, deep gas, and other gas were sequentially uncapped. The sequence, a classic example of regulatory micromanagement, focused excess demand on the gas released from caps, which in turn made release gas prices too high.[31] The subsequent demand for merchant service of interstate pipeline systems decreased as the demand for unpackaged (non-merchant) gas increased in a search for newly priced gas. Excess supplies in certain producing regions contrasted with shortages elsewhere. Industrial buyers wrote their own contracts for new production in spot markets and then put together separate contracts for pipeline space where link capacity was available, switching at hubs to links on other pipelines with available space, to bring that gas to their production facilities.

The next stage in a sequence of regulatory events consisted of a fifteen-year progression of reduced wellhead controls under the Natural Gas Policy Act of 1978 until toward the end of this period final consumers were able to buy gas themselves at market prices and pay for their own transport. Pipelines as common carriers transported gas owned by others over their links to city gate nodes.

In 1985 FERC Order 436 made unbundled gas and transportation service for both wholesalers and retailers an option, requiring the same level of delivery service as pipeline merchant service. In 1992 Order 636 made this unbundled service a mandatory offering of the regulated pipelines and required the creation of market hubs where spot transactions in gas were to be available, as were spot transactions in pipeline space. These two orders eliminated demand for pipeline package service. Long-term contract sales by producers at the wellhead to pipelines for resale of bundled gas plus transportation to the city gate were replaced by the more flexible transactions in new hub markets for gas and transportation priced separately, based on buy-sell relationships among traders, brokers, dealers, and agents of retailers. Spot and future contracts became alternative means for managing price risk for those buying at wholesale for delivery to retail utilities still under traditional cost-of-service price regulation. Two transactions, one at the wellhead and a second at the city gate, were replaced by a half-dozen transactions among producers, brokers, local utilities, or end users in the product markets and three or more transactions for space in pipelines at intermediate hubs. FERC had restructured ownership of product and network services in the same way as had the judgment court in the AT&T divestiture: it separated product ownership from product transport, and switching from one transport network to another was enabled by decree.

This restructuring of basic packages of services and product as a matter of course incurred *stranded costs,* that is, payments on long-term contracts between pipelines and producers that were breached when canceled and replaced by spot-market purchase agreements.[32] That these costs were to be passed on to buyers of pipeline space was based on the Filed Rate Doctrine, which in regulatory rate setting dictated that the supplier pipeline had to have the opportunity under rate regulation to make a return on investment. This transition from bundled service to a spot market had eliminated that opportunity, as a consequence of unexpected change in regulation.

Interconnection of the separate pipeline networks at market hubs created a new market structure. Even with this change, rate control, initially justified by an assumed monopoly structure for transport services, remained; but the commission replaced pricing based on the cost-of-service with caps that froze prices at previous levels plus limited adjustments for productivity gains. For what it was worth, FERC also offered shippers and pipelines the option of negotiating prices free of price control, as long as shippers had recourse to price caps as an option. Newly constructed pipelines were placed under "light-handed" regulation, which allowed them to negotiate prices for their new space at start-up outside of price cap regulation.

Similar changes occurred at the state level, with state agencies requiring that in-state pipeline space be offered on an "open-access basis," particularly for large industrial customers seeking transportation. Although residential and small commercial customers continued to purchase bundled gas and line distribution service from their local utilities, most industrial customers purchased gas from wellhead sources and had it transported through pipelines and local utility lines. Almost half of the states instituted some form of residential customer choice between the incumbent local gas retailer and new independent distributors using the space of that retailer; however, there was no rush to market to new suppliers of gas and transport for retail customers. More than half of these states discontinued the order and the remaining have had participation rates at or below 30 percent.[33]

During the last half of the 1990s, gas trading grew rapidly, with multiple buyers and sellers at several trading hubs in each of the three sectors of the country that contain three or more contiguous pipelines. Transport service at wholesale under firm service contracts subject to price caps made up more than 80 percent of the space at times of peak demand. The capped prices set the maximum charge at peak, but terms were significantly discounted off peak when buyers put them into the secondary market.

THE MOVE TO PARTIAL DEREGULATION
IN ELECTRICITY

Federally mandated deregulation in electric markets began with Congress passing the Public Utility Regulatory Policy Act (PURPA) of 1978. This act created incentives for meeting some part of the demand for generation of electricity through both energy conservation and the substitution of renewable sources of fuels for oil, gas, and coal. PURPA anticipated that producers of electricity from alternative fuels at higher, noncompetitive prices would be able to sell that power into the node-link network for delivery to retailers by averaging it in with lower priced fossil fuels. To this end, PURPA required local retailers to purchase new non-fossil volumes at prices that reflected the utility's opportunity costs of displaced next-generation sources of fossil electricity. Opportunity costs could then be defined as a "political" target higher than the costs incurred in current fossil generation. But new gas-fired, combined-cycle heat and electricity plants began to come online, which were more efficient and less costly than the older fossil sources. Wind, hydroelectric, and refuse power plants could only produce higher cost electricity to put into the wholesale/retail grid.

Thus PURPA was, in implementation, pushing higher cost power into systems, which was inimical to continuing traditional cost-of-service price regulation. Other changes equally hostile to cost of service were occurring as well. Electric utilities had functioned for the most part as one-hundred-square-mile networks, producing their own power and distributing it to their own customers. Advances in technology made transmission over long distances more cost-effective, offering the alternative of "wheeling in" electricity from outside the region for sale at wholesale to industry and, if politically allowed, for purchase by the retail utility. The development of regional high-voltage transmission links allowed the local connection to demand of distant generation supply sources, such as hydroelectric or large-mouth-mine coal-burning facilities, large-volume low-priced supplies for rapidly growing regions of the country. These imported supplies became the source for advantageous regional growth of power-intensive industries. Local utilities began to feel the pressure to buy lower priced wheeled power,[34] given that their industrial customers could buy that power to be wheeled over their network.

Electricity prices were increasing more rapidly in highly populated East Coast and West Coast markets. This was seen to be at least in part due to PURPA; that is, required wholesale purchases from renewable fuel sources created price increase pressures in the cost-of-service regulatory process on the coasts more than in the southern and mid-Atlantic regions. Although, according to the Energy Information Administration of the Department of Energy, prices for residential and industrial electricity together rose only 28 percent in nominal terms between 1975 and 1985, most of that increase was in industrial prices and in the two coastal market regions.

The political forces inherent in regional industrial development worked to displace cost-of-service regulation of vertically integrated power producers with open entry of outside power suppliers at grid nodes and links with access to lower cost fossil fuel and water power. Open entry was initiated in wholesale power markets through the Energy Policy Act of 1992, which increased FERC's authority to order integrated utilities to give nonutility power producers access to transmission. With access to the links of the utility and an independent source of lower cost fossil generation, industrial buyers in the Northeast could match power costs in the Midwest with power-plus-transmission packages of their own creation.

But this open-market option approved by FERC on a case-by-case basis proved to be the result of a very slow and cumbersome process. FERC attempted to accelerate this process in 1997 with Order 888, which required vertically integrated utilities with transmission networks to develop formal open-access transmission service offerings and to file tariffs for those offerings. The tariffs were to establish the rules for access to transmission links to "qualified" independent sources of power.

FERC's approach in Order 636 had opened the pipeline networks to independent owners of gas, but Order 888 still did not provide completely open access in electric transmission. The capacity limits of long distance power transmission, along with limitations on interactions between utilities, made it difficult to establish markets for power across regions larger than those containing the established links and nodes of adjoining utilities. But in December 1999, FERC issued Order 2000 to accelerate the process of wheeling by requiring the creation of regional transmission organizations (RTOs) that would control consolidated transmission grids made up of all the node-link systems in a multistate region. Although utilities were to submit RTO operating plans in late 2000 and early 2001, they failed to file and implement such plans before 2005. The developmental work for operational RTOs as a step in "partial" deregulation was limited to that done in New England, New York/Pennsylvania, the upper Midwest, Texas, and California. The northeast and mid-Atlantic RTOs combined numerous utilities in several states, in systems based on existing regional power pools that already functioned in shifting power across state borders.

The state legislatures in these regions went much further, however, as they passed statutes requiring utilities to sell off generation, splitting integrated distribution companies into independent power producers, an independent transmission grid, and side-by-side retail distributors. California, with three major side-by-side retail distributors, developed a restructuring plan calling for a single transmission grid within the state made up of the three company networks plus a new central dispatch facility under an independent system operator (ISO). The California legislature moved to end the vertical integration of the three retail distributors over six years by requiring them not only to turn over management of their transmission networks to the independent operator but also to sell off their fossil-fueled generating facilities to third-party power suppliers and to develop plans for doing the same with their nuclear and hydroelectric capacity.

Other responsive regional organizations moved more slowly. Midwest and southern organizations similar to RTOs existed, in fact, in concept only. As of 2000 only twenty-four states had passed laws or issued regulatory orders to implement wholesale and retail competition. Then the severe operational blowout of the California ISO during 2000–01, which saw spot wholesale prices increase orders of magnitude beyond capped retail prices, effectively halted further development in that state as well as in most other parts of the country at an early stage.

This process in effect ended with partial "restructuring," or partial deregulation. Where there was any response to Order 888, incumbent retail distribution companies separated their generation, transmission, and retail distribution; sold generation capacity to independent power producers; and, while retaining ownership, turned transmission management over to an independent organization. The remaining power distributors did nothing. Any newly independent generating companies went to wherever auction markets for spot power existed to buy power and wheel it to reach the endgame of competitive supply without regulatory price controls. This put the newly formed regional transmission grid in the control of a nongovernmental, profit or not-for-profit entity, with open-ended commitment not to change traditional pricing for grid services. Retail distribution everywhere continued to be subject to state agencies—with cost-of-service or price cap controls.

In the long run, however, retail deregulation was intended to provide individual customers with a choice of electricity marketers (for example, the incumbent, plus Enron, Green Mountain, and so on) that would compete in service with each other while using the wires of the incumbent utility. The power that independents acquired at auction would be wheeled over the incumbent's retail links. But the incumbent utility still intended to buy electricity for remaining bundled-service customers, partly on the wholesale market run by the grid manager but mostly in long-term supply contracts with independent generators, many of which were formerly part of its integrated network. An historical legacy remained: the single distribution network from the city gate to the end-use customer was not to be replicated twice or four times over, no matter how many service providers chose to contract with customers.

But even if there had been a plethora of new independent retail service providers, regulation would not have disappeared. Independent power marketers, new entities that bought and sold electricity at wholesale but did not own facilities, were considered public utilities under the Federal Power Act. Substantial parts of retail regulation were relaxed, or waived, but each provider still had to have prices approved in FERC proceedings to certify a tariff. If power marketers were to propose to sell at certain retail prices that the buyer had agreed to, they did not need to file "cost-of-service"–based rates in that tariff; but if there was disagreement, then the state regulatory agency had to undertake a rate proceeding, for one of thousands of transactions.[35]

The effectiveness of this mix of generation divestiture, grid separation, and independent retail marketing was controversial from inception as "deregulation." Midwest price spikes for wholesale and retail power in June 1998, the California spikes in 2001–02, and the Midwest blackout of 2003 have all been associated with this restructuring. It has proved difficult to design open markets with numerous sources for providing wholesale power in real time, given the necessity of balancing network voltage with extensive ancillary service (power generated not to be sold but to stabilize voltage across the network at its nodes). It also has been difficult to achieve systematic regional power transfers, given limited capacity at the "seams" between the legacy networks of the separate utilities used to create the regional network. Given that few of the RTO network structures have transmission links and hubs that would allow for choices of routings among generator complexes at distant locations, and that the flow of electricity has to be controlled on the grid, numerous locations have had the potential to become bottlenecks. The informal consolidations of company transmission grids created uncertainty as to pricing and investment in regional capacity, and the regional managements putting together the legacy systems have not been able to expand to meet peak demands, including even some seasonal demands. Introducing alternative supply sources at the city gate node would have required higher levels of system redundancy to allow for alternative pathways in case of failure of the ability to deliver on a contract on a specific route, a need that did not exist under an integrated system.

As operational problems became evident, restructuring slowed; something of a de facto moratorium was put in place on this type of partial deregulation. Many states that had passed restructuring laws delayed undertaking implementation or suspended their efforts to complete it. Those that had not yet separated generation from distribution postponed plans to do so. FERC, which had proposed in 2002 a complete set of RTOs and standard market design for all parts of the country, shelved these proposals in 2005. This situation was addressed in a white paper issued in April 2003. In commenting both on the failure of the restructured power markets in California to achieve its lower price and extended service goals, and on the slow rate of adoption of open wholesale power markets on the state level elsewhere, FERC stated, "wholesale electricity markets do not automatically structure themselves with fair behavioral rules, provide a level playing field for market participants, effectively monitor themselves, check the influence of market power, mitigate prices that are unlawful or fix themselves when broken."[36] This observation was a reaction to or an excuse for problems more than it was an insight into how to proceed. In fact, this restructuring provided a call for increasing regulation. These arguments were that fragmented markets had to be designed to ensure sufficient supply sources, which implied at least transitional price controls by the regulatory agency. Faulty market design that did result in too few suppliers at key times probably did lead to a breakdown of the California system, as did gamesmanship on the part of certain suppliers and brokers. The failure, however, in California was directly attributable to the Public Utility Commission in its lack of response to a situation in which its retail price caps were below wholesale power prices from its required daily spot market, which guaranteed no retail supply responses to excess demand that had built up over at least half of the decade. FERC did not intervene in these in-state wholesale market prices, nor did the newly created ISOs respond, other than to take the position that the state water authority could purchase electricity to balance the system (incurring costs that would be the responsibility of the retail customer) when the retail distributors ran out of liquidity and credit in purchase markets.

Other RTOs, although not failing as completely as the California ISO, were plagued with faults in their operations. One research source assessed the results of electricity regulatory changes as follows: "mediocre designed competitive markets are superior to badly regulated systems (England), but . . . poorly designed markets are worse than mediocre regulation (California)"[37]—which is to put the flagship restructured system second from last.

But this is to assess the effects of these partially regulated systems in terms of the number and scale of their blowouts. The sustained performance of networks is what was at issue. The company network before restructuring provided reliability (that is, electricity across nodes "balanced") and quality (that is, at 120 volts and 60 hertz) when generation was dispatched by private grid managers who operated in vertically integrated systems. When dispatching decisions were transferred to an ISO across multi-company networks, they became less reliable and provided product at equal or less quality. Variations in line and hub capacity, in combinations of new and old links, that made up the ISO network after restructuring were at times responsible for significant variations in quality. But some prices declined, as new low-cost sources of power were distributed over the larger-scale ISO networks.

REGULATION IN TRANSITION IN ALL
THREE INDUSTRIES

Network operations were constrained under cost-of-service regulation in the first seventy-five years of the twentieth century by statutes and agency case decisions specific to each state, as well as by the condition of the economy. During periods of high inflation, the prices that followed from keeping revenues in line with historical costs in case-by-case decisions were too low; and during periods of low inflation and high productivity increases, they were too high. Then, in the 1990s, changes in regulation in all three industries brought on by the agencies and/or courts, acting on new "reform" statutes, required restructuring of the former energy or telecommunications corporation. Their networks were separated from the product being shipped, and prices for transmission were partially decontrolled when there were overlapping networks, but prices were newly controlled where there were link or node bottlenecks.

The change in regulatory process focused controls in a strategic game involving regulatory agency and network operator. Compliance with rule makings or a new statute centered on forcing reductions in prices over time, and entry was encouraged to create a semblance of more competitors. The sequence of regulator versus company pricing can be considered conceptually as a one-round game, with no further rounds. As described by David Newbery, investment from the pre-reform period set the capacity of the network, which then determined product levels and finally prices for those product levels. Where there were caps, at retail, they limited prices, and prices had to decrease when entry took place. The regulator achieved a semblance of a "control process" by caps truncating the high prices (on-peak versus off-peak, high versus low demand, in the business cycle). To achieve "reform," regulators attempted to exclude prices higher than those in past markets during full regulation. The corporation subject to the price cap lost share against the entrant at the cap or lower prices.[38] As Newbery notes, "the outcome is predictably pessimistic"; the network operator takes a loss against investment as the lower price distribution results in an average price between average total and variable costs. Then "the utility confidently predicts that if it invests, it will make a loss, and hence does not invest."[39] When applied to networks with declining cost structures, this sequence has the characteristics of a Bertrand oligopoly, which has price-cost margins insufficient to achieve recovery of the costs of investment.

Chapter 3 Electric and Gas Network Performance and Partial Deregulation

There has been a wide disparity in the partial deregulation process between intentions and results for market performance. The intent had been that, with open entry and access to the facilities of incumbent producers, markets for network services would be populated by independent sources of supply that would generate price reductions, along with service increases emblematic of competitive behavior. New entrants, however, have not flooded into the construction and operation of networks in electricity and gas transmission. After almost ten years of policy implementation, very few links in these networks are owned or operated by independents. Three or four firm incumbents still can be found with the largest shares at key nodes in the two industries in most markets, although there is much more switching of product at those nodes.

Restructuring has created extraordinary regulatory complexities, with an extremely high regulatory burden in pricing and service offerings. As one example, California has had for some years more than fifteen active proceedings related to electricity pricing and distribution management at different state agencies. After the retail distributors sold part of their generation facilities, power supply at the generation level was in the control of few corporations, the state had only one transmission network, and almost all retail customers remained with the single utility service provider.

This is but one example. The review of performance in electricity and gas transmission shows that the performance of network carriers in these two industries became disoriented from norms of "competition" supposed to be associated with deregulation. There were only relatively small numbers of new service providers and limited new service offerings, and lower price levels that did follow failed to track declines in long-run marginal costs of service. These markets were instead characterized by oligopoly behavior, in which the actual few—not the hypothetical "numerous"—service providers were induced to reduce prices by regulatory agency practice, not by competition. The agencies did not deregulate pricing but instead set price limits on peak-period network services, which in turn caused spikes in gas or electricity prices in wholesale product markets. When demands were not on peak, then prices fell to levels approaching short-term marginal costs characteristic of Bertrand behavior. With prices capped on peak and at marginal cost off peak, earnings fell to unprofitable levels, which held back capacity expansion in electricity and gas transmission.

PERFORMANCE OF GAS TRANSPORTATION MARKETS

Initiatives of a legislature, or a regulatory agency, intending to reduce regulation in network service markets, focused first on creating change in market structure. The agency process of imposing rules and deciding landmark cases focused on requiring new open exchange of product at network nodes between the existing pipelines. In gas transmission this "created" more carriers, as links of previously separate incumbent carriers became alternative means for transmission from not only initial but halfway nodes. Whether more service suppliers made price behavior more competitive or simply constituted a more fragmented market structure remained to be seen.

Gas transmission became somewhat less concentrated, in terms of the numbers of transporters of record for gas shipments from East Texas to Boston, for example. But gas delivered to retail distributors and industry in the largest population and industrial centers still converged on three separated markets: the eastern market (Virginia to Maine), the midwestern market (Illinois to Minnesota), and the western market (the Pacific states plus Arizona and Nevada). While these markets all drew on reserves in Texas and adjoining states, plus newly developing sources in the Rocky Mountains and Canada, switching from one to another region was not yet sufficient to even out price differences so as to create a single national market.[1]

The number of carriers in each of these markets during the 1990–2003 period was still limited, ranging from three to five comparably sized sources of pipeline space. In the eastern region, the larger states in the center of the market (Pennsylvania and New York) had the lowest concentration, with HHI equivalent to that of five equal-sized carriers. There, states experienced little or no decline in the concentration of transmission service supply over the thirteen years of regulatory transition, from 1990 to 2003 (Table 1). Both states maintained transmission capacity equivalent to that of between four or five equal-sized service providers. The fringe states (Virginia and Massachusetts) had fewer sources, equivalent to between two and three equivalent carriers; Virginia experienced no change, and Massachusetts had a reduction of concentration equivalent to the entry of one new supplier.

In the midwestern region, the level of concentration was lower, and entry or expansion of smaller lines resulted in the addition of one full-sized source of transmission services (Table 2). The interior states (Illinois, Indiana, and Ohio) had HHI levels equivalent to those of slightly more than four equal-sized sources in 1990, which increased to five equal-sized sources in 2003 (that is, HHI = 1 / n for n number of equivalent firms; HHI of 0.20 for Indiana equals 1 / 5). The fringe states (Wisconsin, Minnesota, and Michigan) had higher con-

Table 1. Eastern region: HHI of interstate pipeline capacity (based on ownership of pipeline capacity into each state)

Year	VA	MD	PA	NJ	NY	CT	MA
1990	0.45	0.40	0.18	0.39	0.19	0.70	0.52
1995	0.44	0.32	0.22	0.38	0.15	0.46	0.56
2000	0.44	0.31	0.22	0.38	0.17	0.44	0.37
2003	0.48	0.41	0.21	0.38	0.18	0.39	0.37

Source: Department of Energy, Energy Information Administration (EIA), Natural Gas Analysis and Publications (Washington, DC: U.S. GPO, various years).

Note: Sample does not include all states in the market (such as Rhode Island). Herfindahl-Hirschman index (HHI) = sum of each line capacity share squared. If each is the same share and there are n number, then $\Sigma(1 / n)^2 = 1 / n$.

Table 2. Midwestern region: HHI of interstate pipeline capacity (based on ownership of pipeline capacity into each state)

Year	IL	IN	OH	MN	MI	WI
1990	0.24	0.26	0.21	0.28	0.34	0.35
1995	0.24	0.28	0.21	0.30	0.31	0.35
2000	0.19	0.31	0.20	0.23	0.24	0.34
2003	0.17	0.22	0.20	0.23	0.24	0.28

Source: Department of Energy, Energy Information Administration (EIA), Natural Gas Analysis and Publications (Washington, DC: U.S. GPO, various years).

Note: See note for Table 1.

centration, with four equivalent service providers and no change from entry or expansion of newer pipelines over the period.

In the western region in 1990, the states had the equivalent of a little more than two suppliers, except California, which had two and one-half (although this capacity was divided unequally among a larger number of pipelines). Only California experienced significant changes, with the addition of the equivalent of one and one-half more equal-sized carriers, resulting in the equivalent of five equal-sized providers in 2003 (Table 3).

Across all three markets, it would appear that there were the equivalent of four to five equal-capacity pipeline sources in the center of markets but only two to three sources on the edge of markets over the period of FERC Order 636 restructuring. There were fewer sources in the eastern and western regions than in the midwestern region. In the thirteen years of deregulatory change, only the Midwest realized the supply growth of the equivalence of a single full-sized service provider.

Table 3. Western region: HHI of interstate pipeline capacity (based on ownership of pipeline capacity into each state)

Year	CA	AZ	WA	OR	ID	NV
1990	0.41	0.71	0.43	0.50	0.54	0.51
1995	0.27	0.68	0.41	0.52	0.59	0.41
2000	0.26	0.65	0.42	0.53	0.61	0.41
2003	0.21	0.61	0.43	0.53	0.60	0.58

Source: Department of Energy, Energy Information Administration (EIA), Natural Gas Analysis and Publications (Washington, DC: U.S. GPO, various years).

Note: See note for Table 1.

With so few sources of service in separate networks and so limited change, the oligopoly behavior of the pipelines, as price controls loosened, should have been marked by high prices. Investigations of margins of individual pipelines indicate that they cannot be estimated directly. There is no measure of price, or of marginal costs, of throughput services for any of these service providers. Although FERC reports have estimated capacity and throughput state by state, estimates of revenue and operating income have not been developed at the state level sufficient to provide a basis for price-cost measures at the market level. Operating earnings as a percentage of revenues on the pipeline level are the only financial performance indicator that provides an approximation for the Lerner index. Financial reports on the pipelines contain operating earnings statements that are a surrogate for an aggregate index P and throughput Q that generates sales revenues R. Then operating income $(P - C) \cdot Q$ for unit operating costs C, where unit costs are constant (as in line networks), generates margin on sales equal to the Lerner index $[(p - c) / p]$.

These operating income margins, averaged across pipelines in each of the three regions, are shown in Figure 3. If regulatory changes that restructure gas contracts to separate ownership from the networks, and increase the number of networks, make a difference, then margins should be higher in the East and West and should be lowest in the Midwest. Also, entry corresponding to regulatory restructuring should make a difference by lowering margins just in the Midwest. There was a pronounced increase in the western margin in the mid-1990s (as the California margin doubled to a level in excess of 40 percent), but margins in that part of the country went to zero during the gas-price crisis in the early 2000s. Margins in the Midwest were not the lowest of the three regions but were between those in the other two regions. Margins in all three markets declined, in response to the downturn of the business cycle in 2000–01, but those in both the East and West fell more than in the Midwest. But still, margins in all three regions were higher in the last half than in the first half of the 1990s, increasing from 5 to 10 percent during 1990–93 to the range of 15 to 25 percent during 1995–2000. These margin changes were not associated with "deregulatory" entry of independent carriers but instead with year-to-year demand shifts for space on the systems of leading carriers. In service from Texas to California, El Paso Natural Gas Transmission, the leading carrier, in three years out of seven before 1996 had margins of less than 10 percent; then for two years margins were higher than 40 percent. The leading carriers in the other two regions had margin increases after 1995 as well—Transcontinental in the eastern region and Natural Gas Pipeline of America (NGPA) in the midwestern region

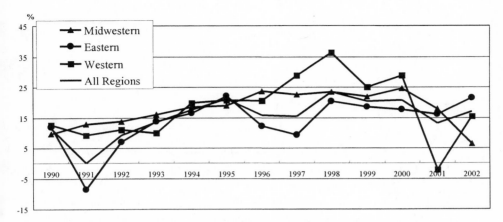

Figure 3. Interstate pipeline profit margins by region (selected companies) (*Source:* As described in the text; FERC Form 11 Annual Reports of Pipelines (2004): Quarterly Reports filed with FERC by the interstate natural gas pipeline companies as required by Chapter 18 CFR Section 203.)

in the range of 15 to 25 percent, whereas earlier they were less than 8 percent. The source was excess capacity in the early years, with margins for space in the summer off peak at zero and at 20 percent on peak. With deficient capacity during the peak in the later years, but with prices constrained by caps, margins were limited to 50 percent for short periods. Long summer periods of transportation at cost were shorter, and the peak period was lengthened with prices capped to allow at least a positive margin.

But performance of the partially deregulated pipelines was also affected by the extent to which they responded to sharp increases in demand for space. Volatile spot prices for space at exit market hubs are indicated by spikes in the "basis differential"—the difference between the gas price at the exit market hub and that at an origin hub where the gas is injected into the initial pipeline node. In a well-functioning transportation market, gas prices at these two points should not differ by more than the charge for transportation, but if there is excess demand for space, as a result of a cap on the pipeline charge preventing it from increasing to clear the space market, the basis differential in gas prices exceeds the transport price and goes to the level that clears the exit gas market.

Based on monthly bidweek prices for spot gas at eighty-five trading hubs for 1986–2003, basis differentials have been constructed for all interesting market periods for space in the three regions. For the eastern region, there are four origin hubs (the Henry Hub in Louisiana, Katy and Carthage in Texas, and the

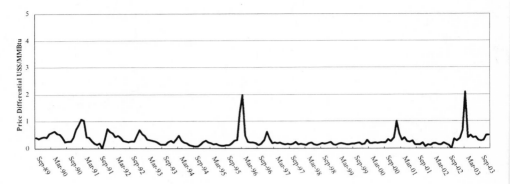

Figure 4. Bidweek basis differential between the Henry and Dominion hubs (*Source:* As described in the text; data from *Natural Gas Intelligence,* Bidweek Historical Prices.)

Texas Eastern entry) and nineteen destination hubs. The midwestern region has eight origin hubs (in addition to the four Eastern hubs, Waha and Oneok in West Texas, Cheyenne in Wyoming, and the Permian Basin of Texas and New Mexico), as well as three Chicago and one Michigan destination hub. The western region has four origin hubs (including Opal in Wyoming and Kingsgate on the Canadian border for the entry of Canadian gas) and nine destination hubs that are transfer points into California to the retail intrastate delivery systems.

Figure 4 shows basis differentials between Henry Hub in Louisiana and the Dominion Hub in Pennsylvania for two bidweeks each year, in March and September, which are "shoulder months" either side of peak winter demand months. These differentials represent nineteen series for the eastern region. The March differentials were generally higher than those in September, as expected from colder weather increasing demand for gas during that month. The increased demand should lead to increases in both origin and destination gas prices, but the destination price more, until the basis differential equals the capped peak transportation price. But on at least four occasions, the differential greatly exceeded the capped price. Origin spot prices for gas and capped firm contract transportation rates of the pipelines, when added together, were less than the city gate destination gas spot price. Spikes in differentials had occurred with the exit gas price more than double entry gas and transportation costs (prices) in 1996 and 2003. Similar patterns are found for Katy and Carthage origin points with the other destination points. But there was an additional spike to $8.00 per thousand cubic feet for March 2001 at Transco zone six destination in New Jersey, when origin gas was $4.00 per thousand cubic feet and capped gas transportation charges did not exceed $1.00 per thousand cubic feet. In all, excess demand for pipeline space was worked off by increases in delivered gas prices for at least three extended periods, during which the increases were four times greater than in other bidweeks.

Capacity in the midwestern market for gas transportation was not as tight; basis differentials spiked only three times, in March 1996, 2001, and 2003 (Figure 5). These spikes were at different times than those in the eastern region and were less in magnitude. As shown in Figure 5, the on-peak differential varied from $0.50 per thousand cubic feet, the approximated margin operating cost of transport, to an off-peak differential of only $0.25 per thousand cubic feet, in the range of, if not less than, half the marginal costs of transport. With that as the differential which would clear gas demand in Chicago at full capacity across the pipelines there, the March 1996 spike between $1.00 and $1.50 resulted in at least $1.00 per thousand cubic feet of windfall for those brokers and dealers able to sell gas at the city gate.

There is less volatility in these differentials on services from Texas to Chicago, reflecting relatively more capacity available for firm throughput services during the frequent peak cold periods around the Great Lakes. But spot price differentials from gas supplies from the new fields in the Rocky Mountains eastern slope to gas deliveries at the Chicago city gate were marked by spikes exceeding $1.50 in March 1996, $2.00 in March 2001, and $3.50 in March 2003 (Figure 6). The newer pipelines from the eastern slope fields ran through available capacity on peak to face excess demand that was dissipated by out-of-

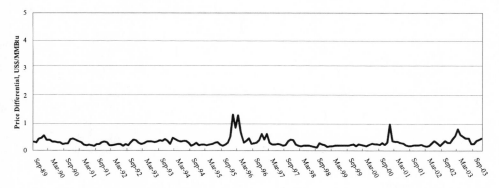

Figure 5. Bidweek basis differential between NGPL Midcontinent and Chicago City Gate (*Source:* As in Figure 4.)

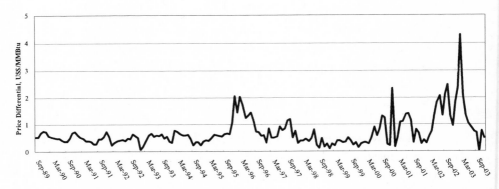

Figure 6. Bidweek basis differential between Rocky Mountains CIG and Chicago City Gate (*Source:* As in Figure 4.)

market increases in gas prices, not by increases in pipeline service prices in the Chicago hub spot market.

The western market for gas delivery experienced extreme volatility in prices for the product (Figure 7). The off-peak bidweek basis differential between Waha and the southern California border varied around $0.50 per thousand cubic feet from 1989 to 2000; the differential increased to $2.00 in September 2000 and then to $10.00 in March 2001, to subside to the $0.50 range in September 2001 through 2003. Spikes were clustered in the 2000–01 crisis period of the electric power delivery systems as the power generation plants called for more gas than could be delivered through full-capacity operations of the interstate pipelines.

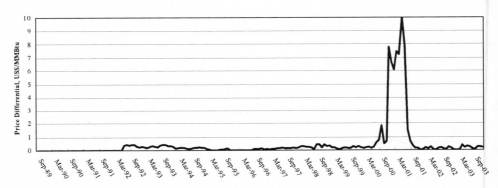

Figure 7. Bidweek basis differential between El Paso Permian (Waha, Texas) and southern California border (*Source:* As in Figure 4.)

The spike of March 2001 in basis differentials was on gas deliveries to Pacific Gas and Electric at the California border, to Southern California Gas at that location, and for deliveries from the Opal Hub for both locations. Increases in demand for gas associated with the blowout of electric power demand in northern California pushed spot gas prices at the state border hubs to $10.00 per thousand cubic feet, a level equivalent to $100 per barrel crude oil.

Then can we generalize about how gas pipelines in oligopoly market structures performed when faced with massive increases in demands for pipeline space in the late 1990s? The metric for answering the question is the price-cost margin. We have aggregate measures of these margins, across the major pipeline systems in three regions; they have extended from the range of 15 to 25 percent in the mid-1990s to 5 to 15 percent in the late 1990s to early 2000s. The determinants were (1) throughput concentration measured in equivalent numbers of pipeline systems in each region, and (2) the elasticity of demands for pipeline services.

With these measures we can estimate the coefficient of conjectural variation, a characterization of the performance of these service providers in terms of Cournot, Bertrand, or collusive oligopoly. That is, with the Lerner index, $L = (p - mc) / p = [HHI (1 + v)] / e$, and values of v, the conjectural variation, equal $(L \cdot e / HHI) - 1$, then values of v that are large positive are associated with a monopoly, and values that are negative are associated with Bertrand behavior (Table 4).

Based on a range of transport demand elasticity estimates, from 0.07 in the short to medium run to 0.7 in the long run, the resulting conjectural variation coefficients are negative.[2] With 0.7 elasticity and concentration such that the equivalent of four to five pipelines provides service, and price-cost margins of little more than 15 to 25 percent, the pipeline interactive price offers for space

Table 4. Estimated conjectural variation coefficients

Demand elasticity/HHI	Lerner index		
	5%	15%	25%
0.7/0.20	−0.83	−0.48	−0.13
0.07/0.40	−0.99	−0.97	−0.96

Note: $1 + v$, the conjectural variation, equals the Lerner index, $(p - mc / p)$, multiplied by demand elasticities and divided by the Herfindahl-Hirschman index (HHI); that is, $([p - mc] / p)(e / HHI) - 1 = v$. All parameter values as discussed in the text.

during bidweeks result in Bertrand performance (for one, a coefficient of −0.83 for margins of only 5 percent). But with less elastic transport demands, as low as −0.07, and high concentration, such as the equivalent of two and one-half pipelines in capacity, the major network transmission companies still did no better in sustaining price-cost margins higher than Bertrand oligopoly. With higher price-cost margins, as high as 25 percent, interactive oligopoly was still Bertrand, given that the conjectural coefficient is estimated to be −0.96, even closer to the classic Bertrand value of −1.00. Pipeline pricing with Bertrand characteristics is not a competitive result in the large, but the resulting margins were the lowest to be achieved from an oligopoly market structure.

While prices exceeded marginal costs, the profit or price-cost margin was not sufficient to generate returns on capital that would generate capacity expansion. The scenario for profitability in the Bertrand model has to be one in which total capacity across all firms is constrained and replacement of stock in pipeline links has not occurred. Off-peak demands still may not fill the links, so interruptible and secondary (resale) space contracts at low prices prevail. Peak demands are contracted at price-cost margins determined by regulatory capped price levels that are too low to make up off-peak shortfalls in returns to capital.

But would uncapped peak prices be enough? Once in five years gas demands could increase to record levels because of a combination of bad weather and high business cycle growth, and price-cost margins for full-capacity transport would increase to twice the 20 percent average or more. At that point, up to six months of full-line delivery at uncapped firm contract prices would generate sufficient cash flow to make up for previous years of operations without profitability.

Examples are abundant in gas markets of hub to hub bottlenecks where the result of low profitability historically has been limited capacity expansion. The profit margins on operations in the eastern region (Figure 3) were less than $0.50 per thousand cubic feet between 1990 and 2003 (that is, the basis differential was less than $0.50 for transport between Henry and Dominion hubs; if that were the actual pipeline service price or rate, then it barely exceeded marginal costs). But five spikes in the basis differential exceeded $1.00 per thousand cubic feet, and two exceeded $2.00 per thousand cubic feet. These were caused by an increase in spot prices for gas at peak at the receiving nodes. The differential, however, equaled the price shippers were willing to pay for delivered gas at Dominion, and therefore what they would have paid in delivery charges for more gas if there were no price cap. Hypothetically, these peaks, in the absence of regulated price caps on space, would have generated the equivalent of $1.50

in margins during the entire peak period, an increase in the Lerner index to 30 percent for the transmission companies. Instead, under regulation, the returns of the high exit price—the spike under price caps—went to those brokers or shippers with gas inventories at the receiving nodes.

In the midwestern region, there were four limited-size price spikes in spot gas for half-years, except from new fields in the Rocky Mountain Eastern slopes, where there were fourteen. In the western region, for production shipped from the Texas Permian Basin to the southern California border, there were five periods during which basis differential spikes were up to ten times the $0.50 realized when there were no excess demands for pipeline space. If considered as separate, equal-length periods, then in sixty half-years the price would have been twice that in the twenty-one periods of 0 to 5 percent margins (see Figure 7 for California). If realized by the pipeline, in the absence of price caps, Lerner margins would have been in the range of 50 percent over the entire sixty half-years. In that case, the additional operating earnings could have financed investment in pipelines and equipment to provide sufficient capacity to prevent any further spikes. Rather than price-cost margins in the range of 15 to 25 percent, falling to 5 to 15 percent, in the newer Rocky Mountain central and California regions, margins could have been in the range of 25 to 50 percent. In the western region, the equivalent to the extreme spike during the winter and spring of 2000–01 could have generated cash flow to increase transportation capacity to levels that would have prevented a repetition of that capacity shortfall.

But pipeline gains could not finance capacity expansion from spikes given the constraints of price-cap regulation. When excess space demand was present during bidweek, the highest price that could be set in the market for dedicated space was the capped firm contract price. This price also capped the secondary space market price, at least for most of the period, before FERC uncapped secondary contracts. Only off-market contracts not subject to FERC review could go to price levels consistent with the spike in gas wholesale prices, and these did not involve enough volume to generate higher average price-cost margins for the pipelines during capacity shortage periods. The revenue in any basis differential spike went to brokers and dealers that had contracts at wellheads that had and could deliver gas in real time under capped firm space contracts; they sent $2.00 gas through pipeline space at $1.00 for transportation and sold gas at $5.00 to $10.00 per thousand cubic feet in unexpected peak markets.

That the FERC regulatory process foreclosed the pipelines from clearing excess demand for space can be seen by examining pipeline financial performance

Table 5. Utilization of interstate pipeline capacity by region
(based on average daily capacity utilization)

Year	Eastern	Midwestern	Western	All
1990	60%	54%	75%	57%
1995	59%	63%	67%	62%
2000	55%	53%	66%	56%
2002	48%	53%	59%	53%

Source: Department of Energy, Energy Information Administration (EIA), Natural Gas Analysis and Publications (Washington, DC: U.S. GPO, various years).

Note: See note for Table 1.

during spikes. If the space market were to function efficiently, then unexpected large increases in demands for throughput would be matched by increases in space contract spot prices. That is, we should observe extreme levels of capacity utilization and increases in transport prices, and subsequently in pipeline revenues, earnings, and investment in capacity. But there were no significant increases in capacity utilization. The eastern region basis spikes were most prominent in 1995 and 2002; capacity utilization in the eastern pipelines in 1995 was slightly less than in 1990 and in 2002 was 7 percent less than in 2000 (Table 5). Closer examination, by comparing flow year to year, indicates a 4 percent increase in throughput above trend in 1995 and no increase in 2002.

In the midwestern region, the increase in utilization in both the 1996 and 2001 spike years was 3 percent. In the western region, the extreme spike in gas demands in 2001 brought forth a 13 percent increase in throughput against flat levels in 2000 and 2002, but since capacity was increasing by 5 percent per year in this region, utilization went up by only 3 percent in 2001. Overall, any percentage increases were small, well within a range that could be attributed to variations in operating conditions and seasonal weather. They do not indicate a response to increased demand for transportation 20 percent or more higher than that in previous seasons.

Detail on capacity utilization in the largest pipelines with the most capacity is even more revealing. Figure 8 indicates monthly transmission volumes and the eastern regional basis differential for gas to the Transco zone six hub in New Jersey. Although there were seasonal peaks in volume transported during 2001 and 2003, spikes in differentials were not coincident with volume peaks.

Large changes in volumes occurred in the eastern region's largest pipeline

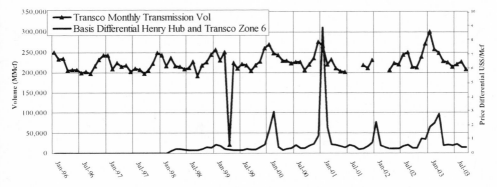

Figure 8. Transco monthly transmission volume and basis from Henry Hub (*Source:* As in Figure 4.)

when the line was down (in 1999) and before a differential spike (in 2003). Most telling is that Transco throughput fell during the quarter when the shortage of space hit its peak in 2003.

The Natural Gas Pipeline Company of America (NGPL) system, the largest from Texas to Chicago, had seasonal peaks in throughput that occurred when there were differential spikes (in 2001 and 2003) (Figure 9). If any change were to be noted, however, these seasonal peaks were less than in earlier years when there were no spikes.

The most startling combination of throughput rates and gas price spikes is that of El Paso Natural Gas Transmission, the original line to California and one of the three largest sources of transmission services from Texas to the West

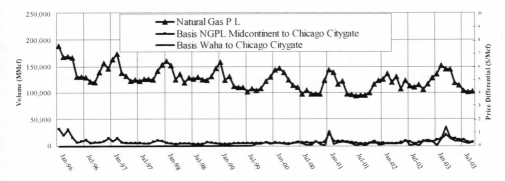

Figure 9. NGPL monthly transmission volume and basis to Chicago City Gate from Waha and NGPL Midcontinent (*Source:* As in Figure 4.)

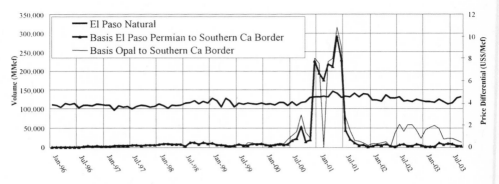

Figure 10. El Paso Natural Gas monthly transmission volume and basis to southern California border (*Source:* As in Figure 4.)

Coast. As shown in Figure 10, El Paso volumes increased in early 2001, after the first large gas price spike in the summer and fall of 2000; but the volumes failed to increase to respond to the $10.00 per thousand cubic feet spikes in early April, July, and October 2001. The increase in throughput that would have caused gas price differences between the Permian Basin or Opal Wyoming hubs and southern California to fall back to less than $1.00 per thousand cubic feet was not forthcoming at or near price spikes.

Limited changes in volumetric deliveries, at constrained (regulated) rates in firm space contracts did not generate price-cost margins at peak sufficient to make pipeline services profitable. Returns on invested capital minus the weighted average cost of debt and equity capital (that is, economic value added [EVA], the amount necessary to return original investment) did not increase at all for the pipelines encountering price spikes.[3] Estimates are shown and aggregated for pipelines in the three regions in Figure 11.[4]

The pipelines in the eastern region generated negative EVA, and the midwestern region lines were at zero EVA in the early 1990s when the economy (and the energy economy) was in recession. The eastern lines were 13 percent short on EVA, that is, of earning to cover their costs of capital; the midwestern lines were from 0 to 1 percent positive. Those in the western region were close 0 percent. While the eastern and western lines converged on zero profitability in the 1993–97 period, the midwestern lines achieved positive returns in the range of 2 to 4 percent (where there were very limited gas price spikes). At the end of the 1990s and in the early 2000s, limited spikes in Chicago, large spikes in New York, and a tenfold increase in the level of the southern California spike all occurred when there were no gains in profits for the pipelines serving any of these

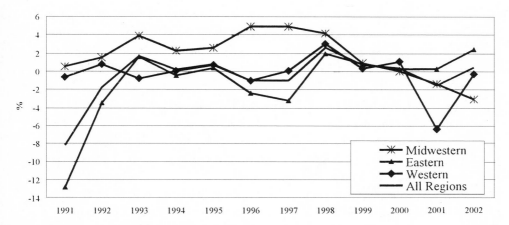

Figure 11. Economic value added (EVA) for selected pipeline companies by region (*Source:* Calculations based on Compustat financial statements of the pipelines. See note 3 for calculation of EVA.)

regions. The EVA rates of all the pipelines fell to zero in 1999 and to negative levels of 2 to 6 percent during 2000 to 2002.

Table 6 shows the condition of three key pipelines. Transcontinental Gas pipeline, the largest and the one with the lowest operating cost, performed the worst of the eastern pipelines by generating large negative returns in two years and averaging only 1 percent returns in other years. But Natural Gas Pipeline Company, the original Chicago line, far exceeded the midwestern average, realizing 17 percent in 1997 and averaging more than 8 percent for the twelve years. El Paso in the western region had negative EVA in nine of the twelve years. Not one of these pipeline companies appears to have been able to turn the spikes in delivered gas prices to its advantage, by increasing net earnings over capital costs in early 2000s.

Table 6. Economic value added by pipelines in the three regional markets (%)

Pipeline (region)	1991	1993	1995	1997	1999	2001
Transcontinental (eastern)	−12.7	0.1	−4.4	1.0	1.5	0.4
Natural Gas Pipeline (midwestern)	13.9	7.4	4.9	17.3	4.8	3.6
El Paso Natural Gas (western)	−2.7	0.1	−0.3	0.1	−0.4	−1.3

Source: The equation and data sources for the estimates of economic value added are as explained in the text.

The test for the effects of partial deregulation of gas networks is to determine whether, while reducing prices, deregulation sustains returns on capital to competitive levels. During periods of normal, off-season demands for gas transport, pipeline service prices did not go to levels where regulatory ceilings applied but were convergent, achieving levels close to operational marginal costs. During periods of demands at the peak, the regulatory caps on prices cut off increases in the price-cost margins. This resulted in price-cost margins that were too low to sustain investment necessary for system expansion. The resulting stagnation in capacity, during periods of very high peak demands, resulted in spikes in gas prices between network origin and destination points. These spikes had little or no long-term effect on pipeline capacity utilization, so there was no relief from high destination prices that would result from the pipeline carrying more gas. In the absence of regulation, in the long run, these spikes in part would have been dissipated by increased line capacity and throughput.

In effect, the regulatory process forced Bertrand oligopoly prices with caps on the pipelines. Emblematic of Bertrand, the major pipelines experienced negative profitability in all but three years during the period from 1991 to 2002. Bertrand interactive pricing, by three or four pipelines, subject to caps on maximum prices in space contracts had to result in price-cost margins that were too low even during peak demand periods to sustain competitive returns on investment (EVA). The lack of capacity expansion was followed by spikes in gas prices at the city gate in the eastern and western regions that caused consumers to experience prices that were higher than they would have been without spikes and thus without price caps.

PERFORMANCE OF POWER NETWORKS

The state-by-state plans for deregulation had initially called for the integrated utilities to divest their generating capacity. The process, whether by auction or bilateral contract, was intended to result in power supply coming from numerous new plant owners making offers in a daily offer/bid auction, providing wholesale and retail customers with the option of buying from other than the incumbent utility company. The intended result was that production would clear market demand at the price that equaled marginal cost of the last selected supplier, so that newer, lower cost facilities would set the price for all power going on the grid. Power made available one day ahead of loading on the transmission grid on such terms would determine the next day's market clearing for the grid manager. When levels of proposed generated power were equal to demands across all nodes, the grid manager would announce to power owners the price for energy and transmission. This process of making a market in close to real time was essential, given that the electricity had to be withdrawn at the same rate from all nodes to balance the network.

The divestiture of plants by the incumbent utility took place, to a significant extent, in most large states on the East and West coasts and also in Texas. The purchasers in large part were integrated utility companies leaving their historic distribution regions to collect capacity across states in other regions. The companies successful in purchasing generation capacity were small in number, had previous histories of plant operations as utilities, and were well financed to buy collections of plants (financed by the required sale of generating capacity within their own service territory). The restructuring of the power grids resulted in few sources of generation and left only one or possibly two sources of transportation services in any geographic market. The few independent power companies left the burden of balancing power across nodes in ready-must-run (RMR) plant services from standby generators to the management of the transmission grid. For these services, the owners of RMR plants were paid prices capped (and guaranteed) by the grid manager according to terms set by the state utility regulatory agency. This collectivized price formation on the supply side, to some extent, because the capacity of various generating companies could be put on RMR status by the grid manager, removing supply priced below the RMR capped price.

Restructuring totally changed grid management. For example, rather than the vertically integrated utility determining the distribution of its own power, and complying with retail power price caps, a systems operator dispatched power across all utilities in the state based on the marginal supply price at the generation point plus transport price plus add-ons to that price for pass through congested locations. FERC empowered the independent systems operator (ISO)[5] to dispatch power to all nodes in the state, after the day-ahead auctions set what power went into the network at what set of purchase prices and level of service quality. The transport charges were based on lease costs for the grid manager for the grid links of the owner-utilities, while the ISO determined where and to what extent the owner-utilities could use their own grid capacity. The system operator-manager generated revenues from grid users to pay for these services, in which it had a monopoly, passing on payment to the owners.

The key to network performance in this type of deregulation was the stream of revenues to those companies that owned the network. The stream was assessed at FERC, which carried out limited "cost-of-service" reviews; and the utilities had recourse to reverse the restructuring if insufficient revenues were generated, that is, they could withdraw their networks from the ISO manager. The relationship then put the ISO in the position of providing service for which it was the only provider, but that service was contestable given that the recipient could take the lease back.[6]

The restructuring process affected the retail distributors by requiring them, like the gas pipelines, to relinquish merchant service. They were no longer to provide transport for electricity from their own generating plants to be sent on their own transmission networks to the circuit breaker of the residence or business establishment of the consumer. But there were significant differences in the structural changes imposed on electricity service. The interstate pipelines had to get rid of all their gas purchase contracts, so they became pure transmission companies. In electric markets, for the most part, the distribution utilities continued to own a significant portion of generation and to be the major purchaser of electricity to serve their customers. Second, while the federal regulatory agency capped only the firm gas transportation price, state regulatory agencies by and large required electricity prices to the consumer either to be capped or to adhere to cost-of-service levels for the grid and retail delivery system plus the purchase price of power. Third, both gas and electricity prices as regulated had to be high enough to cover a "transition cost" of previous capital investments. In California, for example, the legislature froze the retail price on the assumption that the power auction purchase prices for deliveries over the network would be so low that the transition charge plus network costs and purchase prices would be less than the capped price.

The intent of the state legislatures, in the large, was to guarantee retail consumers *no increases in prices* in the long run as the result of deregulation. Deregulation was not supposed to result in higher prices. The scenario for capped prices with stranded cost recovery was both complex and clever: the retail price was frozen, as were delivery costs, and power prices at the plant were to be reduced by reshuffling sources to include only low-cost plant supply in the daily auction market. Frozen delivered prices and reduced marginal power costs would increase the producer's operating income margins, which would generate cash to cancel out losses because plants of the utilities would have to be sold for less than book cost. When these "transition" book costs were fully recovered, the retail cap then would decrease to the average purchase price of power plus the average costs of transmission and distribution. Options for the "post-transition period" included a price freeze at a lower price level rather than a return to cost-of-service rate making. Stranded costs were in excess of $135 billion, accounting for more than 50 percent of book value in half of the country's 114 utilities.[7] It was assumed that it would be years before "transition" recovery would be complete.

The restructuring framework thus set in place three separate levels of statewide or regional markets within the industry. The first level, power generation, provided supply into the state or regional grid at a uniform spot price for all buyers except those receiving product under long-term contracts. The second level, operated by an ISO grid manager, was that of a unified transmission grid made up of a patchwork of company networks that in effect had a monopoly on transmissions (but not a monopoly price, which would have been rejected by the retail distributor that owned the physical capacity). The third level, the retail network distributor, with access to the final consumer, had an exclusive franchise but was operating under requirements for "open access" that would allow other marketers to deliver at retail using that existing retail network. In some areas, such as California, the incumbent retailer prices were capped. Attempts to develop alternative retail distribution networks failed, and even if they had succeeded by using incumbent network elements, they would not have reduced the incumbent system operator's control of distribution unless a second power line were put in place to each residence.

Over the three levels stood the state regulatory agency, with a franchise granting power that allowed it to review distributor prices and service offerings. In partial deregulation, the review process shifted from finding prices that were in line with "cost-of-service" prices to a framework in which performance can be judged in terms of Lerner (price-cost) margins. An ISO/FERC pricing process interacts in the market where the demand side consists of incumbent retail service providers and a fringe of resellers of wholesale purchases from these incumbents. There has been almost no overlay of one retail distribution network over another, so the incumbent is little less than a single source of demand, except where large industrial users built private networks to wheel in power or bring it from their own plants. But where restructuring has required the creation of a single grid across the areas of half a dozen retail distributors, the demand side has had a half-dozen sources. The restructuring process created a single supplier of grid services and as many buyers of those services as retail distributors in the region. As a matter of course, the state regulatory agency has limited the effect of a single source of supply of network services by rolling the network charges in retail price caps. Therefore, while an incumbent retail distributor would not seek to reduce grid charges below cost on its own lines, it would have the incentive to see that power wheeled in over these lines paid higher-than-cost transportation charges. One hypothesis, then, is that the prices for network services should have shown Cournot oligopoly behavior, given that the regulator was acting as price setter for transport at the ISO to system average costs without regard to any of a series of proposed pricing responses from the retail distributor. By assumption, the agency attempted to generate Cournot results from caps on prices at both the network and retail levels. This is the same as assuming that ISO/FERC and the retailer interact as equal sources, or HHI = 0.5, as if the agency "takes" the single provider of network services as given and increases throughput by half through required price reductions, to halve the price-cost margin that would otherwise result from an unregulated single provider of grid services.

Consistent with price caps, seasonal peaks and troughs in power demands, and the basic operating and maintenance costs of the transmission and distribution wirelines, the network ISO sets classifications of service (power delivered to types of users by time of day and volume). These specified price schedules have resulted in Lerner index or price-cost margins in the range of 30 to 35 percent when the distributor was previously a vertically integrated generator/transmitter/distributor. These margins have been reduced to 16 to 18 percent as a result of implementation of other aspects of partial deregulation.

The restructured network service regions that make up partially deregulated markets have in recent years been operating with dispatch systems in which much more than half the generating capacity has continued to be owned and operated by the retail distributors. The deregulatory transition, having slowed or stopped, has caused self-generated power onto the dispatch node to expand relative to power generated by independents. Two ISO regions—New England and Pennsylvania–New Jersey–Maryland (PJM)—had less than 10 percent self-generated power, with 90 percent from other sources as purchased through auction. But New York has had 32 percent self-generated power, California has had 43 percent, and Texas has had 41 percent (see Table 7).

Restructuring has still, in general, resulted in adjoining transmission systems of the retail utilities merging into single organizations with a systems dispatcher (ISO) at all the nodes of the retail distribution utilities. For the independent power put on the grid, there have been transactions in which the utility buying that power and also buying transportation pays for the use of its own network and then receives that payment for the use of its network. Where the grid has been transporting large-volume kilowatt hours that have been independently owned, the ISO has decreed a two-part price system, with access and usage

Table 7. Selected electric generating capacity owned by utilities and others

State/region	Summer capacity (mW)	Utility	Nonutility	Primary energy source
New England				Gas/nuclear
Regional total	28,268	2,506	25,761	
Regional percentage	100%	9%	91%	
New York				Nuclear
Regional total	36,041	11,675	24,366	
Regional percentage	100%	32%	68%	
California				Gas
Regional total	56,663	24,609	32,054	
Regional percentage	100%	43%	57%	
Texas				Gas
Regional total	94,488	38,903	55,585	
Regional percentage	100%	41%	59%	
PJM				Gas/coal
Regional total	70,832	6,200	64,632	
Regional percentage	100%	9%	91%	

Source: Energy Information Administration (EIA), "State Electricity Profiles, 2002," issued January 2004.

charges that together have been intended to cover the cost of the investment in the network and of transmission (the *locational marginal price,* LMP, which includes congestion costs at the sending and receiving nodes).[8] To date, regional network revenues have in large part not included an LMP, and payments for network services have been consolidated with those from the operations of the incumbent power retailer. That is, retail utilities that owned the transmission network in their service regions realized margins for prices over the unit cost of power purchased (or generated) plus operation costs of their networks.

Estimations of these margins have been constructed for the largest distributors in each region, similar to those for approximations of Lerner margins in gas transmission. These margins are shown in Table 8. To the extent that the retail distributors divested most of their generating capacity, in the 1990s, in New England and PJM, the margins were in the range of 13 to 19 percent (New England) and 21 to 26 percent (PJM); but where the restructuring process left more of the generation capacity with the distributors (Texas and New York), margins were in the range of 20 to 26 percent. During the period 2000–04, margins were two to five percentage points higher across almost all regions, most likely as a result of business cycle recovery. The exception was California,

Table 8. Price-cost margins for electricity distribution systems

Selected system	Margin estimate (%)					
	1994	1996	1998	2000	2002	2004
California	26	23	14	(55)	27	47
New England	19	14	13	19	18	18
New York State	19	24	21	23	22	21
PJM	21	23	22	21	26	24
Texas	21	23	22	21	26	24

Source: Data for largest six utilities in each region from corporate Form One Reports to FERC and EIA, annual.

Note: Net operating revenues (revenues minus operating costs) divided by revenues. Both revenues and costs, excluding costs of purchased power.

where the power crisis of 2000–01 resulted in negative profit margins of 55 percent followed by margins of 27 to 47 percent. All these margins were low, driven down by price caps and the newly found costs of operating inefficient grid and wireline networks. The theory is that this "Bertrand" performance of these systems in the RTO regions was responsive to the combined operations of the ISO grid manager and the state regulatory agency.

PERFORMANCE OF REGIONAL POWER NETWORKS, 1990–2004

The measure of network performance of most concern is the stability of generated power price over the period of regulatory restructuring. If the network was providing quality service, the price differential of power between the generation node and receiving city gate node should be equal to the marginal cost of transmission. This basis differential in the 1990s was not stable, and in fact there were significant departures from quality performance so defined at different times in each of the ISO/RTO management regions.

Basis differentials for electricity prices in wholesale auction markets have been estimated for five ISO/RTO regions: (1) the Electricity Reliability Council of Texas (ERCOT), which has transmission rights for 90 percent of the state of Texas and is contained within the state; (2) the California Independent System Operator (CAISO), encompassing the state of California, with links to adjoining states; (3) the Independent System Operator of New England (ISO-NE), which has dispatch rights to and within all five New England states;

(4) the New York Independent System Operator (NYISO), encompassing the state of New York and limited adjoining states; and (5) the Pennsylvania–New Jersey–Maryland RTO (PJM), including all or parts of Delaware, Virginia, Maryland, New Jersey, West Virginia, Ohio, Illinois, Pennsylvania, and the District of Columbia.

Each ISO/RTO region was divided into zones, and for each zone, one node was chosen as the base to form a differential between it and a counterpart receiving node. The differential was positive if the spot electricity price at the base was lower than that at the delivery node, or negative if that price was higher than that at the delivery node. In limited cases, the price at base and counterpart zone was the same. On-the-hour basis differentials were taken for each of the regions at 8:00 a.m., 5:00 p.m., 6:00 p.m., 7:00 p.m., and 8:00 p.m. (PJM data exclude 7:00 p.m.). These times correspond with times of peak usage and accordingly, with higher demands on the grid for power flow.

The Texas (ERCOT) basis differential performance is examined first. Its network management system provides a framework in which producers and distributors complete bilateral contracts that set schedules of power delivery. ERCOT ensures that the transmission network carries the power loads to meet demands at all nodes, given contract scheduled deliveries, and it procures balancing loads at ancillary plants to maintain the regional node balance. Day-ahead schedules with infusions of ancillary power are complemented by congestion charges that have been used to even out loads at key hubs. There is no spot market, but there is a "market clearing price" from bid stacks that suppliers submit for ancillary services. Since ERCOT has operated as an organization that ensures reliability, its board of directors has included generator, marketing, and distribution company representatives. With the Public Utility Commission of Texas, it has reviewed proposals for new investment in transmission by the utilities owning parts of the state grid. It also sets service conditions for independent power suppliers buying at wholesale and selling into retail markets using the lines of the incumbent utility.

Performance of the Texas network in recent years has been relatively free of disruptions caused by deficient transmission operating performance. This has been indicated by the relative absence of large basis differential spikes. The 6:00 p.m. West Texas to Houston basis shows two spikes in January–February 2002 and three lesser spikes in October 2002 and April plus July of 2003 (see Figure 12).

The California experience with CAISO in regards to the quality of power delivery service has been quite different. CAISO managed day-ahead and hour-

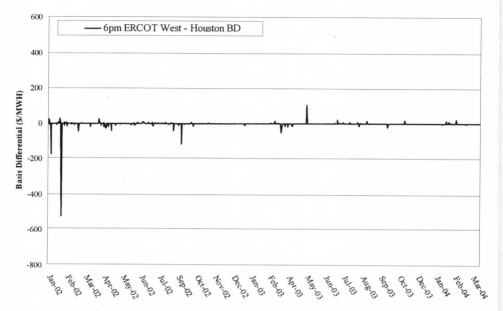

Figure 12. 6:00 p.m. basis differential between ERCOT West and Houston (base) (*Source: ISO web sites.*)

ahead power spot markets by scheduling for a separate "PX" power exchange that cleared excess or deficient supply for both integrated and independent power providers. The network transmission system had multiple zones, each with separate prices depending on the distance from major generating sources to city gates of the major metropolitan area distributors. But the network consisted of the patched-together transmission grids of three regional incumbent retail distributors plus links that took power from hydroelectric and fossil generation plants in Washington, gas-fired combined-cycle plants in California, and nuclear and coal plants in Arizona. Loads from out-of-state sources were in decline over the 1990s, and new generation capacity in state was slow to come online, given the highly uncertain effect on investment of the legislature's plan for restructuring. At the same time, demand increased at a higher rate than forecast so that "the amount of reserve capacity was shrinking rapidly . . . [such that] California's electricity system was facing a very severe challenge."[9] This put the newly configured state transmission system under pressure for capacity to shift power from surplus to shortage locations.

CAISO set the terms and conditions for the use of the transmission network, the component nodes and links of which were still the properties of the three retail utility companies; the California Public Utility Commission capped retail prices (rates) so that the retail power price-cost margin would generate cash flow sufficient to recover stranded costs. But from its inception in the middle 1990s this operating income margin formed a "window" of recovery of stranded investment funds that was at risk, given the fact that it was based on the day-to-day spot price for power in the CAISO auction, and the higher the spot price the less the "window" between wholesale auction price, transmission price, and retail price. That was because the capped retail price level was not responsive to power purchase prices; only after stranded costs were recovered, or after five years had passed, whichever was first, would retail cost-of-service–based price levels be restored.

In this restructuring and tight market, the transmission network, essentially fixed in capacity since the mid-1980s, was pushed to full-capacity utilization. Figure 13 shows the results for transmission service quality; the basis differentials for CAISO north versus south zonal average energy prices at 6:00 p.m. for ten-day periods in 2000–03 show severe price spikes. These spikes resulted from the inability to transmit north sufficient kilowatt hours to clear excess de-

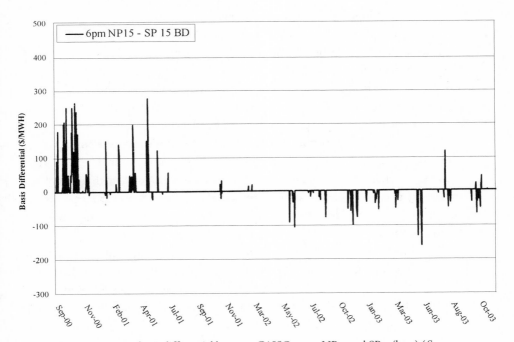

Figure 13. 6:00 p.m. basis differential between CAISO zones NP15 and SP15 (base) (*Source:* CAISO data available online.)

mands, so that marketers in zone NP15 had to pay $200 per megawatt hour more than spot prices in zone SP15. Twice per year during 2002–03 congestion spikes in the opposite direction occurred, causing spot prices in southern California to exceed the basis by $200 per megawatt hour. The capacity-growth "challenge" in generation had been realized in the highest spikes in the country.

The New England, New York, and PJM regions had similar but not as extreme experiences in adapting to divestiture and expanded grid networks. Each had an RTO or ISO that managed power flows on the transmission links and nodes of the large companies in their regions. In New England the new ISO managed the consolidation of company grids across seven states; in New York it consolidated upstate grids with those in New York City and Long Island; and in the PJM region the new management organization had jurisdiction to send power across what were previously company networks in Pennsylvania, New Jersey, and Maryland and to affiliated adjacent states. There, three regional networks had been based on what previously were pooling arrangements and intercompany exchange networks, but the RTO in each treated its region as one entity for managing flows through ancillary service power generators, but less through a day-ahead auction of spot power given that three-quarters or more of volumes were shipped under bilateral contract.

All three RTO/ISOs managed combinations of intracompany grids cobbled together into adjoining but separate transmission networks. They used the wireline properties of the retail distributors, initiated plans but did not build extensions of existing systems, and made returns to grid owners based on charges to all shippers that were carryovers from before restructuring. Performance on the New England grid was marked by the reluctance of plant owners to undertake power export from Maine, which had a surplus, to more populous and power-short retail systems in Massachusetts and Connecticut. The resulting basis differentials for Connecticut to Maine (Figure 14) indicate that lack of grid capacity caused price spikes five times in the range of $100 per megawatt hour in the 8:00 p.m. peaks during 2003, and smaller peaks nearly twenty times up to April 2004.

The eleven zones for power delivery in New York State were similarly subject to price spikes because of the lack of network deliverability to power-deficit nodes in the southern part of the state. From 2000 to 2004, basis differentials between the west zone (bordering Ohio), the lowest priced source of power, and New York City, with higher priced power, show six spikes in the range of $100 per megawatt hour and one at $400 in the 8:00 p.m. time period (Figure 15). The most significant bottleneck in New York State was in link capacity to

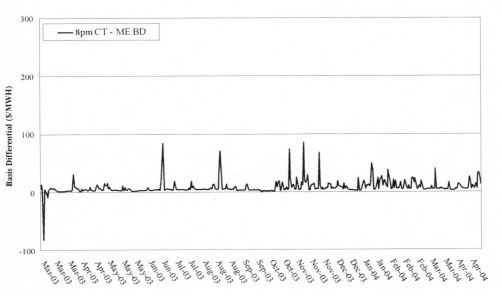

Figure 14. 8:00 p.m. basis differential between Connecticut and Maine (base) (*Source:* ISO web sites.)

Long Island, where there were eight differential spikes of more than $100 per megawatt hour and two of more than $250 during 2000–04. The New York City experience was repeated and then repeated again (see Figure 15).

The most complex process of putting together a regional transmission grid took place in the PJM multi-state amalgamation of twelve corporate systems. The performance of the resulting grid is indicated in the basis differential power prices, as estimated from eleven sets of access node prices against Pennsylvania Power and Light (PPL) receiving node prices. Figure 16 is replete with basis differential spikes in excess of $50 per megawatt hour; one, in 1999, was the result of a breakdown in delivery on the main grid link through the region. Both the frequency and magnitude of spikes declined after 2001, however. More capacity has been available from better management of system operators, not from building new plants and equipment.

THE CONDITIONS DETERMINING
OLIGOPOLY BEHAVIOR

A lack of price responsiveness is indicated by the spikes in the basis differentials across all the major new "reform" power transmission systems. When grid

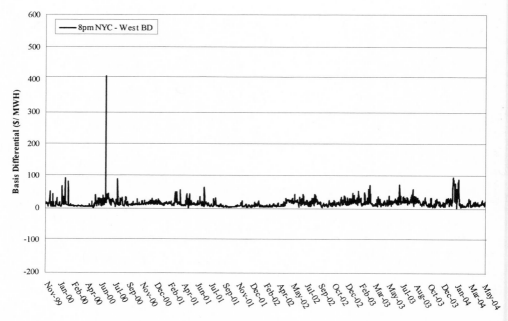

Figure 15. 8:00 p.m. basis differential between New York City and the west zone (*Source:* ISO web sites.)

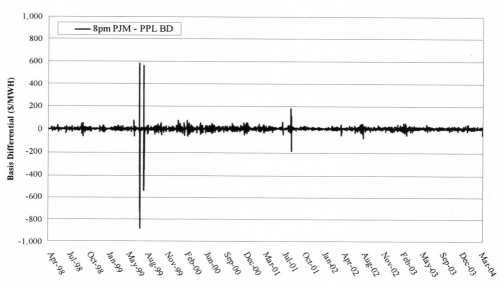

Figure 16. 8:00 p.m. basis differential between PJM and PPL (base) (*Source:* ISO web sites. PJM data available online at http://www.pjm.org/markets/jsp/lmpmonthly.jsp.)

nodes were congested because of excess demand for load at delivery nodes, utilization prices, a day or an hour ahead, were not increased sufficiently there to reduce demand, nor were additional sources of supply at other links able to replace those stopped by congestion. Instead, the bid price at the receiving node increased by two to five times in order to decrease demand for power there by as little as 5 percent.

This is not to imply that demand was perfectly inelastic. Over the period in which spikes were repeated, power users sought alternatives, such as their own standby facilities, plant relocation, and shutdown planning that did reduce demand. The experience of both residential and industrial consumers indicated elasticities in the range of -0.14 in the short run and -0.32 in the long run as compiled by Carol Dahl and Carlos Roman outside of the abnormal spike periods. But in the spike periods, elasticities have ranged from -0.14 to -0.56; that is, the percentage reduction in bid volumes was approximately half the percentage increase in prices.[10]

Demand elasticity of one-half, indicating limited volume responsiveness to price, would be consistent with the pricing of network services in the long run. That is, the regulatory initiatives of historical fixed-line charges, based on cost-of-service price controls, had ISO-allowed charges in the lower range of the demand function for grid services. The operating earnings margins of retail power distributors have been indicative of Lerner index values in the range of 16 to 30 percent. Together, these two measures, for grid transmission plus retail distribution, resulted in extreme transmission pricing exhibiting Bertrand-level performance.

Table 9 summarizes the resulting coefficients of conjectural variation. Bertrand negative values of slightly more than -1.0 predominate over the range of short- to long-run demand elasticities for even the highest margins.

There is remarkably little difference in these measures of Bertrand behavior

Table 9. Estimated conjectural variation coefficients for network service providers

Demand elasticity	Lerner index	
	16%	30%
-0.14	-0.96	-0.92
-0.32	-0.90	-0.81
-0.56	-0.82	-0.66

Note: See note to Table 4.

from one RTO to another. They all indicate that restructuring resulted in high concentration in grid wholesale and distribution retail services. But if it were assumed instead that the state installed price caps in retail distribution, while FERC continued to require cost-of-service–based prices on grid services, then price-cost margins for transmission were different. What is meant by "different" is not clear, but most analysts hypothesize that the incentives in price caps reduce costs and increase price-cost margins. However, PJM margins were the lowest in the first half of the decade when all state regulatory agencies in its region put price caps at retail in place, compared with CAISO, New England, New York, and Texas, where most states still used some form of cost-of-service rate-based price control. In the second half of the decade, PJM margins increased relative to those in the other RTOs, but these margins still implied values of the conjectural variation coefficient not different from the value of -1 associated with Bertrand oligopoly.

The question then remains as to whether Bertrand performance implied losses for both producers of network services and consumers across all the RTOs. The scenario in which the producers did not lose would have consisted of periods of normal demand, when excess capacity and price competition forced network operators to discount line charges down to marginal costs (below average costs) but were then "matched" by periods of extreme price increases during the large spikes. Grid managers were not able to exact spike price differences between origin and destination nodes because of caps in price limits on network service. But were they making up that nonresponse but setting high congestion prices for that transportation? If spikes were continuous over a quarter, then 90 percent or more price-cost margins from congestion prices could have generated earnings at least equal to the losses generated the rest of the year.

The three conditions necessary for Bertrand oligopolists to have in this way generated profits were the presence of wide swings in demands, significant bottleneck periods, and high congestion prices during bottlenecks. First, there were no long periods in which capacity utilization of RTO grids was low, due to low-level demand, and no increase in capacity. Transmission and distribution capacity during restructuring increased in the first half of the 1990s (although at a slower rate than the growth of generation capacity). Transmission investment declined by 5 percent between 1990 and 1996, which was deemed inadequate to ensure reliability and sustain the expansion plans for the merged company grids into "seamless" regional grids.[11] Second, as noted, there have been significant bottleneck periods in power supply in California, the Midwest, and the Northeast. But, third, the practices that FERC installed for pricing during spikes made it all but impossible for grid management to count on large increases in basis differentials during congestion being the source of increased grid revenues. RTOs were authorized as part of their control of grid service pricing to put in place reserve rights to transmission space that would sell for high prices during spikes, but the revenues from these high prices go to holders of the rights purchased before at the normal transmission tariff rate. That is, the increases in revenues from spikes become broker speculative gains.

The proof is in whether congestion payments of any type allowed the networks to realize compensatory earnings. If so, they would have been realized as positive EVA for the transmission-distribution company in that RTO that year in which basis differential spikes were extensive. Figure 17 shows EVA for all large retailers in each of the five functioning RTO regions, averaged for all companies by year. The EVA estimates are close to, if slightly above, zero for the retail distributors of ERCOT and PJM during the last half of the 1994–2002 period. The distributors in New England and New York RTOs had negative EVA throughout the ten-year period. Altogether, the CAISO members experienced a loss of 25 percent of capital value during and after the power crisis in northern

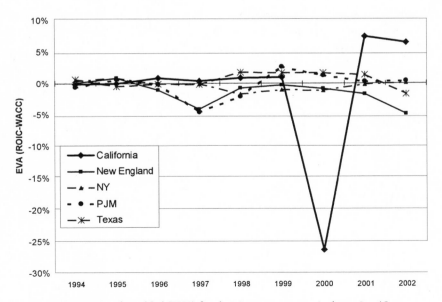

Figure 17. Economic value added (EVA) for electric power companies by region (*Source:* Compustat financial statements. See note 3.)

California during which their retail service prices were frozen (with some makeup of losses from compensatory regulated price increases in 2002).

The first and second quarters of 2002 were spike periods in Texas, but the EVA results for RTO members were negative that year. The California basis differential spikes were in the last quarter of 2000 and first two quarters of 2001, the first when the three retail service providers were reduced to insolvency and the second when asset values (and EVA) had been reduced by 25 percent. The New York City–to–West hub basis differential spiked in the second quarter of 2000, but EVA did not increase then. There was no relationship between congestion-related price spikes and the profits of the network owners/operators in the RTOs. The owners had to rely on the long-term price-cost margins, set by FERC and the state agencies, on grid and distribution network service compensation. These EVA results were of the Bertrand oligopoly type and over the past twelve years were negative at volumes close to the -1 conjectural variation associated with a noncompensatory Bertrand.

A more acute examination of the interaction of a state regulatory agency that had a strict mandate to implement restructuring and a regional power producer, transmitter, and distributor is possible from the state archives of Pacific Gas and Electric Corporation. The next chapter examines the company's strategic response to directives from the California legislature and public utility commission to sell its generating capacity, freeze retail prices, and collect stranded costs from the "headroom" in the Lerner price-cost margin. This was all to take place during the power supply crisis of 2000–01.

Chapter 4 The Strategic Response of Pacific Gas and Electric Corporation to Partial Deregulation during the California Power Crisis

The supply-demand conditions for power in northern California during 2000–01 were in many aspects unlike those in other markets before or since. They may not be representative of future markets there or elsewhere. The coincidence of reduced supply because of lower hydropower availability, and increased demand because of an unexpected surge in the West Coast business cycle, is not likely to occur again. Nor would power distribution companies again be likely to do little or nothing in response to a multiyear decline of the "safety margin" of excess generating capacity. Yet the California scenario, while extreme, contains the essential elements of the interaction of regulation with the distribution companies that determines prices and service. The sequence of actions and reactions of numerous state agencies and bureaus with the distributing companies resulted in price spikes that cut off power supply, given the inability of the retail distributor to finance further power purchases. The response patterns of both agency and distributor were measured, strategic, converging on an inability to provide service, built into the process of what was the most advanced program of partial deregulation.

The Pacific Gas and Electric Corporation (PG&E), retail electricity supplier for most of northern and central California and serving a population of 15 million, developed a comprehensive new strategy in response to California Assembly Bill 1890 (AB 1890) and subsequent implementation by the California Public Utility Commission (CPUC). The new strategy consisted of a two-part plan: first, to focus on "competitive" performance in retail distribution in its region within California, and second, to develop unregulated affiliates to expand capacity in generation markets outside the state as the company was required to sell off its generation capacity within the state. The utility failed on the first part by fully attempting to provide all its services during extreme financial stress caused by price spikes in the wholesale electricity market in which it was a major purchaser. Throughout the price spike period, PG&E carried out the old strategy in compliance with regulatory requirements to provide service to end-use customers, specifically retail residential and business customers in those locations where it originally held the state franchise. But escalating prices in wholesale markets could not be passed on to its customers because the statute had required that retail prices be frozen during transition. PG&E sold power at retail for less than it paid for that power based on the reasonably supported position that the difference between wholesale power prices and retail sales prices could be banked and collected later as the equivalent of a "transition" cost. That regulatory "compact" was not realized; in due course, and absent any signs of recovery of funds already borrowed and spent to pay the excess-price bill, the company lost access to the capital markets and went into bankruptcy. It still continued to buy dear and sell cheap until its cash ran out. To have stayed in the power market as long as it did was not financial mismanagement; rather, it was required under the transition in which it retained regulatory responsibilities as a utility while it was deregulated in the purchase power market.

AB 1890, passed in 1996, set the direction of the restructuring of the industry in California by requiring that the three large power-distributing corporations focus on retail activities, sell off their generating capacity, and turn over management of their transmission capacity to the aforementioned CAISO. The legislation followed years of debate in the state legislature and at CPUC in a quest to achieve lower electricity costs to consumers, principally industrial and commercial consumers, so as to make California more "competitive" while maintaining and expanding the generation, transmission, and distribution systems both in the largest cities and in the complex industrial establishment. The argument was that increasing the number of suppliers would reduce price-cost

margins and thus prices at wholesale, while holding transmission and distribution costs steady through technology improvements coupled with cost-of-service rate making at retail. This led to statute specification of the first step in
phased deregulation, the separation of generation from distribution, the creation of a wholesale day-ahead power auction market, and implementation of
phased price decontrols that allowed recovery of stranded costs.

But the restructuring, from its inception in 1993 through AB 1890 in 1996,
went further, to include the following items:[1]

- The utilities were to divest a large portion of their generation capacity, principally the fossil-fueled generation plants, but would continue to exercise
utility-like responsibilities for safety and reliability for nuclear and hydropower plants in their current portfolios.
- While each of the utilities would still own transmission assets, the statewide
grid would operate as a full dispatched single transmission network, balancing the energy on the grid on a minute-by-minute basis by calling for ready-
must-run plant activity.
- The utilities were to purchase all power, including self-produced power,
through a statewide auction spot market established by CAISO; there would
be only very limited contracts outside the auction market.
- The state-granted retail distribution franchise would remain with the utilities, regulated by CPUC, but retail markets would be open to the entry of
independent service providers outside of CPUC regulation.
- During the transition period, retail pricing would conform to regulatory
caps that were set to give retail consumers some immediate price relief but
were sufficiently in excess of marginal costs to allow utilities the opportunity
to recover transition costs of assets made uneconomic by the restructuring.
After full recovery the utilities would return to cost-of-service rate regulation.

Creation of this restructuring package was initiated in a 1993 CPUC staff report that had the stated purpose of beginning "a dialogue" with the various interests "to better align the state's regulatory program with California's dynamic
and increasingly competitive electric service industries." The report took the
position that California's then-current market structure was "ill-suited" to gov-
ern the electric industry and was incompatible with likely future competitive
conditions.[2]

An investigation by the commission followed, based on wide-ranging pre-
sentations in numerous hearings, which ultimately resulted in a CPUC "Pre-

ferred Policy Decision" that specified a new industry structure based on separating the generation, transmission, and distribution of electricity.[3] That "Preferred Policy Decision" anticipated review and passage of a statute by the legislature, which culminated in a close variant of the CPUC plan being codified in AB 1890, passed in 1996 for implementation in 1998.

The act envisioned the new wholesale market, in which the former generation capacity of the utilities, owned by independent power producers, was to provide power supply and the utilities were to provide demand, that is, to purchase power only in that market. A newly created power exchange (PX) was in real time to match that supply with demand and set the price on an hourly basis, so that voltage balance was achieved throughout the nodes in the state. The act also sought to create incentives for utilities to divest their generation assets quickly and assessed penalties if the utilities did not divest within a defined time period.

In this state plan the high-voltage transmission grid continued under utility ownership but was placed in the hands of CAISO, which, although a nonprofit entity, would levy charges, set under cost-of-service principles, for transmission.

From the perspective of the state's utilities, the new structure was potentially effective in achieving two of their goals. First, AB 1890 would allow them to generate earnings that potentially would be sufficient to recover in full their prior investments in generation, even if sales of plant facilities to independents failed to produce prices high enough to do so. Over a five-year transition period, retail prices would remain frozen at 1996 levels, in the expectation that because the legislature saw these old prices as being quite high, the revenues from sales at capped rates would exceed operating and electricity purchase costs by enough to provide for any remaining recovery. That is, earnings were expected to generate sufficient net cash flow over operating costs to cover interest and book depreciation on any "stranded" generation capital.[4] The earnings, or Lerner index operating income margins, were called *headroom* and were to be credited in newly set up accounts to record the deficiency from sales of generating assets below book value.

In regulatory terms, during the transition period a *competition transition charge* was built into sales-cost margins that would pay down the shortfalls in a *deficiency account* from the sale of generation assets below book asset costs. For PG&E, retail power rates were frozen at an average of 5.4 cents per kilowatt hour, a level believed to be sufficient for recovery of the capital costs of generation assets after also covering unit operating costs and the costs of purchased energy at wholesale.[5]

Although "headroom" was intended to provide the utility with the opportunity to recover investment in generation made before restructuring, it did not guarantee recovery. As AB 1890 stated, "the transition should . . . provide the investors in these electrical corporations with a fair opportunity to fully recover the costs associated with commission approved generation-related assets and obligations." And after a transition period defined by full-cost recovery,[6] retail pricing would be based on wireline and customer service costs, in markets where the utility was envisioned to face competition from numerous independent power retailers.[7] These conditions were supposed to provide incentives for the state's three major utilities to focus on programs to complete the transition period as quickly as possible, so as sooner rather than later they would have greater flexibility in responding to competitive entry.

PG&E's strategy for retail services was to intensify programs that improved service. One new subsidiary, a semi-independent services provider called Energy Services, was to offer consulting on conserving energy and on sustaining quality in the use of its delivered electricity. Another new subsidiary would acquire, construct, and operate power plants and combine these with acquired assets in natural gas, specifically in the "midstream" portion of the gas market (that is, gas gathering, processing, transportation, storage, and commodity marketing). A facility was to be developed for trading in electricity to increase the retail company's access to supplies.

In effect, however, the second part of the PG&E corporate strategic response to AB 1890 was simply to take advantage of opportunities in power markets outside of California that were experiencing the same unbundling process, to utilize "the skill, experience and knowledge we have attained over a century of success in the electric and gas business to take full advantage of profitable opportunities as competitive markets open up."[8] The remarkable, if not strange, focus of strategy was on programs to enhance the company's retail distribution services being pulled all apart by AB 1890. A "Letter to Shareholders" in the 1996 annual report noted that in recent years major spending programs had been undertaken on distribution systems for improving customer service, and that these programs had been sustained "in 1996 to upgrade the systems and facilities of our core electric distribution business. These programs will improve customer service, increase reliability and safety, and hone PG&E's [utility] competitiveness in the more deregulated energy market to come."[9]

Two additional strategic measures were taken to "realize the benefits of AB 1890." First, PG&E sought increases in the amounts of currently authorized retail cost in current rates that would reduce the headroom for recovery of stranded costs. Even though this then reduced the probability of recovering transition costs before the end of the transition period, it would provide additional authorized costs in "cost-of-service" rates going forward after the freeze was lifted.

The second measure taken to extend the benefits of AB 1890 followed from requirements for certain changes in control and operating systems. PG&E had to turn control of its transmission system over to CAISO. It also had to establish systems to sell and then purchase its own generated electricity in the newly organized auction market. It had to have a management organization to bill new marketers for retail wireline services in their independent dealings with PG&E's former customers and to reconstruct its billing process to unbundle these various charges. Making these changes in a short time frame required fast-action management systems that were different from those associated with the delivery of vertically integrated utility services. At the center were measures for increased monitoring of services—for example, monitoring with regard to customer outages, customer calls to the utility, and customer satisfaction surveys. These were new measures of service quality required to be made visible to the public under CPUC's scrutiny. Increasing use of these fast-action systems would in theory increase demand for service and sales revenues, even though initially they increased transaction costs, service delays, and compliance costs.

The foundation for implementing the new strategy was built on a specific financial plan. At inception, the utility was not realizing efficiency levels set out for restructuring; 1997 costs were higher than planned and higher than authorized in earlier rate proceedings, and they did not account for the additional costs of restructuring beginning to take place. The new transaction costs in purchasing wholesale energy, for receiving power from brokers using its transmission facilities, and the like, were yet to be accounted for. The financial plan for improving the quality of service would require increases in outlays in the areas of operations and maintenance (O&M) and administrative and general (A&G), by an amount expected to exceed $450 million in 1999.

In 1997, the implementation began to take place. The initial focus was on the divestiture of generating assets and the financing of rate-reduction bonds. The utility restructured its balance sheet in line with the reduced capital that followed its divestiture of fossil fuel power generation. The cash from the sales of power plants was followed by declarations of extra dividends and repurchases of stock, and there was a new focused effort to undertake the first stage of selling hydroelectric generation facilities.

In appraising utility management during this period, the issue is whether management carried out the strategic plan with diligence and due care for meeting the basic goals of regulation and shareholder interests. But there is still another criterion for assessing conduct. After the fact, CPUC alleged that PG&E's revenues "greatly exceeded its operating costs" in the early years of the transition period, such that PG&E had extra headroom available to offset the subsequent undercollection of wholesale power costs in the crisis of 2000–01. Specifically, the commission stated that PG&E

- Received substantial headroom and other transition revenues in the first two years of transition
- Made cash disbursements to its parent company under its new holding company structure, which then paid out extraordinary common-stock dividends or repurchased stock and retired debt ahead of schedule
- Failed to establish a contingency fund or to retain cash "to cushion its risk"[10]

The CPUC analysis implied that PG&E should have held transition-period excess cash flow received in 1998 and 1999 in escrow, in anticipation of the drain in cash that had to follow from spikes in wholesale electricity prices in 2000–01. But then the question had to be, was it reasonable to expect spikes? Forward-looking conditions in California electricity markets were not so negative that they supported the development of such a contingency fund. Before the first price spike in the wholesale market, beginning in the summer of 2000, the restructured market had not experienced any significant price volatility. Prices had increased during the previous summer's heat wave, and although excess capacity in generation had been limited, overall supply conditions did not support an outlook for sustained price spikes in the next few years. There was no forecast that would have compelled PG&E to abandon implementation of its new strategy to hold cash instead. The actions the utility took over this period were consistent with the regulatory requirements for working out the transition—the larger-than-expected revenues from headroom could not both become a new contingency fund and accelerate the pace to the end of the transition period.

Furthermore, at this initial stage, regulators were already setting boundaries between regulated and open-market services based on the completion of the transition.[11] In May 1997, CPUC issued the first of a number of opinions to enforce the requirement that PG&E operate solely as a purchaser of wholesale electricity through the day-ahead and hour-ahead markets established by the independent PX and run by CAISO.[12] In August 1997, the commission denied PG&E's request both for authority to purchase power outside the PX in long-term contracts, and to employ financial hedging techniques to reduce the risks of increases in the future costs of power purchased in the auction market.[13] Instead, CPUC supported as a "book" hedging process the creation of a new regulatory account; in that account, if wholesale prices in the PX turned out to be higher than frozen retail rates, there would be no change in the transition cost deficit account, but additions would be made there (in the new account) to be recovered by rate increases after the transition was complete.

Adverse future wholesale market conditions were scarcely a matter of concern before 1999. Professor Frank Wolak, chairman of the CAISO Market Surveillance Committee, noted after the fact that participants in the wholesale power auction market did not act as if they gave a high probability to wholesale prices increasing to levels that would result in a sustained negative retail-wholesale margin. As he observed, "it seems reasonable to believe that the three IOU's [investor-owned utilities] believed that if wholesale prices reached this level, FERC would intervene and declare the wholesale prices as unreasonable."[14] In the early years, headroom was between $25 and $30 per megawatt hour, depending on the particular utility, as a result of average wholesale power prices in the range of $30 to $25 per megawatt hour and the retail freeze of $55 per megawatt hour. As Wolak observed:

> Wholesale prices on the order of $70/MWh were difficult to fathom unless one was willing to assume substantial unilateral market power was being exercised, which would cause FERC to intervene, or extremely high natural gas prices, which did not occur in California until early 2001, after all FERC's initial remedies led to a market meltdown. Consequently, as of the start of the market, and even as late as April 2000, it is difficult to see how the IOUs could have forecasted average wholesale prices above $70/MWh for an entire month, which could explain their lack of interest in hedging this spot price risk.[15]

Another indication that wholesale prices would most likely be high enough for utilities to recover stranded costs was provided in forecasts made by the California Energy Commission (CEC). In 1998, the CEC forecast average wholesale prices of $26.50 per megawatt hour for the year 2000, against a freeze retail price average of $54 per megawatt hour. This forecast wholesale price, if realized, would have generated headroom sufficient to allow full recovery of stranded costs in the scheduled transition period. Two years later, in response to rapidly worsening gas prices, and consequently in wholesale power prices, the CEC increased its forecast of the average PX price by $2.00 per megawatt hour, which was not sufficient to preclude full recovery of stranded costs. Even within the year before the crisis period, there were no CEC forecasts involving negative or even substantially reduced headroom.

Other contemporaneous predictions also were that wholesale power prices would be sufficiently low to provide a reasonable expectation of recovery of the stranded cost account. Together, they implied that the utility was not compelled to hedge wholesale power prices against a significant probability that they would exceed the frozen retail rate.

And by 1999 a regulatory automatic hedge against negative headroom was in place, with the establishment of the new book account. This transition revenue account (TRA) booked any negative difference between retail sales revenues and operating costs including wholesale power costs. It was separate from the transition cost balancing account (TCBA), which from inception of the transition tracked the level of stranded costs, that is, the excess of book values over sales values of generating plant and equipment. When current retail sales revenues exceeded operating and power costs, the utility was to transfer the difference (that is, the headroom) to the TCBA, reducing stranded costs to be recovered during the transition.[16] But if retail sales revenues at frozen rates were insufficient to cover operating costs plus wholesale power costs, the undercollection would be accumulated in the TRA. This account's balance would not be added to the TCBA until the TCBA balance was eliminated; then the balance in the TRA would be recovered, that is, reduced, by post-transition retail price increases under cost-of-service rate making—or so it was supposed to go.

The balance in the TRA in fact was to become an asset against which the retail distributor could borrow to fund cash requirements, similar in concept to an accounts-payable account. If a spike in wholesale prices occurred while retail prices were frozen, then the utility would run up negative balances by selling power at retail for less than it paid for that power. It could then borrow against those negative balances in the TRA posted as an asset; if that financing were undertaken, and retail price-cost margins again were positive, the utility could use the margin cash flow to repay the loans against the TRA after using that accumulation to run down the TCBA. The utility could forever repay borrowings against the TRA with an add-on to retail prices after the freeze was lifted. At least, that is what the providers of debt in the national capital markets assumed in order to rationalize their loans against the TRA.

DIVESTITURE OF GENERATION ASSETS

Under AB 1890 and the commission rules implementing restructuring, investor-owned utilities in California were mandated, if not required, to divest at least half of their thermal power–generating plants. The goal inherent in this reform initiative was to sell to independent generating companies, and to sell at prices that were at least equal to book value, so that there would be no stranded costs from those assets to drive up future electric prices. This goal was shared by the utilities, which sought to achieve full recovery of stranded costs before the end of the transition period, so as to lift the transition cap on retail prices and return to cost-of-service–based price regulation.

In October 1996, PG&E began the divestiture, according to plan, of approximately 50 percent of its fossil fuel generation assets. The following month it filed an application with CPUC for permission to sell the first four of these plants. In June 1997, it began the process required to complete the sale of its remaining fossil plants, other than the Humboldt Bay power plant (near Eureka, California). Half a year later, in January 1998, the fossil-fueled Humboldt Bay plant was also put up for sale, so that the process of selling the fossil plants was put in gear in fifteen months.

In September 1997 CPUC approved the sale of the first of these generation plants—the Morro Bay, Moss Landing, and Oakland facilities—and also specified that an auction was required for finding "fair market value" in the sale.[17] The auction was held shortly thereafter, with Duke Energy Power Services bidding the highest prices for all three facilities. On November 18, 1997, PG&E approved the sale of Morro Bay, Moss Landing, and Oakland to Duke for $501 million, considerably more than their total book value of $380 million (this *negative stranded cost,* of $120 million would be used to reduce the TCBA balance). The commission approved the final sales in December 1997, and drawdown of proceeds was completed by July 1998.

In March 1999, the utility offered for sale various other generating assets. The purchasers at auction were Southern Energy (Petrero and Delta), Calpine Company, and Geysers Power Company. The purchase prices in these transactions were again greater than book values, so once again there were reductions in stranded costs in the TCBA accounts. These transactions had all been approved in October 1998, leaving PG&E with ownership of only the two Diablo Canyon nuclear plants and its various hydroelectric facilities.[18] Table 10 summarizes the results of the divestitures, indicating that the dollar amounts from the sales of the fossil plants in both 1998 and 1999 were well in excess of book

Table 10. Divestiture of utility generation assets

Generation asset	Capacity (mW)	Year	Market value (millions)	Book value (millions)
(1) Fossil plants	2,645	1998	$501	$346
(2) Fossil plants	3,065	1999	$801	$256
(3) Geothermal generation facilities	1,224	1999	$213	$244

Source: Pacific Gas and Electric Corporation, *1999 Annual Report.*

values and provided PG&E with roughly $700 million to apply to TCBA account (stranded-cost) recovery.

As a final step in divestiture, PG&E management expected to complete the disposition of the hydroelectric assets by the end of 1999. In September 1999, the utility filed an application with CPUC proposing an auction design similar to that used in the sale of fossil and geothermal plants for making "fair value" on the disposed assets. In response, two separate CPUC regulatory proceedings were scheduled; the first called for an environmental impact report to be completed by November 2000, and the second considered PG&E's auction proposal or some alternative disposition process. The ruling anticipated that a final CPUC decision regarding these conditions would be issued by May 2001.

In October 1999, CPUC confirmed that "[t]he end of the rate freeze occurs on the date the Utility has recovered 'commission-authorized costs for Utility generation-related assets and obligations'" and that "[t]his is the sole criterion for determining the end of the rate freeze."[19] CPUC further stated, "[a]ccordingly, we find that interim or final market valuations [of remaining hydro generation assets], to the extent they remain the Commission's responsibility, will precede the end of the rate freeze."[20] Since PG&E would already have taken down all stranded costs before the approval of the sales plan for the hydro facilities, and thus did not have to complete these sales to complete the freeze period, this position of CPUC specifically delayed the end of the freeze. In February 2000, the commission ordered the utility to estimate the market value of hydro assets and credit it against stranded costs by June 23, 2000, an exercise, in effect, that constituted PG&E self-purchase of the hydro facilities. In August 2000 PG&E completed that valuation, which estimated that there was an excess of market value over book value. The value of the hydroelectric facilities, at $2.8 billion, was greater than their $0.7 billion book value, an amount that would enable PG&E to state that it had recovered stranded costs. The commission did not act on this finding, when its acknowledgment would have triggered the end of the transition to PG&E as an independent retail distributor and the end of the freeze on its retail prices.

MANAGEMENT OF CASH

In this process of asset disposition PG&E's board of directors made key decisions with regard to the uses of the cash and liquid assets that followed. Restructuring was supposed to offer a more narrowly defined set of services—in particular, the utility's exit from generation reduced its demand for cash in operations. The traditional response was to be made as if fully regulated. In the interests of shareholders, cash generated from the sale of plant assets was to be returned to the parent holding company for investing in other business lines or for increasing dividends to shareholders. Whether these were the shareholders' best investment opportunities was not so much the issue, however; after the fact the new CPUC position was that the newly acquired billions of dollars in liquid assets should have been banked to be used later to buy power during wholesale market price spikes.

CPUC RESPONSE TO PG&E BALANCING
ACCOUNTS

The commission made case rulings regarding the TRA and TCBA accounts to keep in place a process of recovery of excess costs incurred in transition. In addition to approving what was to be included and reports of account balances, CPUC held annual proceedings to review the present and future status of these accounts.[21] An October 2000 decision on PG&E's application to issue short-term debt against the TRA stated: "This shortfall in revenues is recorded as an undercollection in PG&E's Transition Revenue Account (TRA) to be financed by a debt issue."[22] A December 2000 decision authorizing a large long-term debt issue explicitly limited the use of the funds to finance recovery of high wholesale power costs in the TRA. As the commission explained: "we grant PG&E's request for authority to issue $2 billion in long-term debt for the purpose of financing its TRA undercollection. PG&E's authority to issue long-term debt to finance its TRA undercollection shall expire six months after the undercollection is paid off."[23] The debt as authorized would extend as long as ten years, well beyond the end of the transition cost recovery period, and it would be discharged by increased sales revenues from future price increases to be confirmed by CPUC at some later date.

A December 2000 CPUC decision made a distinction between borrowed funds backed by the RA and those for financing general operating accounts (with reference to California Public Utility Code Section 817). It authorized borrowing the full amount of the balancing account but restricted the uses to which the funds could be put. Specifically, the commission limited the amount borrowed to that for reducing the balancing account, denied the request for further authorization after the balance was covered, and required that $2 billion in long-term debt be extinguished within six months of the time the account was paid off. However, the authorization did increase borrowing for general operating purposes to $370 million, and it noted other sources of operating cash potentially available to the utility, including reissuing $300 million of utility stock that had been repurchased in 2000 and reissuing $287 million of long-term debt, which would come due in 2001.[24] While these were specific limitations on borrowing to cover general operating expenses, the funds for financing the balancing account were approved in full. However, they were insignificant compared with the large account balance that at that time was being accumulated to pay for wholesale power.

Under generally accepted accounting principles for utilities, balancing accounts were "regulatory assets," or treated as a deferred expense if "probable of recovery." The utility was required by the Financial Accounting Standards Board Statement of Financial Accounting Standards (SFAS) to write off these accounts if assessments of recoverability were to change, that is, if a balance were no longer considered probable of recovery.[25] PG&E noted in its annual reports that the utility made an assessment of recovery on a regular basis, with the knowledge of CPUC. The wholesale power price spikes of the summer and fall of 2000 resulted in close to $7 billion of PG&E wholesale power purchase costs not passed on in final retail sales prices. The $7 billion was subject to "asset" creation, which by late 2000 and early 2001 was written off when borrowings could not be set against them. As PG&E stated in its *2000 Annual Report:*

> The energy crisis has materially and adversely affected the Utility's cash flow and liquidity and has created substantial uncertainty about their prospects for the future. As a result, the Utility can no longer conclude that energy costs, which had been deferred on its balance sheet in accordance with SFAS No. 71, are probable of recovery through future rates. Accordingly, the Utility has taken a charge against earnings of $6.9 billion ($4.1 billion after tax) to write off its remaining generation-related regulatory assets and undercollection purchased power costs. This charge has resulted in an accumulated deficit at the Utility of $2.0 billion as of December 31, 2000. PG&E Corporation's accumulated deficit at December 31, 2000 is $2.1 billion.[26]

Further, the utility did not have authority to recover any excess purchased power costs it had incurred during 2001 Such amounts had to be charged against earnings, as incurred, absent a regulatory or legislative solution that provided specifically for that recovery.

This write-off was the first of many actions that made the financial community aware of an emerging risk of insolvency. The next were, first, an appeal to FERC to cap wholesale power prices in the California PX; second, initiating in the California legislature a "rate stabilization plan" of the same kind as the proposed FERC cap; and third, requesting again that CPUC authorize the use of bilateral contracts for purchasing power outside the PX spot market. These initiatives were all undertaken in the expectation that the unwritten rule of regulation was that the utility still had the opportunity to earn a return on invested capital. PG&E management and the board of directors continued to proceed as if future recovery of past excess wholesale power costs would take place after the freeze was lifted and the company would still be able to borrow to purchase more wholesale power at spike prices during the freeze period on the implicit promise of that recovery later.

FINANCING OF RATE REDUCTION BONDS

AB 1890 had required as the first step in restructuring that PG&E make a one-time reduction in prices, the revenue loss from which was to be recovered immediately from one or more issues of rate reduction bonds to be issued by the California Infrastructure and Economic Development Bank. The revenues produced by the bonds were to make up for a 10 percent reduction in the utility's residential and small business electricity rates through the rate freeze period. On September 3, 1997, CPUC also granted authority to PG&E and other California investor-owned utilities to finance transition costs associated with restructuring through such bonds. From the utilities' perspective, the revenues for recovery of transition costs would be cash in hand, and the bonds would be paid off over time with revenues from a rate increase later. The rate reduction bonds were the political means by which to substitute a near-term price reduction not justified by cost reductions but associated with restructuring for a later price increase (that later price increase greater than the present price reduction by the interest costs of debt).

DECLARATION OF UTILITY DIVIDENDS

On the basis of then-current abnormally large cash flow from asset sales and debt issues, the utility paid the parent company dividends on its holdings in the utility from 1997 almost to the end of 2000.[27] Given the divestiture requirements from restructuring, the utility sold generation assets and passed to the parent cash from these sales. Table 11 summarizes the history (from January 1997 to early 2001) of dividends declared by the utility and paid to the corporation (that is, to the holding company owning the utility shares). In 1997, the dividends of the utility equaled $739 million and thereafter varied between $440 million and $475 million in the following three years. In July 2000, the utility authorized a special dividend of $125 million to be paid to the corporation for the third quarter of 2000, and declared it in September 2000. As of the date of authorization, the utility was still in compliance with the condition that it have "sufficient" equity as defined by the commission's specified capital structure for the company, but in January 2001 it ceased payment of preferred stock dividends in light of its accelerating liquidity crisis. Thus, November 2000 was the last date before bankruptcy in which the utility paid a quarterly dividend.

Throughout the last half of 1999, the utility purchased its common stock from the holding company for an aggregate amount of $926 million and in April 2000 purchased additional shares for $275 million. These purchases were undertaken to maintain the utility's required capital structure, as were repurchases in 1997 and 1998.[28] That is, CPUC established a maximum debt-equity ratio for California utilities, and as PG&E's assets were reduced and its long-term debt redeemed, there had to be a reduction in equity as well. But regulatory requirements aside, these actions were steps in the implementation of corporate strategy. Reducing debt and equity to reflect the sale of assets had the

Table 11. Annual dividends paid by PG&E Utility to PG&E Corporation

Year	Dividends paid (millions)
1997	$739
1998	$444
1999	$440
2000	$475

Source: Pacific Gas and Electric (PG&E) Corporation, *2000 Annual Report* (April 9, 2001), p. 40; PG&E Corporation, *1999 Annual Report* (March 3, 2000), p. 34.

Table 12. PG&E utility income statement (in $ millions)

Line no.	Category	Year ended Dec. 31			
		1997	1998	1999	2000
1	*Operating revenues*				
2	Electric	7,691	7,191	7,232	6,854
3	Gas	1,804	1,733	1,996	2,783
4	**Total operating revenues**	9,495	8,924	9,228	9,637
5	*Operating expenses*				
6	Cost of electric energy	2,501	2,321	2,411	6,741
7	Deferred electric procurement cost	—	—	—	(6,465)
8	Cost of gas	707	621	738	1,425
9	Operating maintenance	2,719	2,668	2,522	2,687
10	Depreciation, amortization, and decommissioning	1,748	1,438	1,564	3,511
11	Provision for loss on generation-related regulatory assets and undercollected purchased power costs	—	—	—	6,939
12	**Total operating expenses**	7,675	7,048	7,235	14,838
13	*Operating income (loss)*	1,820	1,876	1,993	(5,201)
14	Interest income	—	96	45	186
15	Interest expense	(570)	(621)	(593)	(619)
16	Other income (expense), net	127	7	(9)	(3)
17	Income (loss) before income taxes	1,377	1,358	1,436	(5,637)
18	Income tax provision (benefit)	609	629	648	(2,154)
19	**Net income (loss)**	768	729	788	(3,483)

Source: Pacific Gas and Electric Corporation, annual reports and 10K statements.

potential to reduce authorized "costs of service" and increase headroom, depending on the costs of newly purchased power, hastening the recovery of transition costs and the end of the rate freeze period.

The utility's net income and cash flow positions improved slightly over the years 1997 to 1999. During each of these first three years of restructuring, when wholesale power market prices were low enough to result in significant headroom, net operating income (sales revenues minus operating expenses) exceeded $1.8 billion annually (see Table 12). Estimated headroom, however, equal to operating income minus interest expense, depreciation, allowed equity return, and income tax, was $2.3 billion annually, or 30 percent of revenues. But in 2000, headroom turned negative, as the purchase cost of electric energy increased from its prior year of $2.4 billion to approximately $6.7 billion, creating a headroom loss in excess of $4 billion.

The cash flows in 2000 indicate the effects of the wholesale power price spike. During 1998 to 1999, the utility proceeds from rate reduction bonds and the sale of its generating assets provided immediate cash to retire long-term debt, purchase stock, and pay dividends, all in accord with the two-part strategy. These steps together yielded in the end a small net change in cash and cash equivalents. But the increase in wholesale power costs that occurred in the last half of 2000 drained the utility's cash, so the total declined from $2.2 billion in 1999 to $−699$ million in 2000. At that point, cash needed to maintain operations was generated from borrowing from short-term credit facilities and issuing long-term debt, with $2.63 billion coming from credit facilities and $680 million from new long-term debt.

STRATEGIC RESPONSE TO SPIKES
IN WHOLESALE POWER PRICES

From the opening of power markets in April 1998 through the end of that year, the California PX quoted day-ahead market clearing wholesale prices in the range of $12.5 to $44.5 per megawatt hour (see Figure 18). This range corresponded to power costs of 1.25 to 4.45 cents per kilowatt hour, to result in utility price-cost margins of 4.1 to 0.9 cents per kilowatt hour before accounting for network operating costs. For most of this period, positive headroom (after operating costs) allowed limited amounts to be posted into the TCBA, reducing the total required for the recovery of stranded costs, but not by the reductions realized from the sale of assets. Throughout 1997 and 1998, given the combination of sources, PG&E was reducing stranded cost at a rate that would cause the transition period to be complete by the end of 2000.

The goal was to shorten the transition period. Persuading CPUC to accept its valuation of the hydroelectric facilities of $1.8 billion, whether it sold or kept those facilities, would have allowed PG&E to announce that it had successfully reached the end of transition in the fall of 2000, before the price spike in the wholesale electricity market during January to March 2001. Then a return to cost-of-service prices would have resulted in pass through of the spike in the wholesale auction prices to consumers in higher retail prices.

PG&E had both CPUC declarations of intent and a positive market for the hydroelectric facilities in its favor. However, the necessary steps to sale or self-purchase were foreclosed by CPUC in the summer of 2000. Starting in August

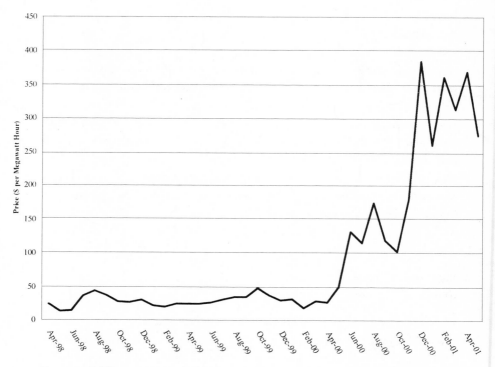

Figure 18. California power exchange day-ahead prices (April 1998 to May 2001) (*Source:* California PX, 1998–2001.)

and continuing to May of 2001, PX prices were outside the range for producing positive headroom. Figure 18 indicates average prices of wholesale power purchased on a day-ahead basis in the PX during that period.[29] The first spike in prices occurred in June 2000, with the average wholesale price for that month increasing to approximately $125 per megawatt hour.[30] An increase was hardly unanticipated, since prices rose as demand increased during the hottest months, but the increase this time was not expected to result in negative headroom and was expected to disappear when the weather cooled.[31] But the PX day-ahead prices stayed high over the course of the fall, at approximately $100 per megawatt hour, and increased to levels in the range of $200 per megawatt hour in November. As Figure 18 shows, prices then rose to $300 per megawatt hour in December, after CAISO, which had the power to set PX price limits, increased its provisional wholesale price cap from $250 to $750 per megawatt hour in an effort to stimulate market supply.[32]

In retrospect, power prices in 2000 were orders of magnitude higher than the CEC had predicted in 1999. The CEC had forecast an average market-clearing wholesale price of $26.50 per megawatt hour; but there was no month after June of the following year in which the average price was less than $100 per megawatt hour. PG&E booked its payments for the excess of these power costs over the frozen retail prices in reserve accounts, to be paid off after stranded costs in 2001 or later.

Wholesale prices spiked once again in November 2000, to approximately $185 per megawatt hour, and in December to $385 per megawatt hour. Before these prices, seven times the forecast level, the utility indicated that the higher prices had not affected its basic financial accounts.

But operating performance was on the decline, given that the retail network was under stress created by operations at or above capacity. By May 2000, CAISO had declared the first of thirty-six "Stage Two" alerts issued during that year, as reserve capacity fell below 5 percent.[33] Demand increases were partly the cause. Unusually warm weather in California during the middle of the year, with temperatures in May and June among the fifteen hottest months of the previous one hundred years, had caused demands for air conditioning and cooling to rise sharply.[34] On June 14, the system was at a demand peak for the year 2000 as the temperature in San Francisco reached 103 degrees. But also PG&E's distribution system went down at various points with supply (voltage) reductions at various nodes in the grid that required it to shed load, cutting off 100,000 customers (the first curtailed service by load shedding).[35] And later that week, rolling blackouts affected another 100,000 customers in the San Francisco Bay Area as a number of northern California generation plants shut down.[36] Demands were increasing beyond forecast levels, and generation supply and distribution capacity were falling short.

Regardless of its practice of placing excess payments for power in deferred asset accounts, PG&E was beginning to be affected financially by the negative cash flow from buying high in the spot wholesale power market and selling low in retail. For the period May through December 2000, wholesale prices for electricity exceeded the $54 per megawatt hour limit on frozen retail prices. The differences between retail and acquisition prices went from positive to negative in May and stayed negative to December 2000. By the end of the first month of the period, the total costs exceeded total revenues in the utility's income accounting. This condition required that reserves of cash and liquid asset holdings had to be called to add to net negative cash from operations.[37]

At the end of June the CAISO's response to the increase in wholesale power prices was to lower a self-imposed wholesale price limit—what it would accept—from $750 to $500 per megawatt hour.[38] As discussed above, in October 1999 it set this higher limit in an effort to elicit more electricity supply, hoping to match excess demand with additions to supply. Given no such response, the $500 new limit was to cut off a spike. A little more than a month later, on August 1, CAISO lowered this price to $250 per megawatt hour.[39]

The company response was to pay whatever was the daily price in the auctions, and post the excess payments to create an asset and borrow against it. The excess power payments increased the TRA balance from close to zero in May to approximately $2.5 billion by August. By September, increases in prices had taken the TRA account to approximately $6 billion. The utility held to its position that this and any further TRA balances would be recovered in higher prices after the end of the retail freeze. This was integral to the "rate-stabilization" plan it proposed at that time, which again called for borrowing in the capital market to finance the excess price in purchased power. The company and regulatory agency had to agree that amounts in these accounts would be recovered with interest in future higher retail prices in order for the TRA account to continue as collateral.

And this plan had credibility. The utilities and other market participants at that time still believed the spike was a limited and mostly seasonal phenomenon. This position was supported by prices in forward three-month contracts traded on the New York mercantile exchange (NYMEX) which throughout 2000 had prices at the end of the year in the PX market below spike levels. The NYMEX contract prices three months out had prices per megawatt hour ranging from the low $20s to the mid-$40s over the next year. Even during the rapid escalation of auction prices in the third quarter of 2000, NYMEX futures continued to show substantial declines in price after the end of 2000.

At the end of the third quarter of 2000, PG&E announced debt issues to cover undercollections of wholesale prices in its power purchases and sales. CPUC authorization was required. The company in September 2000 submitted an application to issue short-term debt of $1.4 billion.[40] As wholesale prices took a second large step upward in October, PG&E was close to exhausting its cash and other liquid reserves; in an emergency motion the company requested that CPUC accelerate approval of its earlier application and decide by the following week, with the obvious implication being that otherwise the company would be foreclosed from buying power in the PX market.[41] On October 19, the commission authorized PG&E to issue the $1.4 billion of short-term debt "for the purpose of financing the purchase of wholesale electricity to its retail customers."[42] But the day before this decision, on October 18, PG&E petitioned for authority for an additional debt issue of $2 billion with a maturity period of more than twelve months, again "to finance a large undercollection in PG&E's TRA."[43] This time, the company took the position that it would be prudent to finance a portion of the TRA using long-term debt since "the sheer size of the undercollection makes it difficult for PG&E to obtain sufficient short-term debt to finance at a reasonable cost" and since "the use of long-term debt acts as a hedge against the risks inherent in the short-term credit market."[44] On December 21, CPUC in response authorized an additional $2 billion in long-term debt until "six months after the undercollection in PG&E's TRA is paid off."[45] The commission noted that PG&E had "demonstrated a reasonable need to issue long-term debt to finance the large and growing undercollection in its TRA" and that "because of the sheer size of the undercollection," it could not charge PG&E's TRA undercollection "to operating expenses or income at this time."[46]

Even so, in December the utility began to take the position that, despite currently financing the power cost undercollections through increased debt, it had to pass these costs through to consumers. The commission had shown no willingness to allow PG&E to recover higher wholesale power prices by increasing retail prices, that is, by releasing the cap on retail prices. Yet short-term debt had to be repaid, and positive cash flow was required to do so, and failing to start repayment in 2001 would foreclose the utility's ability to borrow further.

Eight days after it received the long-term debt approval from CPUC, the utility found it necessary to file petitions to extend both the October short-term debt order and the December long-term debt order for authority to issue an additional $8 billion in debt to finance further undercollection of wholesale power costs.[47] Then in January 2001, while awaiting a response, the utility defaulted on a current short-term debt repayment. Its credit rating was downgraded to below investment grade.[48]

PG&E utility no longer met the credit requirements not only of Wall Street, but of the wholesale power auction market. The retail distributor at PG&E could no longer make spot market purchases of power.

Credit crises spilled over to the utility's gas business as well. Gas suppliers to PG&E's retail gas distribution services throughout northern California were no longer willing to sell for credit, and the utility was close to exhausting storage gas in meeting current demands of end-use customers.[49] The utility informed CPUC that its major suppliers would provide gas only if it pledged its customer accounts receivables to secure payment. It sought permission to pledge both accounts receivables and inventories "for the purpose of procuring gas supplies for its core customers, including storage gas."[50] The authorization was granted for a period of no more than ninety days, as the commission believed that legislation "recently introduced in the State Assembly"—bill ABX118—"would relieve PG&E from much of its financial distress caused by the wholesale electricity purchase price escalation."[51]

These gas supply regulatory decisions were clearly designed to forestall a cash crisis at PG&E from the wholesale price spikes. That is, regulators' responses sought "to avoid the possibility of PG&E being unable to fund its ongoing operations"[52]—but they also were attempts to preserve the status quo in price control at retail.

PG&E went further to contest the continuation of the power price freeze at retail. In November 2000 it filed post-freeze tariffs in an emergency application to increase retail prices to levels commensurate with increases in wholesale power purchase prices.[53] This filing was never approved, and CPUC dealt with other initiatives seeking immediate price cap relief that centered on an October petition of PG&E and Southern California Edison for expedited recovery of $4 billion in deferred purchase power costs.[54] CPUC rejected the petition, and PG&E immediately brought suit against the commission in the state courts seeking to eliminate the CPUC rate freeze justified by its having completed the transition period.

Under the November filing of proposed post-freeze tariffs, transition caps would be set at the level of 6.5 cents per kilowatt hour. This initial cap would have increased retail electric rates an average of 22.4 percent, effective January 1, 2001. The filing also sought renewed assurances from CPUC that all wholesale power energy procurement costs in excess of retail revenues under the freeze would be recovered; that is, the TRA would be drawn down by future revenue generated by increased prices at retail. CPUC did not approve this filing but did authorize an increase in the capped price of 1 cent per kilowatt hour for ninety days, effective January 4, 2001.

By the end of 2000, excess wholesale power costs had added approximately $6.6 billion to the TRA, against which the utility had borrowed $3 billion under its various credit facilities to pay out part of the wholesale purchase accounts. But borrowing further on the TRA as an asset based on a CPUC promise to allow post-freeze price increases had severe credibility limits, as indicated by the January 2001 reduction in bond ratings to below investment grade, precluding further access to borrowings in the national capital markets. The utility then had to default on payouts to maturing commercial paper, and it could no longer pay invoices for wholesale power purchases made a month earlier. Requests for immediate price increases at retail caused CPUC (on March 27, 2001) to allow an addition to retail prices of 3 cents per kilowatt hour, to be collected after May 2001.

On April 6, 2001, the utility was out of cash, and of methods to raise cash, and sought protection from its creditors in Chapter 11 bankruptcy.

To the end, PG&E took the position that the regulatory process to implement AB 1890 required the regulator to approve pass through of wholesale price increases in retail prices, if not in the period incurred, then in drawdown of the TRA account at some later date. CPUC's response was to maintain the price freeze at retail, as the foundation of the commitment to consumers in the act. The commitment to recover the TRA went only as far as its series of approvals for PG&E to borrow, never to stating that regulatory actions would support repayment, that is, until it allowed price increases defying the freeze at the end, too late.

Does this experience indicate a generic pattern in partial deregulation? CPUC supported the development of an auction market for wholesale power, without controls on auction prices, while it maintained to the end a freeze in retail prices. Any deviation from plan, such as from wholesale prices higher than retail prices, that would lead to reduced headroom would be dealt with in reserve accounts. But then to reduce these accounts later by allowing higher retail prices was a separate regulatory decision that might recover $2 billion but quite likely would not recover $8 billion.

In its response to AB 1890, PG&E developed a two-part strategy, to exit the supply side of auction markets at wholesale but to compete in the retail market in its service region after the price freeze. This guiding corporate strategy was consistent with, even required by, the deregulatory initiative established by the California legislature and CPUC. The legislation and its implementation by the commission required the utility to divest its power generation plants, purchase all power at wholesale prices, and sell that power at retail prices that were frozen until the recovery of all booked plant costs not realized in plant sales. PG&E was achieving these goals on schedule until 2000. During that last year, however, this exit from regulated prices was aborted by the utility's complete cash outage, which resulted from purchasing wholesale power at prices in the auction market that were orders of magnitude higher than the CPUC frozen retail prices. These purchases were contrary to its strategy.

How should PG&E have responded? A competitive enterprise, for example in the soft goods industries, would, if prevented from raising prices, have ceased production and sales. But the CPUC regulatory process provided and indeed required a different answer. The utility could not increase retail prices, and could not cease providing power on demand, given its franchise requirement to act in the public interest. It could, however, bank the wholesale-retail price difference for recovery in some future time period, when CPUC would allow retail prices to include the difference as a cost of service. If revenues from frozen rates were insufficient to cover current authorized costs, a negative balance in a regulatory TRA would be an asset to be borrowed against and repaid at some later date when revenues again exceeded operating costs plus power costs. The utility could turn to the capital market for loans against this account. The commission approved of PG&E requests for additional debt for this purpose during the period of escalating spikes in wholesale prices and as such demonstrated the regulatory commitment to the unique regulatory entity of deferred price collection.

A second response to the question as to what PG&E should have done was provided by its response to the CPUC treatment of the freeze under pressure of the wholesale price spikes. Given CPUC terms for ending the transition, the utility tried to execute plans to accelerate the process of ending the freeze by divesting generating facilities rapidly and at prices above book value, thereby eliminating stranded costs that when taken to zero determined the end of the freeze. Given PG&E's success in this process, the transition period should have ended before the price spike in wholesale electricity during the winter of 2000–01. Its accelerated—and successful—efforts to complete the sale of hydroelectric assets should have prompted the end of the transition, so that then the return of cost-of-service retail price regulation would have allowed the pass through of the wholesale power price spikes to consumers. The subsequent massive cash flow deficits never would have occurred. By delaying and rejecting the required hydro facility valuation estimates, CPUC with deliberation prevented this from taking place. PG&E did not adjust its strategy in recognition that this delay and obstruction was rank opportunism on the part of CPUC to force PG&E out of operation. The company's flaw may be that it did not believe that CPUC would default on the implementation of AB 1890 and instead give the retail price freeze a life of its own.

Throughout the second half of 2000 and into 2001, faced with wholesale power prices far in excess of its retail prices, the utility denied its *competitive* strategy, making adjustments to deal with rapidly accumulating cash flow losses. PG&E used all its options for financing the losses of cash, while *staying the course* in utility service at retail freeze prices. This program, what might be termed a nonadaptive strategy, confirmed the company's pre-determined requirement for providing service at retail under a regulatory franchise, even though regulation was in the process of grinding its financial assets into fine dust.

In all, PG&E undertook numerous efforts with regulators to find a solution to the cash crisis unfolding as a result of this brand of partial deregulation. At no time did the company slacken its reliance on the appeals process at CPUC to correct a large and increasing disparity between deregulated wholesale and regulated retail prices. It is difficult to conclude that it should have adhered to its part of the deregulatory process for as long as it did. The same can be said of the regulatory agency. Failure to end the transition period, allowance of the three-cent price premium too late, and prolonged support of the PX as the only source of wholesale power were CPUC positions that made for an accumulation of self-serving regulatory induced economic destruction.

Chapter 5 The Long Distance Telephone Networks and Partial Deregulation

In telecommunications the performance of the incumbent local exchange networks, each in its own franchise territory, along with less than a half-dozen long distance networks, has been dominated by FCC implementation of the Telecommunications Act of 1996. The act, in the tradition of network restructuring, called for the development of additional local exchange wireline networks, most likely to be realized by the entry of the current long distance carriers into markets closed to them by the 1984 antitrust divestiture of AT&T. Then restructuring would take the second step, with the incumbent local exchange networks expanding into long distance in their regions, to put in place connecting nodes so that more than a half-dozen unitary systems provided national all distance service. The goal of TA96 was to expand into a consolidated wireline services market by fostering redundancy in at least twelve wireline systems across the country. But this new structure was based on a quid pro quo. Entry of the regional local exchange companies, the RBOCs, into long distance could take place only after local exchange wireline markets were "competitive" in form and performance.

The opportunity was attractive and was acted on, as indicated by the resources that both local and long distance carriers put into achieving parts of that structure of new independent but interconnected systems in the past decade. The unitary local–long distance network was to provide "one-stop shopping" for telecom services, on one monthly bill, that was to unite for system subscribers the fragments of service resulting from divestiture. Simplification was considered to be a positive change in service by focus groups and in surveys of residential and business subscribers. But there were significant barriers to implementation in the process prescribed by TA96 as "pro-competitive," just as there were in those required by restructuring in gas and electric transmission.

The telecom network in its physical aspects had dimensions similar to those for gas and electric transmission, as well as substantial differences. Network capital outlays made up more than three-quarters of total costs over the lifetime of a telecom wireline facility. Outlays on information control, advertising, and customer services made up the larger part of variable costs. Marginal costs for energy and labor were only a small percentage of total costs. At local exchange service levels in urban and surrounding residential and small business markets, average variable and marginal costs for a network provider were declining over the range of relevant volumes of service provision. But in long distance networks, where links were many times wireless, marginal costs were constant over the range of volumes in services for large communities and manufacturing facilities. The scale of services in the three largest national long distance networks, which aggregated millions of messages per minute for national city pairs, was large enough to cause the average variable and marginal costs to converge to constant and low levels (a few cents per message minute). The capacity of long distance networks increased exponentially, as a result of digitalization and improvements in switching software, so that established carriers encountered constant or declining marginal costs at all volumetric rates of service. Still there were barriers to entry in replication of installed wireline systems, in links from the street to the household, in intercity networks.

The telecom networks faced regulatory barriers to entry as well as these limited technological barriers. A potential entrant in long distance, most likely an RBOC, with the goal of providing a one-stop local and long distance as a service package, had to establish that the three incumbent long distance carriers— AT&T, MCI, and Sprint—could enter its local exchange regional market to complete their offerings of packages as well.

Credit for the creation of barriers to entry goes to Sections 251 and 252 of

TA96, the "Development of Competitive Markets," as well as to Section 271, which specifies a "Competitive Checklist" for RBOCs to comply with before they could be certified in long distance service markets. Section 251 specifies requirements for interconnection, retail resale of traffic purchased from the incumbent by others at wholesale, number portability and dial parity, access to rights-of-way, and reciprocal compensation. This section specifies that incumbent and entrant have obligations to negotiate agreements on the use of existing networks. Incumbents should provide nondiscriminatory access to UNEs and offer wholesale services at prices that allow a retail entrant a margin on retail service prices. There was no dispute as to the implication of Section 251 for access offered to a competitive entrant into local exchange by the incumbent; as Robert Crandall and Jerry Hausman explain, "a competitor could lease everything from its incumbent rival, thereby obviating the need to invest in any network facilities whatsoever."[1] This section of TA96 sought to encourage rapid entry in the local market by relieving potential entrants from having to undertake capital outlays that might have constituted the barriers to entry.

Section 252 of the act outlined procedures for the negotiation, arbitration, and approval of agreements if and when they were made. Most significant was Section 252(d), which set pricing rules for interconnection and for the use of the incumbent's UNEs, to be based on cost and a "reasonable profit." These rules were to be guiding principles for the state regulatory agencies, which had jurisdiction to regulate local exchange wholesale (link and node) as well as retail rates.[2] The "Competitive Checklist" of Section 271 had the intent of assuring that local operating companies would install operating and support systems that would provide for the rapid and complete transfer of services from an incumbent to an entrant requesting such services.[3]

This was not, then, a process of creating open entry where there had been regulatory certification of a franchise holder in local exchange. Regulatory constraint was to be exercised on the pricing of UNEs that determined the ease of entry. Both sides of a lease contract for network elements would be affected by the level of the charge—a low charge would stimulate demand and reduce supply, and a high charge would reduce demand and increase supply. The FCC sought a methodology for determining "cost-of-service" pricing but did not succeed at the informal level for the first five years after TA96; it was not until 2002 that it took a position that a costing system based on hypothetical future expenditures using more efficient technologies was required. The resulting estimates of lease charges were less than the costs incurred by incumbent service providers when providing elements in their actual networks.[4] The position of the incumbent local exchange companies was that total element long-run incremental cost (TELRIC) was less than current operations average cost, the standard for cost of service, and if TELRIC were to be the determinant of prices, it would undermine current network operational services.[5]

THE INCENTIVES IN TA96 FOR COMPETITIVE STRATEGIES

In addition to meeting the conditions of the checklist, TA96 required that local exchange companies seeking entry into long distance take one of two alternative paths, commonly referred to as Track A and Track B. Track A, based on TA96 Section 271(c)(1)(A), stipulated that a local operating company could begin to provide in-region long distance service once that company had entered into binding agreements with a facilities-based long distance carrier to enter its local exchange market under the conditions of Section 252. Track B, based on Section 271(c)(1)(B), stipulated that if ten months passed after TA96 was enacted and no such new local service provider had requested interconnection or access, the potential incumbent local exchange entrant into long distance then had met the requirement for certification and could enter long distance service markets in its region.

These two different tracks created incentives for an incumbent long distance carrier to game the system, first by requesting interconnection within the first ten months, thereby eliminating Track B as an option, then by delaying its entry, to prevent the potential local exchange entrant from satisfying the conditions of Track A.[6] Tim Sloan argues that the FCC took steps in implementing Sections 251 and 252 to mitigate such behavior by requiring good faith negotiations if interconnection were requested, or reopening Track B if such negotiations did not occur in a timely manner. Sloan's discussion of the commission's approach to Section 271 can lead one to believe that the commission anticipated, and adequately addressed, such blocking actions. But a report by the Center for Regional Economic Issues (REI), under contract to SBC Ameritech, the largest of the RBOCs, indicates that litigation-initiated delays complicated any assessment that such a problem was resolved.[7] The REI report described the local/long distance markets as the setting for a game of "prisoners' dilemma," in which the players in both markets enjoy substantial rents from maintaining the status quo.

REI describes two scenarios, one in which one company enters the other's market without facing competition in its own market, and a second in which both enter the other's market, so that each faces competition in its own market from the Section 271 process. Of these scenarios, the best for the long distance service provider was to delay entry into the local market, thereby forestalling competition by the local exchange carrier in the long distance market. The way for long distance carriers to do so, if this game was in fact played out, was to appeal to the federal courts for the enforcement of the FCC-proposed plan for pricing of network local elements, which provided access at too low a set of prices and which was opposed by the local exchange providers of these elements; and in fact, litigation on TELRIC created years of delay in entry into the local market, entry that would have released local Bell companies from bondage to Sections 251 and 252 preventing their entry into long distance.

PRICING WITH PARTIAL DEREGULATION
IN LONG DISTANCE COMMUNICATIONS
MARKETS, 1990–2003

The incumbent long distance carriers were AT&T—an FCC-designated "dominant" firm, consisting of the former long distance division of the Bell System divested in the 1984 antitrust breakup—and two independent carriers, MCI and Sprint, both of which emerged after the antitrust breakup with national wireline networks and access to some if not all the local switches of the basic exchange operating companies. These three carriers made up most of the supply side of national long distance markets; that is, they had switches and nodes over which prices tended to equality and that overlapped regional systems of smaller carriers to make the markets national in scope.[8] As the FCC concluded in 1997, "in general, interstate long distance calling [is] a single national market unless there is credible evidence indicating that there is or could be a lack of [overlap] in a particular point-to-point market."[9] But the test for the existence of one market, that is, prices tended to be uniform for identical service, had been distorted because pricing at all points in a company tariff had to be the same, or uniformly different by a distance gradient as a regulatory requirement. Before July 2001, prices of long distance carriers were governed by tariffs filed with the FCC in which a carrier charged the same price to all its subscribers throughout the country for interstate calls of a given duration and time. The prices of AT&T, the dominant carrier, were determined by FCC-filed and -approved tariffs; before 1996 tariffs were subject to ceilings or caps set to decline at a fixed rate but adjusted for industry-wide expected productivity (downward) and inflation (upward). The FCC eliminated the caps in 1996 as it declared AT&T "nondominant" and dispensed with the filing of all interexchange tariffs of the three carriers in 2001. The unfiled tariff prices of AT&T, MCI, and Sprint after 2002 were communicated to consumers through web sites and mailings. But each carrier was still required to set its same price schedule for node-to-node service at the same distance and subscriber classification at all locations, as TA96 continued what the Communications Act of 1934 had required—"that a provider of interstate interexchange telecommunications services shall provide such services to its subscribers in each State at rates no higher than the rates charged to its subscribers in any other State."[10] Thus the geographic market for long distance telecom services has been national by decree.

With respect to specific services, the primary long distance offerings of the major interexchange carriers within the United States included the following in the 1990s and the early years of the 2000s:

• *Message toll service (MTS),* or switched long distance service, furnished to the general public, that requires local exchange origination and completion. MTS is priced on the basis of per-minute usage for individual calls and is referred to as "standard" service without formal individual contracts. Carriers also have made available "discount" MTS calling plans to which consumers subscribe by contract, with a monthly charge for access plus a price-per-minute usage.

• *Wide-area telecommunications service (WATS)* has been a generic class of network-provided toll services for voice and/or data transmission for business. Connections have been made using either switched or dedicated access, and price, based on bulk (rather than individual call) usage rates, is determined by geographical zone, time of day, and day of the week. WATS was differentiated by whether the service was outward or inward bound: *outbound WATS* offered business customers the opportunity to place long distance voice or data calls using either switched or dedicated access; *inbound WATS* had business customers receive and pay for incoming long distance voice or data calls using either switched or dedicated access on bulk billing plans. Inbound WATS included "800" number services in which firms pay for incoming calls that, from the perspective of the individuals originating the calls, were "toll-free."

• *Integrated services* were "combined services" of both inbound and outbound voice and data traffic to business customers using switched or dedicated access facilities.

The FCC defined two markets in which the three long distance carriers were primary suppliers: the *mass market,* for residential and small business customers, and the *large business market.*[11] In terms of carrier service offerings, the mass market consisted of standard and discount MTS and the large business market consisted of outbound and inbound WATS and Integrated services. Customers purchasing MTS were unlikely to switch to WATS or Integrated services, given that the volumes required to qualify would not be consistent with household or small office demands; similarly, customers that qualified for business service did not consider mass-market plans a substitute, given their volume limits.

After TA96 several specialized carriers established high-capacity networks across the country to provide facilities-based wholesale service, principally to the large business market. At the time of WorldCom's 1998 acquisition of MCI, those independents offering wholesale service of this type included Qwest, Excel, and Frontier, as well as numerous smaller providers offering limited service in a few states. Even the largest of these other carriers, however, did not have the capacity to offer the range of services of the three large national multi-service carriers. Consider, for example, the access to customers of AT&T, MCI World-Com, and Sprint versus that of Excel or Frontier. Customer awareness of AT&T was based on eighty years of the company advertising itself as the country's single supplier, while customer awareness of Frontier was limited to links and hubs in upstate New York, with the majority of subscribers in business markets and not having access to a national network except by switching from one of the three national carriers. Second-tier carriers tended to focus marketing efforts on specific regional targets, particularly large business customers through providing special services such as Internet and last-mile digital subscriber line services.[12]

In the two national markets, the three incumbent interexchange carriers over the past fifteen years underwent significant changes in relative position. At the time of the 1984 divestiture, AT&T had more than 90 percent while MCI and Sprint had 5 and 3 percent, respectively, of long distance revenues. (These were not exactly "market shares," because revenues were a mixture of national and regional market revenues.[13]) By 1990, as shown in Table 13, AT&T's share was 65 percent, a reduction of 25 percent; 15 percent of that had been gained by MCI and Sprint, with an additional 11 percent gain distributed among the independent wholesale service providers in regional markets. This redistribution of revenues largely resulted from FCC practices favoring the relative growth of MCI and Sprint.[14]

Table 13. Shares (%) of toll service revenues, 1990–2004

		Long distance carrier				
Year	HHI	AT&T	MCI WorldCom	Sprint	RBOC	Regional
1990	0.45	65.5	14.2	9.7	—	10.7
1992	0.41	57.7	15.6	9.1	—	17.6
1994	0.34	52.7	16.5	9.6	—	21.2
1996	0.28	44.5	18.5	9.0	—	28.0
1998	0.26	42.5	23.2	9.7	—	25.9
2000	0.19	37.0	21.9	8.8	1.1	28.1
2002	0.18	34.9	22.4	9.0	1.9	26.1
2004	0.15	30.7	21.6	8.5	2.4	28.7

Source: Federal Communications Commission (FCC), *Statistics of Communication Common Carriers* (annual editions), Table 1.4 (Washington, DC: U.S. GPO).

Note: Herfindahl-Hirschman index (HHI) is equal to the sum of squared shares, except "Regional," the sum of all specialized carrier shares not providing common carrier services on a national facility-based network. MCI WorldCom estimates combine separate MCI and WorldCom estimates for 1998–2004. RBOC equals the average of the shares of the regional Bell operating companies as a proxy for national share of one local exchange company.

By 1991 the shift of revenue share from the leading to the second- and third-place carrier was substantially complete. For the next six years (until World-Com acquired MCI), collective share growth by MCI was only four percentage points and by Sprint was zero to slightly negative. MCI's share then exhibited substantial growth to 23.2 percent as a result of its acquisition by WorldCom. Sprint's share of toll service revenues in the last half of the 1990s was essentially flat, fluctuating between 9.7 and 9.0 percent. The combined share of MCI WorldCom after the merger in 1998 declined from 23.2 percent to 21.6 percent by the beginning of 2004.

MCI and Sprint were not able to gain share at the expense of AT&T after 1996; instead, the gains against AT&T were by the independent regional carriers. Then, after 2000, the local exchange Bell companies, granted FCC authorization to enter these markets, were able to acquire up to 3.8 percent (Qwest) or 3.2 percent (Verizon) and across the four averaged gains of 2.4 percent. These shares on the whole indicate stability among the largest three carriers after 1990, and limited gains by a noncompetitive fringe, at least until the entry of the RBOCs.[15]

In a competitive market, share increases would result from price or product-quality strategies of carriers able to attain an advantage. The stability in the

1990s of MCI WorldCom and Sprint market shares suggests that MCI World-Com and Sprint made only a very limited effort to develop takeaway strategies vis-à-vis AT&T. Over the period 2000–04, AT&T gave up six percentage points of share of long distance toll revenues. Nevertheless, MCI WorldCom and Sprint claimed none of these percentage points of share as of the end of 2003. RBOCs, entering interexchange markets with new state-by-state approval granted under the TA96 procedures of Sections 251 and 252, each achieved on average less than 3 percent of toll revenues. At present, the three incumbent interexchange carriers control 60 percent, with the remainder going to a host of regional carriers and to new operating company entrants (that is, local Bell carriers, each with limited access or delivery scope within separate service territories, have taken a limited percentage of the national collective share). In the relevant national mass and business markets, the three carriers of national scope collectively have had all except the fringe business and have given up systematic share only marginally to new RBOC entrants.

The HHI values in Table 13 provide a summary measure of these trends in the restructuring process called for in TA96. HHI levels were around 0.45 (the equivalent of two equal-sized firms) and fell to 0.15 (six firms), but only as a result of counting the revenue shares of the fringe of specialized carriers as if they were side-by-side alternative carriers. This structure is "concentrated" when compared with those in other national service markets. As Paul Samuelson and William Nordhaus note: "In some industries, there are only a few firms. In others, there are many firms, but only a few dominate the market. Oligopoly is consistent with a large number of small sellers, called a 'competitive fringe,' as long as a 'big few' dominate the industry's production."[16] As shown in Table 13, for HHI, the long distance carriers exhibit the structural characteristics of an oligopoly dominated by three large sellers with a fringe of specialized, regional, and wholesale service carriers. The HHI estimates overstate the capacity of the fringe to offer substitute services to those three large national carriers. An oligopolistic market structure of three service suppliers determines the framework for analyzing the performance under partial deregulation as defined by TA96.

FIRM CONDUCT IN MASS AND BUSINESS
LONG DISTANCE SERVICE MARKETS

With annual declines in HHI, principally in the share of the largest service provider, it was expected that price-cost margins would decline, at least those of the three large incumbent service providers. But the price-cost margin, that is, the Lerner index, $[(p - mc) / p]$, adjusts to changes in three parameters, not only to HHI but market demand elasticity, e, and firm conduct, v, the coefficient of conjectural variation (that is, Lerner = HHI $[1 + v] / e)$, so lower HHI and v lead to lower values for the Lerner index. If conduct was becoming more disciplined (that is, if v was increasing) and demand was becoming more elastic over time, then the decline in price-cost margins should be less than that in concentration. The evidence from the 1990s through 2004 is mixed.

PRICE-COST MARGINS FROM TARIFF DATA

The three incumbent long distance carriers had submitted to the FCC tariffs setting out individual price schedules since the AT&T divestiture in 1984. After a long and tortuous history during which the FCC questioned the posting of tariffs as a pricing scheme incompatible with market competition to follow from deregulation, and had questioned whether collusion was more likely with posting, the carriers, in compliance with TA96, had to abandon posting. But they continued to issue tariff information on web sites and through other public outlets; in any event, subscribers to specific services were to determine what they would pay from referring to one of a number of price indexes for each period. Here we construct such an index by assuming a generic transaction, made up of calls conforming to the pattern in standard or discount mass-market transactions for MTS and business market offers by the three incumbent long distance carriers. The standard and discount plan tariffs filed with the FCC or posted by the companies that have been collected by telecom industry research groups then serve as the source for estimating that price index on a single call according to that generic calling pattern relevant in each plan.[17]

Table 14 presents the index price in dollars per minute for mass-market MTS to subscribers. With regard to the prices of AT&T, MCI, and Sprint, a characteristic pattern emerged over the period. MTS prices fell until 1995 and then stabilized to increase in 2000 to a level that exceeded the level initially available. Through the early period, prices of AT&T and Sprint were nearly identical, as Sprint tended to match changes in AT&T's price. During the first years of the new century, however, the Sprint price rose from $0.22 to $0.32 while AT&T's price stayed at $0.18 before rising to $0.24, short of Sprint's price by $0.08 per minute. This dispersion between AT&T and Sprint prices was not matched by MCI. AT&T and MCI prices became almost identical in the 2000–04 period. In all, until the turn of the century, AT&T was price leader, but since then it set

Table 14. Interstate standard message toll service price ($/min)

Period	AT&T	MCI	Sprint
Q1, 1990	0.1795	0.1742	0.1760
Q1, 1992	0.1748	0.1687	0.1748
Q1, 1994	0.1790	0.1785	0.1805
Q1, 1996	0.2008	0.2008	0.1970
Q1, 1998	0.1986	0.2211	0.2198
Q1, 2000	0.1861	0.2211	0.2198
Q1, 2002	0.2430	0.2475	0.2250
Q1, 2004	0.2430	0.2475	0.3250

Source: HTL Telemanagement, Inc.; Telecommunications Research and Action Center, *TeleTips* (various issues).

Note: Quoted prices are for the start of the stated period.

the price for MTS at levels that were followed by MCI (WorldCom), while Sprint went to levels one-third higher, most likely as a step toward leaving the MTS market, which it announced in 2005.

For the entire period from 1990 to 2004, not only did the three major long distance carriers offer standard or "no plan" service but also a series of discount plans in the mass market. Table 15 shows the price series for such plans of the incumbent interexchange carriers, from "best" available discount plans.[18] After an initial decline prior to 1990, best available discount prices remained steady

Table 15. Interstate discount message toll service price ($/min)

Period	AT&T	MCI	Sprint
Q1, 1990	0.1618	0.1600	0.1631
Q1, 1992	0.1575	0.1562	0.1490
Q1, 1994	0.1604	0.1374	0.1540
Q1, 1996	0.1506	0.1450	0.1576
Q1, 1998	0.1196	0.1198	0.1500
Q1, 2000	0.0936	0.0857	0.1196
Q1, 2002	0.0780	0.0539	0.0855
Q1, 2004	0.0780	0.0539	0.0855

Source: HTL Telemanagement, Inc.; Telecommunications Research and Action Center, *TeleTips* (various issues). See text for additional details regarding discount plans used to construct the price indices.

Note: Quoted prices are for the start of the stated period.

up to 1998.[19] The discount price level, approximately $0.12 per minute, was then subject to a substantial decline to $0.09 per minute at the end of the period. Both standard MTS and discount plan prices demonstrated more dispersion in these later years, as MCI quickly responded to changes by AT&T, with Sprint lagging behind. These reductions in prices could have been initiated in response to changing market structure as HHI declined or to more elastic demands due to the increased adoption of cell phone services. But our conclusion is that they have been driven by cost reductions and were not large enough to cause decreases in the Lerner index.

The costs of providing interexchange services consist almost entirely of access charges levied by local exchange carriers on the initiation and completion of calls when these calls are switched to the long distance networks. There were operating expenses for traffic on the long distance networks but at much lower levels than those access charges as they were set by state regulatory agencies as part of the tariff of the local carrier for services rendered to the long distance carrier.[20] Operating expenses did not exceed $0.01 per minute, and productivity increases likely resulted in halving that amount in the past five years; then the total traffic-sensitive charge per conversation minute borne by an interexchange carrier was fixed for the most part by the access charge.

Table 16 summarizes originating and terminating access charges to the long

Table 16. Interstate traffic-sensitive access charge (cents/min)

In effect		Per-minute switched access charge		Total charge per conversation minute
From	To	Originating	Terminating	
01/01/90	06/30/90	3.75	4.03	7.78
07/01/92	06/30/93	3.41	3.35	6.76
07/01/94	06/30/95	3.43	3.46	6.89
07/01/96	06/30/97	3.03	3.01	6.04
01/01/98	06/30/98	2.23	1.73	4.04
01/01/00	06/30/00	1.57	1.27	2.85
01/01/02	06/30/02	0.90	0.78	1.69
07/01/03	06/30/04	0.73	0.70	1.44

Source: Federal Communications Commission (FCC), Industry Analysis and Technology Division, "Trends in Telephone Service" (May 2004), pp. 1–6, Table 1.2 (citing local exchange carrier access tariff filings).

Note: This table estimates average (weighted by minutes of use) for local exchange carriers filing tariffs to state regulatory agencies and the FCC. They do not include subscriber line charges levied directly on consumers of basic exchange services.

distance carriers over 1990–2004. These charges were substantially and continually reduced, so by 2004 they were 18 percent of what they had been in 1990. Compared with the price series shown in the previous two tables, the local exchange access charges fell more, and more rapidly, than did prices charged by the large interexchange carriers for standard and discount MTS.

The three large carriers did not report operating expenses associated with interexchange networks, but one or the other disclosed them in regulatory proceedings. For outbound and inbound WATS, AT&T reported in 1990 long-run network operating costs of approximately $0.010 to $0.013 per minute.[21] These estimates were in the range reported in a 1996 study of Strategic Policy Research which concluded that AT&T's incremental network costs were from $0.0043 to $0.0129 per minute.[22] Wharton Econometric Forecasting Associates developed an estimate, equal to $0.01 per minute, consistent with AT&T's estimates.[23] On the basis of these estimates, the network operating expenses for major incumbent interexchange carriers are assumed to have been approximately $0.01 per conversation minute.[24]

Adding access charges to interexchange network operating costs results in estimates of per-minute operating costs for switched interstate MTS; since both elements of these costs are constant over the range of service volumes, they can serve as that for both marginal and average operating costs.[25] Subtracting these costs from the price series and dividing by the price series allows us to generate tariff-based estimates of the Lerner index. Tables 17 and 18 indicate that stan-

Table 17. The price-cost margin for standard message toll service, 1990–2004

Period	AT&T	MCI	Sprint
Q1, 1990	0.5109	0.4960	0.5011
Q1, 1992	0.5441	0.5276	0.5441
Q1, 1994	0.5721	0.5709	0.5756
Q1, 1996	0.6434	0.6434	0.6365
Q1, 1998	0.7457	0.7716	0.7702
Q1, 2000	0.7937	0.8263	0.8253
Q1, 2002	0.8897	0.8917	0.8809
Q1, 2004	0.8984	0.9002	0.9240

Sources: HTL Telemanagement, Inc.; Telecommunications Research and Action Center, *TeleTips* (various issues) (long distance service rate data); Federal Communications Commission (FCC), Industry Analysis and Technology Division, "Trends in Telephone Service" (May 2004), pp. 1–6, Table 1.2.

Note: Price-cost margins are for the start of the period.

Table 18. The price-cost margin for discount message toll
service, 1990–2004

Period	AT&T	MCI	Sprint
Q1, 1990	0.4573	0.4513	0.4617
Q1, 1992	0.4941	0.4896	0.4651
Q1, 1994	0.5223	0.4424	0.5028
Q1, 1996	0.5246	0.5062	0.5456
Q1, 1998	0.5779	0.5786	0.6633
Q1, 2000	0.5898	0.5518	0.6790
Q1, 2002	0.6564	0.5031	0.6866
Q1, 2004	0.6833	0.5420	0.7112

Sources: HTL Telemanagement, Inc.; Telecommunications Research and Action Center, *TeleTips* (various issues) (long distance service data); Federal Communications Commission (FCC), Industry Analysis and Technology Division, "Trends in Telephone Service" (May 2004), pp. 1–6, Table 1.2 (network access cost data).

Note: Quoted price-cost margins are for the start of the stated period.

dard plan Lerner margins were in the range of 50 percent in 1990–94 and rose in two steps, to 70 percent in 1994–98 and to 85 percent in 2000–04. Discount plan Lerner index values were at 45 percent in 1994, then went to 55 percent in 1998, and finally to 63 percent in 2004. MTS carrier margins were strikingly similar across carriers and, in the mid-to-late 1990s were nearly indistinguishable. Margins varied more among the three carriers with regard to the provision of discount MTS plans than with the MTS plans for residential consumers. But margins of the three large interexchange carriers' discount plans nevertheless increased from 45 percent to in the range of 65 percent from 1990 to 2004 in what passed as discount and/or "competitive" offerings.

For both sets of plans, the price-cost margins for the three large incumbent interexchange carriers increased at the same time that subscribers were shifting en masse from standard to discount plans. The high-margin standard plans were in effect abandoned. The increased margins in standard plans were designed to price those plans out of business. Indeed, at the end of this period both AT&T and Sprint announced that they were no longer offering standard plan services to new customers.[26]

An alternative perspective on long distance carriers' pricing strategies can be derived from the examination of average revenue per minute (ARPM) as an indicator of price level. As reported by the FCC, ARPM is derived from dividing total interstate switched service revenues by total interstate domestic conversa-

Table 19. Average revenue per minute for all switched toll services

Year	Interstate domestic switched revenues ($ millions)	Interstate domestic conversation minutes (millions)	Average revenue per minute ($/min)
1992	28,323	190,417	0.1487
1993	30,965	208,743	0.1483
1994	31,610	233,481	0.1354
1995	32,100	256,982	0.1249
1996	35,509	286,849	0.1238
1997	33,664	312,381	0.1078
1998	38,071	335,398	0.1135
1999	39,507	352,147	0.1122
2000	34,364	380,734	0.0903
2001	30,840	371,245	0.0831
2002	23,427	333,826	0.0702

Sources: Jim Lande and Kenneth Lynch, Federal Communications Commission (FCC), Industry Analysis and Technology Division, Wireline Competition Bureau, "Telecommunications Industry Revenues 2002" (March 2004), Table 9; FCC, "Universal Service Monitoring Report," CC Docket No. 98-202 (May 2004), Table 7.8.

tion minutes, including both residential and business interstate switched services minutes.[27] Although it is not an estimate of any one price year to year, ARPM does reflect changes in weights in the average for different services due to the shift of customers to the discount calling plans. The ARPM for long distance services, shown in Table 19 for all long distance carriers reporting to the FCC, fell steadily from 1992 through 1997, then stabilized from 1998 through 1999, before falling again in 2000 through 2002. The decline is consistent with sustained movement of customers from standard to discount MTS plans; for example, in 2002, the standard and discount MTS prices for the three major carriers (see Tables 14 and 15) were approximately $0.24 and $0.07 per minute, respectively, while the ARPM was approximately $0.07 per minute. The ARPM however, included substantial revenues derived from business services, which were priced less than mass-market services; also, ARPM included revenues from independent carriers that offer more limited regional discount plan services at prices lower than those of the three major carriers.

As with standard and discount MTS tariff-based price indexes, we can construct the price-cost margin using ARPM as an approximate Lerner index.[28] Again, the marginal costs to AT&T, MCI, and Sprint of providing interexchange service were estimated from the same network access charges levied by

Table 20. Average revenue per minute–cost margins for long distance carrier revenues

Year	Average revenue per minute (ARPM) ($/min)	Unit cost ($/min)	ARPM less unit cost ($/min)	ARPM-cost margin (%)
1992	0.1487	0.0787	0.0701	47.1
1993	0.1483	0.0771	0.0712	48.0
1994	0.1354	0.0778	0.0576	42.6
1995	0.1249	0.0753	0.0497	39.8
1996	0.1238	0.0710	0.0528	42.6
1997	0.1078	0.0661	0.0417	38.7
1998	0.1135	0.0493	0.0642	56.6
1999	0.1122	0.0427	0.0695	62.0
2000	0.0903	0.0338	0.0565	62.6
2001	0.0831	0.0281	0.0550	66.2
2002	0.0702	0.0258	0.0444	63.3

Sources: Federal Communications Commission (FCC), Industry Analysis and Technology Division, Wireline Competition Bureau, "Trends in Telephone Service" (May 2004), Table 1.2 (access charges); Jim Lande and Kenneth Lynch, FCC, Industry Analysis and Technology Division, Wireline Competition Bureau, "Telecommunications Industry Revenues 2002" (March 2004), Table 9; FCC, "Universal Service Monitoring Report," CC Docket No. 98-202 (May 2004), Table 7.8.

Note: Average revenue per minute (ARPM) from Table 19 above. In addition to originating and terminating access charges, operating costs of $0.01 per minute have been assumed (see text). ARPM-cost margin equals ARPM less access plus operating cost per message minute, divided by ARPM.

local exchange carriers and the same unit operating expenses as for the tariff-based price index. Table 20 shows yearly "ARPM-cost margin" values, obtained by subtracting per-minute costs from ARPM and dividing by ARPM. This Lerner index averaged 43.1 percent during the period 1992 through 1997, then increased substantially to 62 percent during the period 1998 though 2002.

As with the standard and discount tariff-based price-cost margins, the ARPM-cost margins increased over the period in which marginal costs and industry concentration were declining. In 1992, tariff-based and ARPM margins were roughly identical (comparing discount plan margins in Table 18 and ARPM margins in Table 20). By 1994, however, the ARPM margin was 42 percent while the three incumbent carrier margins were between 44 and 52 percent. In 1996, the ARPM margin was the same as in 1994 while the long distance carrier tariff margins had increased to between 50 and 54 percent. It was not until 1999–2000, when the ARPM margin had increased to 62 percent, that it was within the range of the tariff margins, from 55 to 68 percent. By 2002, ARPM margins had stabilized in that range. In all likelihood the shift of

Table 21. Earnings margins on revenues (%)

Company	1990	1992	1994	1996	1998	2000	2002
AT&T	4.8	5.8	6.3	10.7	9.8	7.0	2.3
MCI WorldCom	6.3	−0.02	−5.5	−48.8	−14.4	11.4	—
Sprint PCS	3.7	4.6	6.9	8.4	9.6	7.3	6.8
Average	4.9	3.4	2.6	−9.8	1.6	8.6	4.7

Source: Company annual reports, 1990–2002.

Note: Averages weighted by percentage of total revenues.

subscribers to discount plans was essentially complete, and the average price was then made up not of the usage weight of standard and discount plan charges but of those of discount plans alone.

Still another estimate of the Lerner price-cost margin can be constructed from the financial statements of the three large incumbent long distance carriers, using the same procedure for estimation as for the gas pipeline and electricity distributor margins. Revenues from sales of telecom services minus operating costs equal operating earnings from sales; this estimate divided by revenues constitutes an approximation to the price-cost margin. But in this industry, operating costs include outlays on marketing and customer services not found in power and gas transmission and are not strictly marginal costs. If all service costs are not excluded from the Lerner index, however, earnings over revenues, as shown in Table 21, are a lower bound for the index estimates.

For this period, margins were within the range of 0 percent to 10 percent, except for MCI WorldCom in 1996, just before the merger, when large write-offs of costs attributed to options were posted, and costs exceeded revenues by more than 40 percent. All these margins were low compared with those from tariff data and ARPM statistics; treating MCI as an outlier, price-cost margins doubled over the period 1996–2002. They are much lower than estimates from the same process for price-cost margins in gas network and power distribution companies. But they are biased downward because sales and distribution costs were incorrectly included as reported unit costs. For long distance carriers, Lerner margins, to be comparable to those of the other regulated network companies in the gas and electric industries, would have required marketing costs that were marginal with respect to message minutes, less than one-quarter of actual marketing and distribution outlays.

Then what was driving price-cost margins during this fifteen-year period? Considering all three sets of estimates of the Lerner index, but giving greater weight to those from tariffs for discount and business plans, Lerner margins were in the 40 percent range in the early 1990s and rose by at least 10 percent at the end of the decade. With carrier concentration, as measured by HHI, declining and demand elasticity increasing, then increasing Lerner index values are positive conjectural responses in new oligopoly initiatives.

Estimation of the conjectural variation coefficient requires not only estimates of values of the Lerner index and HHI, but also the elasticity of demand.[29] The research literature shows a range of elasticity values. As in Table 22, historical and econometric analyses from 1987 to 1990 generated e values from -0.36 to -0.75 for markets from short-haul Midwest to long-haul Canada. The most recent estimate for 1997 results in a conservative value of $e = -0.51$, based on data for MTS, and $e = -0.70$, which may better reflect the shift to discount plans by subscribers more sensitive to price.

The values of the conjectural variation coefficient from tariff-based Lerner

Table 22. Estimates of long distance service price elasticities

Author	Study	Own-price elasticity
Weisman (1990)	Southwestern Bell	-0.75
Appelbee et al. (1988)	Telephone Canada	-0.36 to -0.75
Gatto et al. (1988)	Developed by AT&T	-0.723
Train et al. (1987)	Intra-LATA, short haul	-0.47
Taylor and Taylor (1993)	U.S. Interstate Toll	-0.63
Taylor and Rappoport (1997)	U.S. Interstate Toll	-0.51 to -0.70
Zona and Jacob (1990)	United Telecom System	-0.41 to -0.70

Sources: Weisman, D. L., and D. J. Kridel. "Forecasting Competitive Entry." *International Journal of Forecasting* 6 (1990): 64–74.

Appelbee, T. W., N. A. Snihur, C. Dineen, D. Farns, and R. Giordano. "Point to Point Modeling: An Application to Canada–US Long Distance Calling." *Information Economics and Policy* 3, no. 4 (1988): 311–331.

Gatto, J. P., J. Langin-Hooper, P. B. Robinson, and H. Tryan. "Interstate Switched Access Demand." *Information Economics and Policy* 3, no. 4 (1988): 333–358.

Train, K. E., D. L. McFadden, and M. Ben-Akiva. "The Demand for Local Telephone Service: A Fully Discrete Model of Residential Calling Patterns and Service Charges." *Rand Journal of Economics* 18, no. 1 (1987): 109–123.

Taylor, W. E., and L. D. Taylor. "Post Divestiture Long Distance Competition in the United States." *American Economic Review* 83, no. 2 (1993): 185–190.

Taylor, L. D., and P. N. Rappoport. "Toll Price Elasticities from a Sample of 6500 Residential Telephone Bills. *Information Economics and Policy* 9, no. 1 (1997).

Zona, J. D., and R. Jacob. "The Total Bill Concept: Defining and Testing Alternative Views." Paper presented at the Bellcore Industry Forum on Telecommunications Demand Analysis, Hilton Head, SC, April 22–25, 1990. Cambridge, MA: National Economic Research Associates.

Table 23. Estimated conjectural variation coefficients for the three incumbent long distance service providers

Period	AT&T	MCI	Sprint
Q1, 1990	−0.65	0.59	1.37
Q1, 1992	−0.57	0.57	1.55
Q1, 1994	−0.51	0.34	1.62
Q1, 1996	−0.41	0.37	2.03
Q1, 1998	−0.32	0.13	2.41
Q1, 2000	−0.21	0.26	2.85
Q1, 2002	−0.06	0.12	2.81
Q1, 2004	0.11	0.25	3.18

Note: Given that the price-cost margin or Lerner index, L, equals [HHI ($1 + v$) / e], then v, the coefficient of conjectural variation, equals [Le / HHI − 1]. Each observation is for one year, with values of L (Lerner index), e (demand elasticity), and HHI (Herfindahl-Hirschman index) as shown in the text and designated tables.

margins (Tables 14 and 15), carrier revenue shares (Table 13), and demand elasticity at −0.51 are shown in Table 23 for mass-market discount plans. Lerner margins on discount plans for each of the three carriers each year for the fifteen years were low; given that demand elasticities were also low, the conjectural coefficients were in the negative-to-zero range for AT&T or the zero-to-positive range for MCI.

These values suggest that interactive pricing of AT&T and MCI was following a Cournot strategy or was on the boundary of Bertrand strategy.[30] AT&T had negative values of v from 1990 to 2002, starting at −0.65 in 1990 and increasing to −0.51 in 1994 and −0.32 in 1998. (Only in January 2004 did the value of v become positive at 0.11.) Negative conjectural variation indicates that the largest service carrier followed a Bertrand strategy. Prices were lower than those characterized as Cournot, or necessary to stabilize market shares across the three carriers. As AT&T attempted to hold share, MCI had a more cooperative strategy of matching share, as indicated by positive conjectural values. Sprint's values indicate extreme supportive responses to share and price leadership, with values from 1.37 to 3.18 over the fourteen years. When AT&T reduced prices on discount plans in its semiannual tariff announcements, the (Bertrand) initiative was followed later with positive, that is, affirmative, responses by the second and third carriers that prevented prices from falling further.[31]

Table 24. Estimated long distance conjectural variation coefficients for all long distance carriers based on average revenue per minute

Year	Lerner index	HHI	e	Conjectural variation coefficient
1992	0.471	0.41	−0.51	−0.415
1994	0.426	0.34	−0.51	−0.361
1996	0.426	0.28	−0.51	−0.224
1998	0.666	0.26	−0.51 (−0.71)	0.110 (0.154)
2000	0.626	0.19	−0.51 (−0.71)	0.680 (0.952)
2002	0.633	0.18	−0.51 (−0.71)	0.793 (1.110)

Note: Lerner index equals average revenue per minute (ARPM) less average access plus operating costs divided by average revenue per minute; Herfindahl-Hirschman index (HHI) from Table 13. Figures in parentheses are based on an assumed higher elasticity of demand in the last half of the period.

Because of the movement of subscribers out of standard plans to discount plans, and of larger business subscribers to tailored deep-discount contracts, these values of the coefficient of conjectural variation in the later years could be misleading indicators of the changing nature of the interactive behavior of the three. To gauge how much more weight should be given to discount plan pricing strategies and to Tariff 12 (tariffs individually written for large business clients), the conjectural variation can be estimated on the basis of ARPM-cost margins.

Table 24 provides a sample of conjectural variation estimates based on the Lerner index from ARPM; HHI for all carriers, not just the large three incumbents; and a market elasticity of demand that increases from −0.51 to −0.71 in the last half of the period. In the early to mid-1990s the conjectural variation coefficient was negative, as associated with Bertrand oligopoly. But in the later years of that decade, and in 2000 to 2002, the coefficient was positive and increasing, as associated with more collective price increasing strategy across carriers than implied by Bertrand behavior. The determinant of the shift of the conjectural variation coefficient from negative to positive in later years was increasing price-cost margins in both the mass and business markets.[32] The explanation for rising margins was most likely a move by the FCC to increase index values for the incumbent carriers, the gains from which were to advance congressional and regulatory social policies.

TELECOM MARKET CONDITIONS, 1998–2000

The end of the 1990s brought market conditions that made it increasingly diffi-cult for the incumbent long distance carriers. Information regarding prices of leader and follower carriers is critical to any strategy seeking to maintain shares, and that information had become less available following rejection by the FCC of further filings of long distance tariffs in 2001. The RBOCs started entering the long distance service markets after the FCC finally approved a Section 271 request for authority in New York State in 1999. Toll service revenues of the three large incumbent interexchange carriers had begun to decline as con-sumers shifted to wireless (cell phones) for long distance services. Last but not least, the end of a long business cycle expansion took place in late 2000 or early 2001. The incumbent interexchange carriers had to face entry and product sub-stitution challenges during a nationwide downturn in demand for telecom ser-vices.

But of all these factors, the greater challenge was the detariffing of interex-change service. Until 2001, the three interstate long distance carriers had set out new price schedules in tariffs filed with the FCC. Tariffs represented "legally binding contracts that outline[d] the rates, terms and conditions of long dis-tance companies' services" and were a guarantee to subscribers as to what they were to pay for service.[33] The three incumbent long distance carriers relied on the tariff to disclose proposed price schedules before they went into effect. By going to the filing, a carrier could determine the price for every variation in ser-vice of the other carriers. This was to establish close to perfect information about prices and as such it could to prevent "mistakes" in price matching that would cause breakouts of discounts that reduced price levels.

That is, the filed tariff process provided the three large carriers with a service by which to become informed so as to respond quickly—before tariffs went into effect—to one another's price movements. Early and effective matching maintained shares and thus Cournot price levels. The exception, however, in large business services was Tariff 12, a tailored offering to large business users not filed but negotiated privately, and it is in Tariff 12 services that prices fell to marginal cost levels in the use of excess fiber-optic capacity in the wired links.

From divestiture in 1984 until the late 1990s, AT&T's status of dominant carrier required the company to file tariffs, which it did first, with MCI and Sprint filing voluntarily after so that the FCC was the central clearinghouse on prices on all three national market incumbents. Any prices designed to increase share were known and matched, or would be complained about in FCC proceedings against the carrier that filed. And the FCC itself understood that while not collusive, tariff filing supported cooperation on price levels that would not have occurred in its absence. In pursuit of competition, inherent in TA96 "reform," the commission sought to deny filing to those that were voluntary, requiring only the dominant firm to continue. Before TA96, the FCC could not prohibit the filing of the voluntary tariffs by nondominant carriers. Efforts by the commission to do so had been challenged successfully in the federal courts by MCI on the basis that the then-prevailing Communications Act of 1934 required the FCC to review the tariff rates of all telecommunications carriers, whether dominant or not, for "reasonableness."

With TA96, however, the commission had the authority to forbear on accepting tariffs if in the "public interest." The FCC sought to apply this new discretion to the interexchange tariff-filing process, and in April of 2000, a federal appellate court confirmed the FCC's initiative to forbear.[34] Beginning in July 2001, interstate long distance carriers (including AT&T, since the FCC had declared it no longer to be a dominant carrier) no longer filed tariffs with the commission. This so-called detariffing process had the effect of making it more difficult for companies to interact to stabilize prices, just at the time when all three incumbents were to encounter the effect of entry into long distance by the RBOCs.

ENTRY OF REGIONAL BELL OPERATING COMPANIES

TA96 set out the conditions by which the RBOCs could offer in-region, long distance services in markets with the incumbent interexchange carriers. Authorization from the FCC had to be secured as well as from (and prior to) the state regulatory agencies.[35] For several years, this authorization process was not successful as the FCC rejected all petitions brought by the operating companies even after state agency approval had been won; it was not until December 1999, that Bell Atlantic (now Verizon) was successful in a Section 271 petition to offer long distance service across all parts of New York State. SBC then received authorization for service in Texas in June 2000, and a flood of successful petitions followed in the major states for Bell South and finally Qwest (as US West). By the close of 2003, the FCC had granted permission for the local Bell companies to enter long distance service in point-to-point markets between and in all forty-eight continental states and the District of Columbia. The four RBOCs with that authorization then began to provide in-region service for nearly 100 percent of long distance domestic service markets. This did not result in four new long distance carriers each covering the national mass and business markets, but instead, in four regional companies each in its own local exchange territories, so as to layer one loosely coupled new network on the three incumbents.[36] But the RBOCs had unused authority to enter long distance out of region as well; and the blueprints were in place for extension of one or more new carrier networks to offer one-stop service to the national mass market. This extension plan was put in effect in 2005–06 by means of RBOC plus long distance carrier mergers, in which two of the entering operating companies acquired national networks by taking over MCI and AT&T. There were still three, but perhaps four, national carriers in wireline mass and business markets by the end of 2006.

Given the history of long distance performance before 2000, one could expect that price reductions would result from this pattern of entry of subnational local exchange companies into these long distance service markets. The local carriers had facilities in place to deliver long distance services across calling areas in which they previously provided service. In effect, each Bell company formed a subnational long distance network, and by leasing national capacity from the fringe wholesalers, each had the potential to form a new national network. These carriers' brand names were familiar to mass-market subscribers, having long been associated with the provision of local service, at least in region. Nonetheless, establishing share on entry would take place at the expense of the incumbent long distance carriers at the long distance switch. To take share, the new carriers would have to adopt pricing strategies counter to those that had developed among AT&T, MCI, and Sprint. Given some entry price strategy, the incumbents' price-cost margins had to be lower.

These expected changes were to take place when two other changes of similar magnitude were in the offing. Table 25 shows these conceptual changes or challenges to received performance. The business downturn as it affected long

Table 25. Conceptual changes in price-cost margins

Market conditions	Change in price-cost margin
Detariffing of prices at the FCC	Negative
Downturn of market demand	Negative
Entry of Bell local exchange companies	Negative
Addition of USF charges to residential monthly bills for service	Positive

distance communications markets should have been reflected in reductions in demand for the full range of services, which had to have an adverse effect on prices and price-cost margins. Entry should have reduced price-cost margins; but the regulatory initiative to finance the Universal Service Fund (USF) should have increased price-cost margins.

THE BUSINESS CYCLE AND CHANGES IN
INTEREXCHANGE CARRIER PERFORMANCE

Telecommunications fared worse financially throughout the 1999–2001 general economic downturn than most of the rest of the economy. This was partially the result of having been the object of overly positive forecasts in the early 1990s of the growth of data communications and the use of the Internet, which led to a telecommunications stock price bubble that broke with the influx of realistic forecasts in the general downturn. Table 26 shows NASDAQ's North American Telecommunications stock price index relative to that of the S&P 500 and the Dow Jones Industrial Average over this eight-year period.[37] In these series, the daily adjusted closing prices have been converted to index numbers, with prices as of November 16, 1995, set equal to 100. The telecom stock price peaked in March 2000, when the daily adjusted closing value of the index was approximately 4.8 times its November 1995 level (that is, approximately 1,750 in nominal value). It declined sharply to a ten-year low in October 2002 at approximately 80 percent of its November 1995 level. This was more

Table 26. Relative performance of indices of common shares, 1996–2004

Period	North American Telecommunications index	S&P 500	Dow Jones Industrial Average
Q1, 1996	108.2	103.9	104.2
Q1, 1997	113.0	123.4	129.6
Q1, 1998	161.3	163.2	160.3
Q1, 1999	247.9	205.6	184.8
Q1, 2000	427.6	243.6	228.6
Q1, 2001	281.0	214.8	214.2
Q1, 2002	230.5	193.3	202.7
Q1, 2003	130.4	152.2	173.2
Q1, 2004	158.1	185.6	209.5

Source: Yahoo Finance.

Note: November 16, 1995 = 100. Quoted indices are for the first day of the stated period.

volatile than that of any of the major indices in the securities markets. The S&P 500 and the Dow Jones Industrial Average both exhibited peaks similar to that of the telecom index, rising steadily from 1995 to the first quarter of 2000 and then falling for the next three years before recovering over 2003 and 2004, but the spike in the telecom index was twice as high.[38] While some carriers fared better than others, telecommunications companies were strongly afflicted, losing roughly 80 percent of market capitalization.

In 2002, FCC Chairman Michael Powell characterized the industry as being in "utter crisis."[39] Various theories have been advanced to explain this "crisis," but excessive investment in telecom securities based on optimistic but erroneous forecasts of traffic growth was commonly cited as the root cause; these forecasts were explained by the widely accepted "fact" that Internet and other broadband traffic on the wireline network would double every two to four years. Wireline capacity, based on fiber-optic transmission technologies and message digitalization with limited investment in loops and switches, was supposed to expand at a comparable rate. In the presence of these predicted rates of traffic growth, even with the internal growth of capacity, predicted earnings would have supported increased investment in fiber-optic cable, switching and routing equipment, and other transmission-related capacity that was focused on network systems for routing high-speed Internet service from the local exchange through the long distance carrier.[40] Over 1998–2001, the amount of fiber-optic cable deployed did increase fivefold, and with advances in compression technology, a rule-of-thumb "500-fold" increase in transmission capacity was said to have occurred.[41] Over the same period, however, the demands for service that would effectively utilize such capacity increased only by a factor of four, so the country had "ten times to twenty times as much fiber as it is using."[42] As this condition was realized, new investment slowed, installed fiber was "darkened," and network support equipment orders were canceled. This slowdown caused the share prices of leading growth companies to plummet. Exacerbating the stock decline was the fact that much of the new investment was financed through debt, so the most highly leveraged carriers saw their debt/equity rates go to unacceptably high levels. As a trade press source observed, the resulting insolvencies tended to shift incentives to short-term cash maximization.[43] Major carriers responded by seeking bankruptcy protection or, in the cases of WorldCom, Qwest, and Global Crossing, by resorting to manipulation or misstatement of financial accounts so as to avoid bankruptcy for as long as possible. Whatever the countermeasure, the sales and earnings of telecom firms turned downward in the first years of the new century, and worsening performance in the telecom industry as a whole was reflected in downturns in the specific performance of AT&T, MCI, and Sprint.

Despite the entry by the RBOCs, and this downturn in demands for service, the three incumbent carriers did not reduce prices. They had reduced the price in certain discount plans after entry, but if there was a strategy at all, it was that of raising prices on standard plans while holding prices on discount plans, seeking to accelerate the transfer of subscribers to these discount plans. Price-cost margins on standard service increased relative to those for discount or business services, but the trends observed in price-cost margins before RBOC entry also continued.

Long distance revenues of the incumbent carriers steadily declined. AT&T's toll service revenues fell from $38.1 billion to $27.5 billion over the years 2000 to 2002, a decrease of approximately 32.6 percent. Toll service revenues of Sprint and MCI each declined by approximately 24 percent over the same period. Overall, total toll revenues in the United States fell from $109.6 billion in 2000 to $83.7 billion in 2002, a decrease of 27 percent, as carriers other than the three large incumbents collectively also experienced reductions in revenues from long distance services (Table 27). These reductions, to the extent they were unexpected, added to the pressures on the pricing strategies of these three companies.

The revenue declines had to have taken a toll on carrier profitability. Table 28 presents estimates of the earnings before interest, taxes, depreciation, and amortization (EBITDA) of the three incumbent carriers over the ten years from 1994 to 2003.[44] As the table shows, AT&T earnings peaked in 2000 and then declined. MCI earnings turned negative just before the company undertook restructuring associated with fraud charges in its financial accounting and the ensuing bankruptcy.[45] Sprint's earnings increased over the period, although much of this increase was attributed by the company (in filings with the U.S.

Table 27. Annual toll service revenues ($ billions)

Company	2000	2001	2002	Decline, 2000–02 (%)
AT&T	38.1	33.9	27.5	32.6
MCI	22.6	21.3	17.7	24.4
Sprint	9.0	8.4	7.1	23.7
All carriers	109.6	99.3	83.7	27.0

Source: Federal Communications Commission (FCC), Industry Analysis and Technology Division, "Trends in Telephone Service" (May 2004), Table 9.6.

Table 28. Interexchange carrier EBITDA ($ billions),
1994–2003

Year	AT&T	MCI WorldCom	Sprint
1994	12.58	—	3.08
1995	8.70	—	3.30
1996	11.50	—	3.86
1997	10.56	2.05	4.16
1998	11.87	1.35	2.90
1999	16.60	12.24	3.35
2000	17.33	13.03	4.43
2001	12.39	(5.37)	3.69
2002	9.25	(0.88)	7.01
2003	8.53	3.56	5.87

Source: Company annual reports and quarterly and annual filings with the Securities and Exchange Commission (various years).

Note: EBITDA, earnings before interest, taxes, depreciation, and amortization, is assumed to be equal to operating income inclusive of taxes, depreciation, and amortization. MCI WorldCom earnings are reported beginning in 1997 with the acquisition of MCI by WorldCom.

Securities and Exchange Commission) to increased revenues in its wireless operations and to various accounting adjustments. Indeed, in its Form 10-K filing for the year 2002, Sprint stated that reported depreciation and amortization estimates were largely obscuring operating revenues in its "FON Group"—that is, its wireline operations, as opposed to its wireless "PCS Group"—which were declining: although operating earnings for the FON Group increased, the group had "experienced declining revenues for the past several quarters."[46] After adjustments, Sprint reported falling operating income from 1999 to 2001, posting a loss of $254 million before recovering somewhat in 2002.[47]

In terms of measures of economic performance, all three carriers struggled during those years. Our focused measure in evaluating the performance of the gas and power transmission network has been EVA, as discussed in Chapter 3.[48] Table 29 shows estimates of EVA for the incumbent interexchange carriers, as percentage returns on investment, from 1990 though 2002.[49] While estimates vary considerably by company and from year to year, the interexchange carriers in general exhibited destruction of shareholder value. WorldCom, for instance, had negative EVA in 1996, with more than 47 percent of its investment value eliminated that year. And EVA was negative for each year thereafter, with returns to shareholders of at least 20 percent less than its cost of capital in

Table 29. Interexchange carrier economic value added (%)

Year	AT&T	WorldCom	MCI	Sprint
1990	3.0	92.0	7.0	(7.0)
1991	16.0	82.0	6.0	(1.0)
1992	2.0	40.0	2.0	(5.0)
1993	(16.0)	14.0	1.0	1.0
1994	20.0	(14.0)	(1.0)	(1.0)
1995	7.0	64.0	(2.0)	(3.0)
1996	1.0	(47.0)	(2.0)	1.0
1997	19.0	(3.0)	2.0	10.0
1998	6.0	(3.0)	(28.0)	(7.0)
1999	97.0	(7.0)	—	(1.0)
2000	25.0	(20.0)	—	(8.0)
2001	(26.0)	(1.0)	—	(8.0)
2002	(53.0)	(22.0)	—	(7.0)

Source: Compustat data, as used to estimate economic value added (EVA) in the process described in the text.

Note: The MCI security was delisted in 1999 following WorldCom's acquisition of that carrier.

both 2000 and 2002.[50] Sprint did not do better, with only three years of positive EVA since 1990 and consistently negative EVA since 1998. In 1999, AT&T had a 97 percent EVA after a one-time increase in earnings following an accounting adjustment. Much the same type of adjustment resulted in a moderate increase of 25 percent in 2000. But since 2001, AT&T's performance has been substantially negative, causing the company to lose more than three-quarters of the book value of operating invested capital. In 2002 alone, AT&T in its operations destroyed approximately 53 percent of that capital.[51]

Most striking across these companies was the fact that EVA was consistently negative with the downturn in the business cycle in general and the telecommunications sector in particular. As a matter of course, the stock market value of shares in these companies had to decline given such reductions in earnings. There were other reasons for declines, from injudicious acquisition and costly divestitures at AT&T to fraudulent accounting scandals at MCI and Sprint. The share price of AT&T increased from $113 in 1994 and $147 in 1996, to peak at $211 in 1999, only to decline to $40 in 2002 and $14 in 2004. Sprint share price was at $10 in 1996, then $57 in 2000, to fall back to $9 in 2002. These firms were riding the bubble of excessive expectations as to returns; at AT&T, cash flow discounted to present value, based on current cash at increasing industry growth rates, was worth approximately $3 billion in 1999, while stock market capitalization was $199 billion; Sprint's present value cash flow was worth roughly $134 million, but its shares were worth $63 billion that year.

The change in mass- and business-market conditions, which determined these changes in financial markets, could hardly have been more negative. After half a decade of regulatory delay, the entry of the RBOCs into long distance created a situation in which the potential existed for further transfer of demands for services away from the three large interexchange carriers. Partial deregulation at the scene, just when incumbent carriers were realizing negative profitability, could have resulted in Bertrand oligopoly results, in the form of low and declining price-cost margins.

PASS THROUGH OF THE UNIVERSAL SERVICE FUND

To comply with TA96 implementation requirements, the FCC in 1998 established an elaborate process by which the long distance carriers would pay earmarked revenues into a nonprofit organization to disburse and to achieve "universal service." The FCC set the terms and conditions on such payments. From the beginning, these USF contributions had to be collected from final consumers, in then-current sales revenues of the incumbent carriers. Before the program began, AT&T stated that all its contributions should be as a separate charge on the monthly bill of a mass-market or business customer. Sprint took the position that its USF contributions would be passed through from its consumers to the fund as well. Doing so required that if the revenues generated specifically to make USF target contributions were falling, then the percentage surcharge on customer billings would have to increase.

The long distance carriers were to make contributions to USF beginning in January 1998. AT&T, MCI, and Sprint did not initially charge USF recovery to residential customers but instead opted to charge business customers. This was not a decision driven by regulatory policy but one collectively made for achieving full pass through. At the beginning, AT&T stated that it would "assess the results during the first half of 1998 to determine whether a different pricing model would be more appropriate going forward."[52] But in the second half of 1998, the three carriers simultaneously switched funding sources and began charging residential customers. AT&T used a monthly flat fee, and MCI and Sprint used a percentage fee applied to customer charge rates.

During the half-year when USF charges were collected from business customers, there was underrecovery (AT&T reported negative $356 million for the first half of 1998, which it attributed to businesses charges bypassing mass-market tariff rates). After the switch to a charge on residential customers, AT&T decreased underrecovery to $24 million for the second half of 1998. Then, despite the fact that uncollected USF contributions for the first half of 1998 constituted classic "sunk costs," the carriers took steps to recover the undercollections with higher USF surcharges on residential customers in 1999. This was so successful that both AT&T and Sprint had surplus USF contributions in that year. AT&T estimated that for the first half of 1999, it had an overrecovery of $28 million on residential customers, and Sprint estimated that it was overrecovering by 120 to 130 percent.

This pattern continued. In succeeding half-year periods, the USF surcharges set by the three carriers changed several times. When one carrier adjusted its surcharge, the other carriers adjusted their charges commensurately. In August 1998, when carriers first passed through the USF charge to residential customers, MCI charged a fee of 5.0 percent and Sprint charged 4.5 percent (AT&T was charging a flat rate during this time). In November 1998, both carriers lowered the fee to 4.1 percent. In December 1999, MCI raised its surcharge to 6.0 percent, with Sprint raising its surcharge to 5.8 percent one week later. This process was repeated in 2001, after AT&T changed from a flat-rate to a percentage-rate fee structure. During the first week of January 2001, AT&T, MCI, and Sprint were charging 8.6, 8.3, and 8.6 percent, respectively. One week later, AT&T raised its rate to 9.9 percent, and in response Sprint raised its rate to 9.6 percent. In February 2001, MCI raised its rate to 9.9 percent.

From this initial period, when charge rates were variable and changed frequently among the three carriers, to the first three quarters of 2004, when charge rates were the same across the carriers, this process of dynamic tax rate formation converged to following AT&T, and the surcharges generated the full amount of required cash inflow to pay the bill to the Universal Service Administrative Company. That all three carriers succeeded in attaining full pass through was indicated by an April 2003 FCC order to the effect that carriers could not charge recovery rates in excess of 100 percent of the required contribution.[53]

The 100 percent pass-through limit was achieved as a result of a new shared strategy, different from that previously resulting in Bertrand price-cost margins. When marginal costs are constant and demand functions are linear, no interactive Bertrand pricing process would result in complete pass through. That is, Bertrand prices exclusive of the USF charge would be lower in order to absorb some of the USF charge. Although they might note on the monthly bill the full USF surcharge, the underlying price would be reduced so that the total would be less than the old price plus USF charge.[54]

Then to deal with the USF requirement to "tax" on top of current Bertrand prices, which were too low, the three larger inter-LATA carriers had to become more collusive. The involvement of the FCC, seeking full payment of USF charges, must have facilitated agreement across the carriers not to absorb the USF charges. The three incumbent carriers were enabled to set higher prices, not only fully inclusive of USF charges but beyond a Bertrand strategy to a collective monopoly strategy during this period.

Did they, in effect, overtly collude to meet the regulatory goals of having high-income residential subscribers generate revenues to subsidize so-called universal service? Lerner price-cost margins based on average revenue per minute increased from less than 40 percent before the USF program to between 56 to 62 percent in the first stages of USF collection and then 63 to 66 percent in the later stages (Table 20). Prices for all services increased by more than the USF tax during the USF recovery program. Lerner margins were increasing because conjectural variations were increasing.

Table 30 shows average conjectural variations for 1987–97 before USF tax recovery and 1998–2003 after USF recovery was in operation. Given that subscribers were shifting out of standard plans to discount programs most heavily during the second of the two time periods, the table shows averages by carrier only on conjectural variation estimates based on discount plans (for twenty-five observations: sixteen before and nine after the USF charge was initiated). AT&T conjectural variation estimates for the first period were negative, in the range of −0.192 to −0.417 and for the second period were positive in the range of 0.161 to 0.371. In the USF recovery period AT&T conjectural variations were 0.35 to 0.89 higher, at levels indicative of strategy in which others responded positively to its price changes. AT&T in general set price levels and MCI and

Table 30. Average conjectural variation coefficients before and during Universal Service Fund charge recovery

Carrier	1987–97	1998–2003
AT&T	−0.312	0.043
MCI	0.863	0.517
Sprint	2.900	4.05

Sprint followed. In the USF period Sprint exhibited a larger increase in conjectural variation level (of 1.15, as required for it to confirm a price level that was not strictly in its self-interest). MCI stayed in the range of 0.86 to 0.52. These values together confirm that interfirm strategy changed during the USF recovery period. They indicate for the full array of services covered in ARPM that, given the occasion of USF, the three carriers put in place higher net prices, beyond the separate USF recovery tax required for pass through.

But the question is whether the greater extent of pricing coordination achieved cartel status, albeit by FCC facilitation. The "perfect" cartel would operate to restrain individual carrier price initiatives so that resulting price-cost margins would achieve the monopoly level. Since there would be no conjecture between firms and concentration would be as if there were only one firm, the Lerner index would be that of the monopolist: $(p - mc) / p = -1 / e$. For the USF period, to mirror this monopoly behavior, however, the elasticity of demand for long distance wireline services would have to have been in the range of -1.67, given that the reversal of margins put the leading carrier margin at 60 percent. That would appear to be too high an elasticity to sustain, since USF determined surcharges and pass through along with perfect cartel price-cost margins.

Suppose, however, that the FCC's intervention was intended to allow the carriers to pass through the USF charges but not in addition to achieve monopoly price levels. Lerner indexes that approximated 50 to 70 percent in discount plans of the three carriers, after USF began in 1998, would be the result of more collusion, if not of cartelization. That is, the USF pass through plus higher net prices were not the realization of "perfect" cartel pricing, which was not attainable even with the tighter organization of carriers that the USF program put in place.[55]

SHORTAGES OF BROADBAND CAPACITY
AND DEREGULATION

Markets for both gas transmission and power distribution, when subject to restructuring and price caps, manifested Bertrand patterns of conduct in pricing and profitability that shut down the investment process. That produced shortages and price spikes during periods of peak demand for services in the basis differential between prices of the product being shipped at entry and those at the exit nodes on the network. Other parts of the telecom systems than that of the three long distance carriers were subject to limited restructuring—after divestiture, for one, in the programs to add local exchange carriers to the regional incumbents—and those other parts were also subject to complex direct price controls designed to move along the restructuring process. But if the telecom network fits the deregulatory response pattern of the gas and electric networks, where were the shortages and differential spikes due to lack of capacity expansion?

In telecom networks the divestiture in 1984 followed by a plan for more open entry in TA96 constituted partial deregulation, but differences in networks and in the remaining regulation reduced the similarities. The FCC and state agencies focused on the maintenance of price controls on local exchange, including on the use of local network elements and access to long distance. This regulation of charges at the retail node of transmission is not different from FERC regulation of gas and electric transmission at retail. The access charge set by the FCC to compensate local exchange carriers for the loss of cash flow from long lines after divestiture decreased from 12.4 cents per minute in 1987 to 6.2 cents per minute in 1995 and to 1.4 cents per minute in 2004. These reductions were the basis of price reductions of incumbent long distance carriers in service offerings in the mass and business markets, but they also were the basis for increases in price-cost margins. The continuation of price controls in the local exchange service was an exogenous force for motivating the local carriers to vertically integrate into long distance, but that was impeded by regulatory barriers to entry imbedded in the details of TA96. And here, threads of motivation become crossed. To the extent that FCC-set access charges were inefficient, the local exchange carriers were motivated to enter long distance markets. These markets were Cournot in behavior, devolving to Bertrand behavior in pricing strategies; with FCC help they became marked to cartel pricing level in the USF recovery program.[56] But to enter these markets, the local exchange carrier also had to qualify under TA96 Sections 251 and 252, along with the Section 271 checklist that required, in effect, earlier entry of the three large incumbent long distance carriers into local exchange. That earlier entry turned out to be determined by the FCC-set prices of the local exchange carriers for the use of unbundled local network elements; that is, the long distance carriers promised to layer their facilities over the local link and node networks, but their initial entry into local exchange would be on the existing elements of the Bell networks. The key to opening the supply side of both local and long distance markets was then the price to be charged to long distance entrants for the leasing of local network elements.

The UNE-P prices of the FCC for the unbundled elements and platform became the bottleneck that cut back capacity expansion of transport in and out of

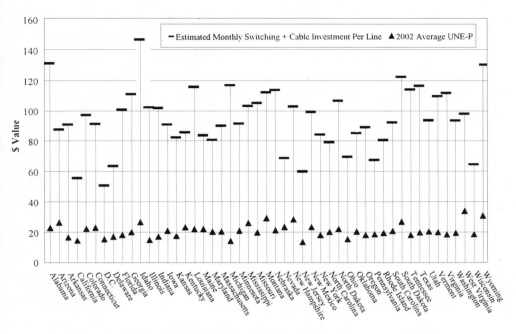

Figure 19. Unbundled network element full platform (UNE-P) versus marginal costs of network services (*Source:* FCC Armis database, annualized; also see text. UNE-P charges are as announced by the state regulatory agencies.)

the expanding long distance network. These prices were set after months, even years of rulings based on gross distortions of the historical principles of utility regulation. The FCC went beyond cost-of-service and price cap methodologies to invent TELRIC, a concept and estimation process that approximated long-run incremental costs of future technologies for caps on charges for leasing network elements. TELRIC-based element prices stopped the forward movement of the local exchange companies into investments for new wireline capacity that would transmit voice, data, and emerging Internet traffic.

TELRIC prices varied from state to state depending on population, urban/ rural mix, and business activity, but they were below current direct (variable) unit costs for providing element services. The monthly average charges were from $15 to $30 per UNE full platform while the bare-bones current costs of transport and switching, including replacement costs of hardware annualized on a monthly basis, were from $55 to $140 for that platform (see Figure 19).

The local carrier had strong negative incentives against leasing its equipment below marginal costs. The long distance carrier had mixed incentives; although clearly to its advantage to enter and in its one-stop package to charge consumers local service prices less than the incumbents' marginal cost for that service, it faced two challenges. The entrant had to force the lease transaction on the local carrier; and it had to rely on the FCC to keep TELRIC prices in effect in the face of intense political opposition in the courts and the agency. In this contest, as it developed, the rate of network element leasing increased, but as a last resort after the bypass of Section 271 checklist requirements allowed Bell local exchange carriers into the long distance market in 2000.

The advent of broadband high-speed Internet access was lost in this process. The shortage of subscriber lines for fiber-optic message transmission from the home was met by the development of high-speed modem service of cable television service providers. As a result the digital subscriber line (DSL) service of the telecom operating companies came later and was slower to be adopted. In 1998, halfway through restructuring basic exchange networks to the Internet, only 32 percent of the access lines of RBOCs had "pair gain"—that is, could carry more than one voice message simultaneously.[57] The FCC regulatory process still loomed on the operating company horizon. The concern was that the FCC would declare any advanced Internet access capability in the local exchange as a "network element" subject to lease terms and conditions set on TELRIC principles. The rate of installation stalled, to such an extent that twelve nations currently experience higher rates of broadband utilization in mass markets than in this country (an increase from three at the beginning of the decade; see T. Beeha, *Foreign Affairs* [2004]).

The "shortage" or bottleneck in telecommunications has been the fact that services over high-speed links are missing from local exchange/long distance networks. There was no price spike, as in electric power transmission, in 2000 and 2001. The "spike" was hypothetical, equal to what potential subscribers would have been willing to pay for fiber-optic transmission of Internet-based information on lines that were being used for telephone messages, fax, and fire alarm simultaneously at speeds equivalent to those, say, in Finland.

In that sense, the process of partial deregulation in telecommunications has produced spikes comparable to those in power and gas transmission. Price caps reduced investment, which then put significant limits on capacity, as in Bertrand market performance when partially regulated. In this industry, the TELRIC caps affected the development of the information transmission sector of the knowledge industries in highly adverse ways. So-called deregulatory control of networks by both FERC and the FCC produced Bertrand price-cost margins that sustained bottlenecks that caused price spikes.

Chapter 6 The Singular Result
of Partial Deregulation and
What Can Be Done

Chapters 3 and 5 explored the effects of a generic plan of partial deregulation on the incumbent large carriers that operate networks in the
natural gas, electricity, and telephone service industries. Chapter 4
provided a case study of the financial impact of the California plan for
partial deregulation on a leading network carrier of electricity during
the state's power crisis of 2000–01. What was common in these appraisals was that large network systems, independent or linked together, operated by four or fewer companies in regional or national
markets, made up the market structures. There was an initial stage of
deregulation, the restructuring stage, that attempted, mostly without
success, to increase the number of service providers of the product
and/or transportation. Then a second stage had the regulatory agency
implement new pricing regulations to replace cost-of-service rates
that had been fifty years or more in the making. The interaction of the
network systems with restructuring did not result in significantly
more service providers, nor did the new, partial price controls reduce
the scope of regulation in these industries. Through the 1990s, the
networks did not break out into competitive supply, even though re-

structuring separated the products that were transported—gas, electricity, and telephone calls—from the interstate spoke/hub systems.

Even with limited change in structure, the regulatory agencies moved away from comprehensive cost-based price limits to focus price controls on bottleneck and peak supply of services, with price caps on contract services or on the largest carrier. Various methods were used to focus these price limits on a multiplicity of transactions. Caps were set to prevent price levels under deregulation from going higher than they were under regulation, but they worked to prevent prices from increasing only during periods of peak demand, whether for gas in cold weather, electricity in hot weather, or UNEs in the largest switching centers. They did not change off-peak prices, particularly where there were wide swings in demands from hour to hour, as well as season to season, that left substantial excess capacity on the market for many off-season months of the year.

The logic of divestiture and capped prices at peak made it inevitable that average prices were too low. The peak price was capped at average total costs at full capacity (most often the previous cost-of-service price), and the off-peak price was not capped, but market demands would have it go far below that level; together, these realities guaranteed that any average of realized prices across seasons would be lower than average total costs. As a result, price-cost margins in the 1990–2004 period were below levels required to fund the replacement and expansion of network capacity. In gas transmission in three subnational markets, price-cost margins were consistent with those for a five-network oligopoly following Bertrand rules of conduct, in which prices were below average costs and within range of marginal costs (Figure 3). In power-grid operations, where transmission costs were rolled into retail distribution, price-cost margins were in the range of 20 percent (Table 8), a level far below Cournot behavior but that as in Bertrand behavior. The three large long distance telephone service providers had margins, before 1999, that were consistent with Cournot behavior, with low demand elasticities and widely disparate revenue shares. The shift of residence service subscribers to discount plans and of business subscribers to bilateral contracts, both at higher demand elasticities, and at prices lower than tariff, should have resulted in falling margins. But as the price schedules were detariffed, and markets made subject to entry by local exchange carriers, resulting margins were more characteristic of a Bertrand oligopoly. By the turn of the century, all three industries, given few large firms under restructuring and partial price controls, had cash flows that would not sustain the expansion required of capacity to meet peak cyclical and growing market demands for transmission services.

The results in terms of performance of the networks can only be described as adverse. Earnings were insufficient to attain EVA in many if not all years. Because negative EVA, year after year, implied a lack of resources to replenish and expand capacity, during high-demand periods differentials between prices at entry and those at exit in gas and power networks rose to levels far in excess of capped transport prices. These basis differential spikes as a matter of course destroyed consumer surplus from service on peak and off peak. The effects on final consumers of the product shipped are illustrated in Figure 20. With a capacity shortage, the amount q_1 is shipped and repriced at p_1 to clear excess demand $q_0 - q_1$. The price increase takes place not in pipeline space services, which are capped, but in the shipped product, which is now in more scarce supply (that is, by Δq, given that q_0 would normally flow if capacity were available).

In Figure 20, DD indicates demand for line transmission; q_0 is total on-peak product demand and one-to-one for line capacity; q_1 is total on-peak available product (equal to available capacity); p_0 is price at the regulated cap; and p_1 is the exit price of shipped product at peak. The consumers of shipped product pay the line exit price, in a pass-through transaction, and lose consumer surplus, $(p_1 - p_0)(q_0 - q_1) / 2$, as a result. For gas transmission service users, for example, these losses can be estimated, in order of magnitude, as shown in Table 31.

For services that had caps of $0.50 per thousand cubic feet of gas delivered, the lost surplus from the gas price increases at delivery point on a spike of $1.00 per thousand cubic feet was approximately 1.4 percent of expenditures over the period 1990–2003 on gas from Henry Hub to the Dominion Hub in the Northeast—not an extensive percentage given that the price-cost margin as a percentage of consumer and producer surplus was in the range of 15 to 25 percent. But two other spikes of $2.00 per thousand cubic feet canceled out 52 percent of the consumer surplus during that period. The Henry to Transco system experienced a spike of $8.50 per thousand cubic feet in 1999 that took the basis differential losses to more than 400 percent of all surplus for nine years of network operations. This experience was replicated on service from Henry Hub to other terminals; any net gains for consumers were wiped out by basis spikes to the Transco, Telco, Algonquin, and Tennessee Six exit nodes.

The midwestern region experienced less damaging spikes because of greater

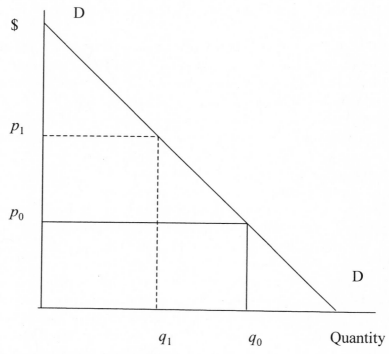

Figure 20. "Basis" spikes and lost consumer surplus

capacity relative to peak demands in the older pipelines from Texas; but in the newer spokes from more recently discovered fields in the Rocky Mountains, an exceptionally damaging spike of $4.50 per thousand cubic feet in 2001 canceled consumer gains from that service since inception in 1989 (as indicated in Table 31, lost surplus was 93.3 percent of revenues). But the narrative history of basis differential spikes in natural gas was written large in the spikes that California gas consumers experienced during 2000–01. Spikes began appearing in the summer of 2000, to reach levels of $2.00 per thousand cubic feet and then over the winter of 2000–01 to exceed first $7.50 and then $10.00 per thousand cubic feet. The impact on consumers exceeded that of any other gas spike, with losses of more than 285 percent from the spike at $7.50 and 525 percent from the one at $10.00 per thousand cubic feet. These percentages are difficult to grasp; what was paid out for gas shipping services from 1989 to 2003 was only one-fifth of the dollar negative impact of these basis spikes on consumers in 2001.

In the five regional electric power networks subject to FERC operating and pricing rules in partial deregulation, the disruptive incursion of excess demand

Table 31. Lost consumer surplus from gas price spikes, 1990–2003

Region, basis link	Basis differential on spikes ($/mcf)	Lost consumer surplus (% of expenditures for entire period)
Eastern		
Henry to Dominion	1.00 (1)	1.4
	2.00 (2)	26.1
Henry to Transco	2.50 (3)	70.0
	8.50 (1)	406.7
Henry to Tetco	2.50 (2)	46.7
	3.50 (1)	52.3
Henry to Algonquin	1.00 (3)	4.3
	2.50 (1)	23.3
	4.50 (1)	93.3
Henry to Iroquois	3.50 (1)	52.5
	1.00 (1)	1.4
	2.00 (1)	13.1
Henry to Columbia Gas	1.50 (1)	5.8
Henry to Tennessee Six	1.00 (1)	1.4
	4.00 (1)	69.0
	2.50 (1)	23.3
Midwestern		
Midcontinent to Chicago	1.00 (2)	2.8
Midcontinent to Joliet Hub	1.00 (1)	1.4
Rocky Mountains to Chicago	2.40 (4)	13.1
	4.50 (1)	93.3
Western		
Transwestern to Southern California Border	2.00 (1)	13.0
	7.50 (1)	285.8
	10.00 (1)	525.8
El Paso to PG&E Connect	1.50 (1)	5.8
	3.00 (1)	328.3

Source: See text.

Note: Numbers in parentheses are the frequency of occurrence of a spike of that size over the relevant period.

for transmission was not different from that in gas transmission. The consumer surplus lost from power price spikes, estimated on basis differentials, was not more than 30 percent of 2002–04 power sales revenues, but from the spike of $500 per megawatt hour, the ERCOT West system lost all gains for customers for the three-year period. New York State experienced a basis differential of

Table 32. Lost consumer surplus from electricity price spikes, 2002–04

Region, basis link	Basis differential on spikes ($/mwh)	Lost consumer surplus (% of expenditures)
Texas		
ERCOT West to Houston (base)	500 (1)	160.0
	200 (1)	22.5
	100 (2)	6.9
California		
Zone 15 and SP 15 (base)	200 (7)	145.5
	300 (7)	54.5
	150 (3)	35.1
	100 (2)	6.9
New England		
Connecticut and Maine (base)	75 (6)	12.6
	50 (2)	1.3
New York State		
New York City and west (base)	450 (1)	128.4
	50 (4)	2.6
Pennsylvania		
PJM (center) and PPL (base)	600 (2)	467.2
	200 (1)	22.5
	50 (2)	1.3

Source: See text.

Note: Numbers in parentheses equal the frequency of spikes in the 2002–04 period.

$450 per megawatt hour and PJM in Pennsylvania had a basis "event" of $600 per megawatt hour. Estimates of losses to consumers during such spikes indicate that they increased exponentially, encompassing 128 percent of revenues when the spike was $450 but 467 percent of revenues at $600. Replication of at least part of this experience in other regional networks indicates that these grid systems operated by new ISOs failed to achieve an acceptable level of reliability. Power systems restructuring left the consumer across the country worse off (see Table 32; only the New England ISO operated to experience limited spikes "worth" negative gains in the range of 14 percent of revenues).

Then what were consumer gains and losses from the partial deregulation of local exchange and long distance telephone service markets? Unlike gas and electric, there were no observable basis differential spikes in these telecom services due to limits in line capacity at peak demands. One might have expected such spikes, given the negative EVA resulting from state regulatory price caps at retail in local exchange and FCC below-cost ceilings on charges for UNEs leased to long distance carriers. But with digital technologies increasing the capacity of already installed link systems and making it possible to substitute wireless for wireline links, the options for consumers expanded vastly outside the wireline network. Substitution was not perfect—the high-speed modem of cable systems was not high-speed enough to match that of the fiber-optic technologies that the local exchange carriers did not put in place. The conceptual spike in essence dissipated into demands for alternative service outside the partially deregulated networks. The incumbent systems were not short of capacity because advances in information technologies allowed new systems in other networks to substitute for constraints on new investment.

But that may not have gone far enough. To have offered subscribers to wireline network services in broadband—that is, links with the capacity for high-speed Internet as well as telephone and video—was not an option of the RBOCs during 1990–2005. It was as if the demand function in Figure 20 was planned but never achieved reality. The stopping point was FCC price caps (TELRIC) on service from local exchange UNEs below current element replacement cost, which curtailed local exchange carrier investment in the required high-speed fiber-optic links. Domestic adaptation rates for broadband were in the range of 10 to 15 percent of line subscribers, but they would have been higher if there had been capacity to offer the service.

Then what was the extent of lost consumer surplus from the spike in nonexistent broadband? Since the measure of surplus in this case is the entire area under the demand function, and only 10 percent of that area of potential demand is being met by fiber to the door of metropolitan businesses and residences, we can provide an approximate answer based on Figure 21. In the first five years of the new century, the demands for broadband were channeled into DSL (of the local exchange carriers) and high-speed modem (of cable television service providers). Together they provided approximately 31 million lines by 2004 that provided inferior service at $30 per month lease charge. That combination of price (p) and quantity (q) in Figure 21 provides a depiction of a "spike," or what consumers had to pay for low speed in the absence of advanced DSL (ADSL) from fiber-optic lines to the office or residence door (which would have been p_1, a lower-price equivalent, for example, to the $30 price for superior service, q_1, rather than q). On the assumption that the least improvement would have been a one-for-one substitution of ADSL for the existing dual systems if the local exchange companies had made the investment, then what the consumer lost from the nonexistence of broadband was approximately $38 billion (the

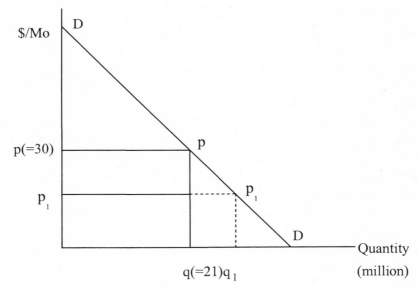

Figure 21. A hypothetical basis spike in broadband services

amount $[p - p_1]q$, where p_1 is conservatively $15 per month equivalent and the capitalization rate at $15 per month is 10 percent).

This is not an outsized estimate of what was lost from a spike never observed. An earlier estimate of the economic costs of delay to U.S. consumers was $33 billion (in 1994 dollars).[1] While this value measures costs for an unknown long period going forward, it does not count the costs of previous years in a prolonged adoption period. It would be less if q were known, because then a more conservative assessment would be the deadweight loss of $(p - p_1)(q_1 - q) / 2$. But if the rate of adoption would have been twice what it has been, so that $[(q_1 - q) = q]$, then the deadweight loss was $20 billion from the spike that consisted in consumers having to take second or third best in Internet access.

The effects of partial deregulation on the networks, in dollars of lost consumer surplus over the past fifteen years, are the major part of the story, if not the whole story. The gains from day-to-day adjustment to partial deregulation also consist of those from price reductions becoming more competitive. Price-cost margins fell because of the business cycle and the reductions in demand for services due to the innovations in wireline services from other unregulated markets. They increased as the reward of the FCC to carriers for providing the USF. Price-cost margins were not competitive but were Bertrand in behavior, and it was the FCC decrees that increased margins.

ROADBLOCKS IN THE PROCESS
OF DEREGULATION

Looking across the three industries, one can see that partial deregulation has not gone as far as anticipated. Corporate performance subject to partial deregulation has resulted in limited benefits and large costs in price spikes. And reality points to the achievement in the telecom industry of more and better service on the fringe by providers outside of regulation, in terms of capacity expansion through the introduction of new technologies and services. But in the gas and electric industries, the lack of entry from outside supports the view that no structural "reforms" can be expected. Increased volatility in product prices associated with partial deregulation, that is, out-of-scale price differentials between the network basis and delivery node, has wiped out consumer gains from the deregulation process.

FERC and the FCC have taken steps to move back up the regulatory path to reimpose utility-style limits on prices. FERC would do so for charges on power retailers that ship over their own lines, not trusting the strategies of not-for-profit grid operators to enhance consumer welfare. FERC would impose delivery node price caps on spikes when they were "too high." The FCC would move toward some variant of cost-of-service justification for the local exchange provider to charge the long distance carrier for the use of UNEs, having given up on TELRIC in the face of multiple federal court rejections. These are not new initiatives. We have seen the results that follow from traditional caps at bottlenecks. We can picture service providers imploding, following the inevitable path of PG&E to illiquidity or just classic long-term Bertrand earnings margins that cannot replenish investment funds.

If spike-style instability from capacity constraints were to continue, and were to become larger and more frequent, then the deregulation process may be forced to turn back toward more regulation. The proposals as to that direction are far-flung—nationalize the grids, replace the investor-owners with nonprofit management entities, complete the installation of price caps wherever there are bottlenecks, replicate the restructuring in foreign privatization experiments. Without volumes of critical appraisal on each of these options, it goes without saying that the process would still have to allow service suppliers, private or public, to expand capacity. They would have to be able to achieve positive EVA levels of profitability or use tax money to motivate expansion into new services—an opportunity not available during the past decade and a half for partially regulated private service providers. Pricing of network transmission has to ration excess demand at peak and motivate investment in cases where deficient capacity is causing the excess demand in the older gas fields, the East Coast and West Coast power grids, and broadband fiber to the home. None of these requirements is being met in the initiatives to add "better" regulation.

Two proposals for forward movement of regulation do confront these requirements for improving performance. These plans may require more regulation, rather than being deregulatory. One is structural, involving changes not in numbers of firms but in the ownership patterns in the assets of these firms. This can be called *Alger restructuring,* after a paper by Dan Alger circulated in the mid-1990s titled "Open Ownership—Not Common Carriage."[2] The second alternative, developed by Ingo Vogelsang building on a series of papers by Hogan et al., can be called *Vogelsang pricing.*[3] The Vogelsang alternative is behavioral, requiring management of the decision-making organizations to set two-part access and usage prices that follow certain optimization rules for capacity expansion.

Alger restructuring would require network owners to offer for sale space in the link systems to all comers that in turn would offer link space services in secondary markets. Purchase prices for space and switching in the link-node system would be regulated so that a "unit" would be sold at replacement cost, and prices for service on sold links would be capped to cover variable costs of network operations.[4] The resulting service offerings in the secondary market would predictably include three to five new service providers inside the subcontinental gas pipelines, that is, in each of four or five pipelines between Henry Hub and any final market set of exit nodes. Given the current overlap in these pipelines, there would be, for example, no less than a dozen separate service providers in the northeast regional market.

The conceptual design of Alger restructuring, for example, in the existing regional power grids would be quite different, since the parts of a current grid now consist of company-specific networks of nonoverlapping retailer service provider/owners. For example, if there were six equal-sized nonoverlapping retailers in a regional grid, they would turn in their six ownership pieces to grid management and receive ownership rights for one-sixth of the space in the newly organized unitary regional network (that is, each of the six would have common property rights to space over the whole network). Except for California, where three owners would result, in most regions there would be at least six owners of space in the power grid. Use of the space would be managed by an

ISO to provide day-to-day balance of generator input with power take rates. In the telecom industry, with extremely numerous path options in long distance fiber-optic systems, the analogy would be for AT&T or Sprint to sell pathways to twelve or fifteen independent long distance companies at a maximum price level set by the FCC.

Such restructuring of ownership, but not management, does not immediately cause the problem to be solved. The problem is supposedly that current grid management implies control of service in a well-defined market for transmission. Alger's thesis is that "unconcentrated joint ownership may induce the efficient outcome."[5] For this argument to be convincing, one has to consider that the problem has been that capacity not used to provide throughput services at any given time has been withheld to increase transmission prices. But that is not the recent situation. The problem of the past decade and a half has not been unused capacity, but deficient capacity, triggering at-peak product spikes in response to space demands that are not worked through capped transmission charges. Then potential purchasers would not offer to bid for space at replacement cost. Furthermore, if their bid prices were lower than replacement costs, then they would not take part in plans to expand capacity that require investments at replacement costs. The Alger solution would not increase prices for pipeline or grid space unless FERC or FCC caps on these transactions were removed. Continuance of these caps in the Alger market structure still results in Bertrand prices, which would still be below levels required to give investors the incentive to expand capacity.

And even if the Alger process were attempted, the restructuring required might very well be quite limited. The target deconcentration levels in Alger were close to HHI values of 0.25, equivalent to four equal-sized firms. Without requiring joint ownership in single lines, markets the size of Pennsylvania, New York State, Illinois, and even California for gas pipeline space have been marked by so many separate link systems with common nodes that HHI levels have been driven down below 0.25 (see Tables 1, 2, and 3). Only the fringe states in each of these regional markets would experience reductions of HHI to that level. The power grids now restructured in RTOs have been owned by multiple retailers, so Alger restructuring would result in six or more retailers hawking their services in combined networks. This would not reduce the level of concentration in supply, since the combined service availability would still be determined by the ISO (competition, if any, would be limited to billing, advertising, and complaint management). Whether this would reduce grid space prices would be the problematical question; more shippers proposing to deliver power to some one retailer cannot reduce price-cost margins for that grid service.

The adoption of Alger rules in telecom markets would have limited effects on corporate performance. The licensing of long distance fiber-optic line capacity by the large three incumbent networks reduced concentration in recent years further than indicated by HHI levels in Table 13, which were in the range of 0.20 by the turn of the century. Resulting price-cost margins were in the range consistent with Bertrand interactive strategies, that is, lower than Alger would have found consistent with the proposed results from his restructuring plan. The only exceptions to prices at Bertrand levels, and therefore lower than long-run cost levels, have been associated with FCC-supported collective efforts in the collection of USF to set joint prices at higher levels. The capacity expansion or lack thereof in broadband can be attributed to bottleneck price caps of the FCC on local exchange network elements; applying Alger rules to these network elements would require the four Bell operating companies to sell rights to use links to the long distance carriers. This would not spur investment in elements and in long distance links and nodes as long as these sales prices in turn were set on TELRIC principles.

Vogelsang pricing, in contrast, could be deregulatory if that were to replace current regulations that make prices too low. But as pricing rules go, it is not adaptable to rule makings by FERC, the FCC, and state agencies because it triggers prices that differ depending on the dynamics of demand growth and on how much direct intervention there is in agency price intervention. In general, however, it requires that network prices be in three parts: an *access price* to get on the network, a *usage price* for each unit of the product shipped over the network, and a *congestion premium* to usage set at a level that eliminates any excess demand for link space. But if there is a regulatory cap on these latter two price components, rules would have the network company maximize its returns subject to that cap, which requires it to expand capacity as long as the congestion charge exceeds the access charge.

Adopting this approach requires the regulator to move away from network element pricing to overall caps. These caps differ if there is excess or deficient capacity, and "only if weights correspond to the quantities traded in the optimal state will investment under constraint be immediately optimal."[6] To be realistic, the performance of FERC and the FCC to date does not support the case for a shift to universal overarching price caps, adjusted for such complexities in the price cap and for company-to-company changes in demands for services.

Vogelsang-style adjustments can be made, however, depending on the industry. In gas transmission, if FERC rule making extended from the current two-part "straight fixed variable" to three-part tariffs, then the Vogelsang essentials would be in place. The trade-off to achieve lower congestion charges would add capacity wherever basis differential spikes have devastated line performance in recent years. FERC would have plenty to do in monitoring congestion charges to determine that they were no more than required to clear market hubs of excess demand. But FERC would also have to take the next step in deregulation, that of rule making along the lines of Order 636, to eliminate price controls on contracts of long distance market participants. That predictably would result in Cournot behavior, an improvement over current conditions derived from Bertrand conduct.

In electric power grid operation, FERC would require the three or four owners of the transmission network to give responsibility to the ISO not only to manage day-to-day operations but also to make strategic decisions on the three-part pricing mechanism, so as to generate cash flow for optimal grid expansion. Rather than dispersed decision making among the owners on whether to add to capacity when doing so reduces congestion costs, the system operator using the Vogelsang model would make these trade-offs. There need not be and should not be an overarching FERC cap on profits of the grid based on cost of service when the decision maker disperses returns to the owner—retail distributor. The superiority of a three-part tariff when there have been serious deficiencies in capacity expansion, leading to basis differential spikes ten times any reasonable usage charge, is so great that the case for eliminating FERC cost-of-service–based profit limits is overwhelming. The case for doing so with the ISO following Vogelsang decision rules but still subject to FERC caps is problematical because it requires that FERC be involved in the capacity expansion decisions, an involvement that has failed during the restructuring period. This would consist of reregulation, a failed initiative.

In the telecom industry, a combination of Alger and Vogelsang initiatives would make up reregulation versus deregulation. The FCC focus has been on regulating pricing of usage in local network elements; breaking down ownership to meet Alger structural specifications confronts the efficiency of single-source ownership of network links in local exchange such that gains in reduced price-cost margins cannot be expected. The gains from allowing the local exchange carrier to use or lease its elements at market-determined contract prices would increase price-cost margins to levels that predictably would reflect Cournot behavior. Whether released prices on network elements would rise to monopoly levels is a question scarcely worth asking, since margins have been negative since the implementation of TA96, and during that period most of the growth has occurred in markets that shifted out of agency jurisdiction. Price caps on wireline local exchange network elements can only increase the growth rates of cable and wireless networks, which are not now subject to price regulation of any consequence. The problem of partial deregulation has not involved containing monopoly pricing by price limits on these and other local exchange services but releasing the downward pressure of price controls on the earnings of local carriers. There has always been a cap on local exchange carrier prices, in cost-of-service rate levels set by state public utility commissions. By eliminating price caps on UNEs, that is, on access charges, reform would set loose the growth of broadband.

THE PROCESS FOR COMPLETE DEREGULATION

To get partial deregulation unstuck and complete the policy change required to accomplish improved network performance, including expansion, it is helpful to examine the network once again. Partial deregulation, remarkably, in all three industries, began with restructuring incumbent networks to open nodes to traffic from entrants. Adding requirements that network links had to provide common carriage services where they had not was a major step, since it vertically separated ownership of the product being shipped from that of the link and node system.

These steps created the potential for node congestion, as more foreign sources of demand called on the incumbent system to create new routes through its links. This created service congestion, to which regulators reacted by requiring more switching capacity (in telecom first before 1990) and then by capping prices at key service nodes (in gas hubs on firm transport, in electricity by setting transport congestion charges). This did prevent market clearing of the congestion during periods of peak demand at frequent intervals.

The fifteen years of congestion in these three industries has provided the basis for judgment on the effectiveness of restructuring, and of resort to the micromanaged price controls that followed. Cutting off further steps in the deregulatory process to invoke price controls was what had to be done from the view of the regulatory agency. The caps on prices were necessary to achieve the goals inherent in the process. Prices in the deregulation transition always had to be lower than they were under utility cost-of-service rates. But that limit on network service pricing in turn led to price volatility in the products transported—in out-of-scale basis differential spikes in gas and electricity and in costly spikes of demand for nonexistent broadband service to the Internet.

Restructuring did not change the configuration of the networks in any fundamental way. Opening the switch to create an exchange of product between carriers increased the number of sources of services at nodes beyond the entry node, but not the number at the entry or exit nodes. From the early 1990s, when this experiment to reduce supply concentration was under way, to the mid-2000s, when the results could be seen in some detail, the number of full network service providers with scale and scope remained in the range of three (electricity) to five or six (gas and telecom). The process of partial deregulation itself has not significantly added to sources of transport. The next deregulatory step is to abandon restructuring.

The abandonment has begun and is in progress, with the regulatory agencies not responding to acquisitions and disbursements that reverse the direction of the "deregulatory" structural change in the networks. The pipelines have expanded their self-owned gas divisions that provide a significant position for them in the product and allow them to participate in the windfall revenues from the basis differential spikes which are precluded by caps on transportation rates. This return to "merchant service" is an acknowledgement by FERC that long positions in gas tend to hedge their uncovered positions in transportation created by price controls. By creating such a hedge the network service provider can make a case for adding capacity. The reversal has not been as straightforward in power transmission because companies that own transmission have slowly and at great expense supported the substitution of local generation for long distance transmission, given that deregulated power plants have a profitability scenario not available to price-capped power grids. This breaks up the regional market into local markets, each with its own generation and limited transmission.

But it is in telecommunications that restructuring is in the process of reversal. The two largest long distance carriers have been acquired by local exchange service providers, thus closing down the artificial dividing line between local and long distance markets at the long distance switch. And with penetrations into both long distance and local revenues by wireless (cellular) service providers that do not have significant link costs related to distance, prices have begun to lose any relationship to local and long distance. And with FCC potential "forbearance" in structuring and pricing routing services to the Internet, the now-integrated local/long distance service provider has begun to pick up the technology and investment to create the capacity expansion into broadband predicted a decade ago.

The immediate concern in controlled, or partial, deregulation is that prices will rise if the caps are removed on firm pipeline space or power transmission or UNEs, not only at peak but on all services, because of the market power of the providers. But at this point in deregulation, such providers are instead locked in Bertrand conduct, which cannot change as a result of the removal of price caps. The Bertrand prices have been too low for more than a decade; they would increase only because of the elimination of the caps at peak, not at other times. They are now not regulated at other times. The elimination of caps should cause spikes to decline in magnitude, since incentives to increase network space would be present that are not now present given that returns from the spikes go to product owners and brokers not the networks. The spikes will decline in magnitude and number as investments would be triggered by some variant of the Vogelsang rule in the uncontrolled market. Without controls on bottleneck prices, most but not all spikes will become seasonal peaks in transportation charges, so that the final prices to consumers over the five-year period would gain a measure of stability at a lower average level.

The last step in deregulation is being taken first in telecommunications by the service providers themselves, most likely because of technology and the entry taking place outside the sphere of regulation. The key to FCC price controls was always the position that the market had to be protected from the full use of the price-setting power of the "dominant" wireline local exchange service provider. When AT&T was found to be no longer dominant, price caps were removed and the Cournot process among three carriers pushed prices down to levels more consistent with a Bertrand process (which was reversed only in the regulatory USF recovery process). Now the combined local/long distance carrier networks overlap and are layered by their own and other wireless networks of national scope, so local charges can scarcely be higher than long distance. If long distance fails the "dominance" test and is marked by more than three and less than six service providers, the inability to discriminate prevents dominance in local exchange. We are now close to having telephone service from the cable company and three or more cellular service providers; the incumbent local carrier will not and perhaps does not now have the structural hold in its markets required for it to be termed the "dominant" service provider that requires price caps.

On March 2, 2006, the Indiana state legislature sent the governor a bill that would end state agency controls on local retail telecom rates in 2009. In the interim, the local exchange carrier could increase the monthly access charge on basic service by $1.00 per year if it offered broadband service to at least 50 percent of the local exchange area within eighteen months of the first increase in that area.[7] The beginning of the end of a price control regulatory regime based on network technology is in place. While not as dramatic as the toppling of the statues of Stalin in Red Square, it is in the same direction.

Notes

PREFACE

1. Roger Noll, *The Slowdown in Regulatory Reform,* p. 2.
2. Energy and Environmental Analysis, *An Updated Assessment of Pipeline and Storage Infrastructure for the North American Gas Market,* p. 8.
3. Ibid., p. 9.
4. Ibid., p. 11.
5. Lynne Kiesling and Adrian T. Moore, "Movin' Juice: Making Electricity Transmission More Competitive," p. 1.
6. Ibid., title page "Conclusions and Recommendations," Part Four.
7. Roger Gray, "The Long-Term Consequences of California's Electricity Deregulation Experiment," pp. 3–4.
8. Michael. J. Boskin, "Reflections on the Bush Regulatory Period: The Good, the Bad, and the Ugly."

CHAPTER 1. INTRODUCTION TO NETWORK TECHNOLOGY AND MARKET STRUCTURE

1. As discussed later in the chapter, a key measure of market effectiveness is a measure of the concentration of ownership, calculated as the Herfindahl-Hirschman index (HHI). The use of the term *equivalence* indicates that the

HHI index, the sum of the squares of market shares, is equal to $1 / n$ for n equal-sized firms. When, for example, HHI equals 0.20, it is equivalent to five firms of equal size.

2. The price-cost margin has been used as the empirical measure of market power for more than sixty years. See Abba Lerner, "The Concept of Monopoly and the Measurement of Monopoly Power"; Keith Cowling and Michael Waterson, "Price-Cost Margins and Market Structure"; Roger A. Clark and Stephen W. Davies, "Market Structure and Price-Cost Margins"; William Landes and Richard Posner, "Market Power in Antitrust Cases"; Dennis Carlton and Jeffrey Perloff, *Modern Industrial Organization,* 2nd ed., pp. 352–354, 360–366. Carlton and Perloff cite numerous empirical studies that have used the price-cost margin to measure monopoly power.

3. If there is one source of supply, a monopoly, HHI is 1; if there are two equal-sized firms, then HHI (the sum of the squares of their shares) is 0.50 and the duopoly price-cost margin (equal to the inverse of the demand elasticity) is reduced to 0.50 of the previous level. This relationship between the price-cost margin and HHI is the monopoly margin times HHI, with HHI between 1 and 0 when the interactive strategies of the firms is what is termed *Cournot* (see below).

4. See, for example, Luis Cabral, *Introduction to Industrial Organization,* Chapter 9.

5. The conjectural variation can be represented as the partial derivative of all other firms' output with respect to a change in that firm's output. See Stephen Martin, *Advanced Industrial Economics,* Chapter 2; James Brander and Anming Zhang, "Market Conduct in the Airline Industry: An Empirical Investigation," p. 56.

6. For this particular form of the Lerner margin equation, I am indebted to Dr. Richard Lee Schmalensee in correspondence dated February 24, 2006.

7. Values of the conjectural variation parameter v that are sufficiently large to prove the existence of overt collusion are discussed in the text below.

8. Jeffrey Church and Roger Ware, *Industrial Organization: A Strategic Approach,* p. 314.

9. Dennis Carlton and Jeffrey Perloff, *Modern Industrial Organization,* 3rd ed., p. 121.

10. Paul W. MacAvoy, *The Economic Effects of Regulation: The Trunk-Line Railroad Cartels and the Interstate Commerce Commission before 1900,* Chapter 2.

CHAPTER 2. THE REGULATION OF NETWORKS

1. Diane Katz and Theodore R. Bolema, "Crossed Lines: Regulatory Missteps in Telecom Policy."

2. Franklin Perez, "The Case for a Deregulated Free Market Telecommunications Industry," p. 66.

3. William H. Melody, "Designing Utility Regulation for 21st Century Markets."

4. Janet Guyon and Jeanne Saddlers, "The AT&T Breakup—One Year Later."

5. "AT&T's New Strategy," p. 17.

6. Ingo Vogelsang, "Network Utilities in the U.S.—Sector Reforms without Privatization," p. 3.

7. See Federal Communications Commission, "Promotion of Competitive Networks in Local Telecommunications Markets," and Third Further Notice of Proposed Rulemaking in CC Docket no. 96-98.

8. *Telecommunications Act of 1996,* Section 251.

9. Rebecca Beynon, "The FCC's Implementation of the 1996 Act: Agency Litigation Strategies and Delay," p. 32.

10. *Telecommunications Act of 1996,* Section 251.

11. Ibid., Section 252.

12. Ibid.

13. Timothy J. Tardiff, "Pricing Unbundled Network Elements and the FCC's TELRIC Rule: Economic and Modeling Issues," p. 134.

14. Ibid.

15. Robert W. Crandall and Jerry A. Hausman, "Competition in U.S. Telecommunications Services: Effects of the 1996 Legislation," p. 85.

16. Ibid.

17. Reed Hundt, *You Say You Want a Revolution: A Story of Information Age Politics,* p. 125.

18. Crandall and Hausman, "Competition in U.S. Telecommunications Services," p. 81. See also Federal Communications Commission, "Federal Communications Commission Authorizes Bell Atlantic to Provide Long Distance Service in New York."

19. Peter W. Huber, "Local Exchange Competition under the 1996 Telecom Act: Red-Lining the Local Residential Customer," p. 42.

20. Laurence J. Kotlikoff, "Broadband: Breaking the Logjam."

21. Beynon, "The FCC's Implementation of the 1996 Act," p. 29.

22. Ameritech, Section 271 Application to the Federal Communications Commission.

23. *USTA v. FCC,* U.S. Court of Appeals, D.C. Circuit, March 2, 2004, D. 00-0102, p. 62.

24. See Robert W. Crandall, Allan T. Ingraham, and Hal J. Singer, "Do Unbundling Policies Discourage CLEC Facilities-Based Investment?"

25. Katz and Bolema, "Crossed Lines," p. 9

26. *Federal Power Act of 1935,* Chapter 687, Title II; *Public Utility Holding Company Act of 1935,* Title 15, 2C; see also Energy Information Administration, "The Changing Structure of the U.S. Electric Power Industry 1970–1991."

27. The developing federal regulation of private utilities accompanied the expansion in government power generation through large federal projects such as the Tennessee Valley Authority and Hoover Dam and through government subsidies of cooperative development through the Rural Electrification Authority. These large government projects brought down the price of energy and extended electric power to regions of the country that had not been served by private investor–owned utilities.

28. There are less important responsibilities, such as review of rates set by the federal power marketing administrations of exempt wholesale generator entities, and certification of qualifying small power production and cogeneration facilities. See note 26 for sources.

29. As disclosed in reports of the Federal Trade Commission made pursuant to S. Res. 83 (70th Congress, 1st sess.) and other reports made pursuant to the authority of Congress, the business of transporting and selling natural gas for ultimate distribution to the public is "affected with a public interest."

30. Federal Power Commission, *Annual Report for 1955,* pp. 106–107.

31. For more detail, see Paul MacAvoy, *The Natural Gas Market: Sixty Years of Regulation and Deregulation.*

32. State restructuring efforts typically required utilities to sell their generation assets. As many have argued, divestiture was motivated by the desire to lessen the ability of utilities to exercise market power in the new markets for generation. (See, for example, Severin Borenstein and James Bushnell, "An Empirical Analysis of Market Power in a Deregulated California Electricity Market"; Severin Borenstein, James Bushnell, and Christopher R. Knittel, "Market Power in Electricity Markets: Beyond Concentration Measures"; Scott M. Harvey and William W. Hogan, "Market Power and Withholding"; James D. Reitzes, Robert L. Earle, and Philip Q. Hanser, "Deregulation and Monitoring of Electric Power Markets." Since many utilities had not recovered the costs of these regulatory assets from customers before divestiture, however, restructuring legislation imposed a temporary "competitive transition charge" on consumers to pay for remaining stranded costs [that is, the costs were stranded by changing regulation]. In California alone, these costs were estimated to be $21 billion to $25 billion. See S. Keith Berry, "Generation Search Costs and Ramsey Pricing in a Partially Deregulated Electric Utility Industry.") Moody's surveys estimated that nationally, stranded costs were on the order of $135 billion and that half of the nation's 114 largest utilities had a stranded cost exposure exceeding 50 percent of their book value. (Mark S. Johnson, Marcia Niles, and Stacey Suydam, "Regulatory Changes in the Electric Utility Industry: Investigation of Effects on Shareholder Wealth.")
33. According to the Energy Information Administration, as presented in Edison Electric Institute, *Natural Gas Procurement Survey,* twenty-one states had residential choice. Of those, ten had discontinued or had less than 10 percent participation; four states had 10 percent to 20 percent participation; two states had 20 percent to 40 percent participation; and five had more than 40 percent participation.
34. This comparison makes sense only under cost-of-service regulation. The retailer can self-generate at average variable cost, which is higher than wheeled average cost; but by self-generating it also can recover fixed costs on its own generation plant plus the allowed profit return in the cost-of-service regulated price.
35. There were more than 600 entities with market-based rates filed at FERC by the close of 2004. There were 467 independent power markets, 128 marketers that were affiliated with utilities, 401 marketers that were affiliated with power producers, 83 incumbent utilities with market-based rates, and 169 other utilities with market-based rates. Federal Energy Regulatory Commission, "Market Based Rate List."
36. Federal Energy Regulatory Commission, "Wholesale Power Market Platform: Remedying Undue Discrimination through Open Access Transmission Service and Standard Electricity Market Design," p. 1.
37. Frank Felder, review of Steven Stoft, *Power System Economics: Designing Markets for Electricity,* p. 113.
38. David M. Newbery, "Playing the Game."
39. Ibid., p. 39.

CHAPTER 3. ELECTRIC AND GAS NETWORK PERFORMANCE AND PARTIAL DEREGULATION

1. Vadim Marmer, Dmitry Shapiro, and Paul W. MacAvoy, "Bottlenecks in Regional Markets for Natural Gas Transmission Services."
2. Natural gas demand elasticities have been compiled and analyzed by Carol Dahl and Carlos Roman, "Energy Demand Elasticities—Fact or Fiction: A Survey Update." Based on this work, the elasticity estimated for the industry as a whole had a mean (simple average) price elasticity of −0.069 in the short run and −0.419 in the long run.

   This result was based on industrial and residential usage figures, as follows: The industrial short-run price elasticities had a mean of −0.03, standard deviation of 0.58, minimum of −0.51, and maximum of 0.86 based on seven separate studies. The industrial long-run price elasticities had a mean of −1.35, standard deviation of 1.92, minimum of −4.27, and maximum of 1.78 based on nine estimates. For residential short-run price elasticities, the mean was −0.13, standard deviation was 0.07, minimum was −0.29, and maximum was 0.03 based on twelve studies. For residential long-run price elasticities, the mean was −0.56, standard deviation was 0.44, minimum was −1.37, and maximum was 0.24 based on thirteen studies.

   Based on the assumption that these are estimates of elasticities for delivered gas demands at wholesale or retail, not gas transportation, we find the elasticity for transport is in fixed proportion, and transportation prices range from one-third to one-half of city gate wholesale prices. Based on these assumptions, transport demand elasticities equal residential and industrial estimates multiplied by one-third to one-half.
3. *Economic value added* (EVA), a copyrighted tool of financial consulting firm Stern Stewart, is equal to "net operating profit minus an appropriate charge for the opportunity cost of all capital invested in an enterprise." James Grant describes EVA greater than 0 representing "the company's after-tax operating profits exceed[ing] the dollar cost of [its] capital" and its managers thus "add wealth to shareholders." By contrast, when EVA is negative, "the firm's managers destroy value by investing in capital projects that fall short of the returns required by both debt and equity security holders." See Stern Stewart, "About EVA," and James L. Grant, "Foundations of EVA™ for Investment Managers," pp. 41–42.
4. Based on Compustat compilations of the financial statements of the pipelines and Ibbotson calculations of industry risk, EVA was determined as follows:

   Net operating profit less adjusted taxes (NOPLAT) = earnings before interest and taxes (EBIT) less adjusted taxes plus or minus change in adjusted taxes
   Return on investment capital (ROIC) = NOPLAT / last year's operating invested capital
   Weighted average cost of capital (WACC) = return on debt and equity times relevant debt/equity
   EVA = ROIC − WACC

5. Although there are differences in terminology at FERC, the independent system operation, or ISO, is similar enough to a regional transmission organization, or RTO, to use the terms interchangeably.
6. Federal Energy Regulatory Commission, Notice of Inquiry, "Oversight and Recovery Practices for RTOs and ISOs."

7. Moody's Investors Service, "Stranded Costs Will Threaten Credit Quality of U.S. Electrics." Moody's survey cited in Margaret Jess, "Restructuring Energy Industries: Lessons from Natural Gas." Jess stated that "many experts have estimated a value of about $135 billion with other estimates ranging from $50 billion to $300 billion. In 1995 as a percent of the value of final electric industry sales ($208 billion), these amounts would be equivalent to 65, 24, or 144 percent, respectively."

8. See Paul L. Joskow, "Patterns of Transmission Investment," for a description of the two-part pricing schemes along these lines of the PJM system operators in Pennsylvania, New Jersey, and other eastern states. The PJM administers a tariff that requires owners of the grid to charge cost-based prices for access (including financial transmission rights, or FTRs, that are assignable) and for usage (the locational marginal price, or LMP).

9. James L. Sweeney, *The California Electricity Crisis*, p. 128.

10. Electric demand elasticities have been compiled and analyzed by Carol Dahl and Carlos Roman, "Energy Demand Elasticities—Fact or Fiction: A Survey Update." Based on this work, the elasticity estimated for the industry as a whole had a mean (simple average) price elasticity of -0.14 in the short run and -0.32 in the long run. This result was constructed on industrial and residential usage, as follows: The industrial short-run price elasticities had a mean of -0.14, standard deviation of 0.15, minimum of -0.33, and maximum of 0.11 based on eleven separate studies. The industrial long-run price elasticities had a mean of -0.56, standard deviation of 0.43, minimum of -1.88, and maximum of 0 based on forty-four estimates. For residential short-run price elasticities, the mean was -0.23, standard deviation was 0.22, minimum was -0.95, and maximum was -0.12 based on thirteen studies. For residential long-run price elasticities, the mean was -0.43, standard deviation was 0.5, minimum was -1.5, and maximum was -0.65 based on thirty-eight studies.

The assumption is that these are estimates of elasticities for delivered electric demands at wholesale or retail, not solely transportation. We stipulate that the demand for transport is in fixed proportion to the demand for gas, and transportation prices range from one-third to one-half of city gate wholesale prices. Based on these assumptions, transport demand elasticities equal residential and industrial estimates multiplied by one-third to one-half. We use the combined average for the purpose of estimating an aggregate coefficient of conjectural variation.

11. U.S. Department of Energy, "National Transmission Grid Study."

CHAPTER 4. THE STRATEGIC RESPONSE OF PACIFIC GAS AND ELECTRIC CORPORATION TO PARTIAL DEREGULATION DURING THE CALIFORNIA POWER CRISIS

1. See California Public Utilities Commission, Division of Strategic Planning, "California's Electric Services Industry: Perspectives on the Past, Strategies for the Future," p. 1.

2. Ibid.

3. See, for example, California Public Utilities Commission, Decision no. 96-01-009 (January 10, 1996).

4. An exception to the frozen 1996 levels occurred on January 1, 1998, when rates for small commercial and residential customers were reduced by 10 percent and remained frozen

at this reduced level. As discussed later in the chapter, this reduction was financed by the substitution of long-term bond debt rates for the higher full rate of return for divested generation facilities.

5. The legislation also authorized accelerated depreciation for high-cost nuclear power plant facilities, which were expected to remain under utility ownership. These transition charges were "non-bypassable." Customers who chose alternative energy providers were required to continue to pay a share of these costs so that cost recovery would not accrue only to those customers remaining with utility bundled service. Paragraph 367, Article 6, of AB 1890 ("Requirements for the Public Utility Commission") states in part:

> 367. The commission shall identify and determine those costs and categories of cost for generation-related assets and obligations, consisting of generation facilities, generation-related regulatory assets, nuclear settlements, and power purchase contracts, including, but not limited to, restructurings, renegotiations or terminations thereof approved by the commission, that were being collected in commission-approved rates on December 20, 1995, and that may become uneconomic as a result of a competitive generation market, in that these costs may not be recoverable in market prices in a competitive market, and appropriate costs incurred after December 20, 1995, for capital additions to generating facilities existing as of December 20, 1995, that the commission determines are reasonable and should be recovered, provided that these additions are necessary to maintain the facilities through December 31, 2001. These uneconomic costs shall be recovered from all customers on a nonbypassable basis and shall:
>
> (a) Be amortized over a reasonable time period, including collection on an accelerated basis, consistent with not increasing rates for any rate schedule, contract, or tariff option above the levels in effect on June 10, 1996; provided that, the recovery shall not extend beyond December 31, 2001, except as follows: (1) Costs associated with employee-related transition costs as set forth in subdivision (b) of Section 375 shall continue until fully collected; provided, however, that the cost collection shall not extend beyond December 31, 2006. (2) Power purchase contract obligations shall continue for the duration of the contract. Costs associated with any buy-out, buy-down, or renegotiation of the contracts shall continue to be collected for the duration of any agreement governing the buy-out, buy-down, or renegotiated contract; provided, however, no power purchase contract shall be extended as a result of the buy-out, buy-down, or renegotiation.

6. CPUC's order of December 20, 1995, regarding "The Preferred Policy Decision" described the utilities' recovery of generation costs in the following manner: "To assure the continued financial integrity of the utilities, and give them an opportunity to be vital market participants in the restructured market following the transition, we will allow them to recover completely costs associated with contracts for power and prior regulatory commitments, called regulatory assets." California Public Utilities Commission, Decision No. 95-12-063 (December 20, 1995), p. 77.

7. The legislation also created an immediate 10 percent rate reduction for small customers to be financed through rate reduction bonds. To pay for the 10 percent reduction, the utility refinanced the expected revenue reduction from the rate decrease on its service level with the proceeds from the sale of these bonds. The bonds allow for rate reductions

by lowering the carrying costs on a portion of the transition costs and by deferring recovery of a portion of these costs until after the transition period. The long-run scenario in the legislation had the "anticipated result" that the "subsequent, cumulative rate reduction for residential and small commercial customers [would be no less than 20 percent by April 1, 2002]." Other features of restructuring, such as consumer protection requirements for new market entrants and job protection of utility generation employees, are not addressed here.

8. Pacific Gas and Electric Corporation, *1996 Annual Report.*

9. Ibid.

10. See California Public Utilities Commission, Decision no. 01-01-018 (January 2001), pp. 15–16. See also this decision, Order on Summary Judgment, p. 52.

11. In April 1997, CPUC issued an order opening a rule making and investigation to establish "standards of conduct" governing relations between California gas and electric utilities and their affiliated, unregulated entities providing energy and energy-related services. CPUC was also intent on accelerating the development of competition in retail services, in which PG&E had operated with a franchise monopoly for decades. In May 1997, CPUC issued its opinion allowing direct access for all alternative service providers for these services to customer classes beginning January 1, 1998, and it established rules regarding the terms and conditions of service of the proposed alternative providers.

12. The opinion focused on the treatment of PG&E's two nuclear power plants at Diablo Canyon. The commission determined the plants' original investment cost for purposes of recovery in forthcoming revenues from power they produced; after that amount had been recovered, power from these plants was subject to market pricing.

13. Similarly, in December 1997, the commission denied a request of the San Diego Gas and Electric Company to purchase power via bilateral contracts with producers outside the California PX.

14. Frank A. Wolak, "Lessons from the California Electricity Crisis," p. 8.

15. Ibid.

16. The original accounting rules promulgated by CPUC in 1997 in Resolution E-3514 provided that balances in the TRA would be transferred to the TCBA each month during the rate freeze. In 1998, the commission changed this rule when it adopted Resolution E-3527, which specified that only positive balances in the TRA would be transferred to the TCBA at the end of each month.

17. PG&E had also sought commission approval at this time to sell its power plant at Hunters Point in San Francisco, but issues associated with the facility's air-quality permits led instead to it being included in a later auction of PG&E's Bay Area facilities. See California Energy Commission, "Electric Generation Divestiture in California."

18. The Protrero Power Station, PG&E's second power station in San Francisco, was ultimately returned to PG&E primarily because of political pressure and local concerns about reliability. Only the utility geothermal generation facilities sold for less than book value, generating stranded costs of approximately $31 million, more than offset by the excess booking of purchase prices on the fossil plants.

19. See California Public Utilities Commission, Decision no. 99-10-057 (October 21, 1999), p. 16.

20. See Ibid., p. 18.

21. PG&E energy purchase costs in excess of rate revenues did not affect corporate earnings because balancing accounts were treated as investments. It was not until the release of PG&E's annual report for 2000, and its fourth-quarter earnings report for 2000, both of which were issued after the announcement of PG&E's bankruptcy, that undercollections in the TRA affected corporate earnings to a significant degree.

22. California Public Utilities Commission, Decision no. 00-10-065 (October 19, 2000), p. 2 (hereinafter October 2000 Short-Term Debt Order).

23. California Public Utilities Commission, Decision no. 00-12-064 (December 21, 2000), p. 5 (hereinafter December 2000 Long-Term Debt Order).

24. Ibid., p. 9.

25. The determination of the generally accepted accounting standard is found in Financial Accounting Standards Board, "Accounting for the Impairment of Long-Lived Assets."

26. Pacific Gas and Electric Corporation, *2000 Annual Report,* p. 49.

27. The holding company regularly declared dividends to common stockholders, consistent with the intent to distribute to shareholders the recovery of former invested capital in the power plants. Whether to reinvest in the newly focused two-part strategy, to underwrite generation investments in other states, or to withdraw altogether and return money to stockholders can be conceived as "investor's choice," as evidenced by the relative share price increase.

28. See Pacific Gas and Electric Corporation, *2000 Annual Report,* p. 65.

29. The PX initially established one-day-ahead and day-of markets for power. Most sales were made on a day-ahead basis; that is, wholesale power was purchased in transactions involving next-day delivery. To the extent that day-ahead purchases did not match actual demand on the day of delivery, additional power was bought and sold on an hourly basis on that day.

30. California Public Utilities Commission, "Report on Wholesale Electric Generation Investigation," p. 10.

31. Prices in 1999 had followed this pattern, rising over the summer to generate negative headroom only in October, then declining to generate positive headroom throughout the subsequent winter.

32. Edison Electric Institute, Staff Summary, "California Travails: A Chronology of Events in California's Energy Crisis" (hereinafter EEI Staff Summary on California Energy Crisis).

33. See, for example, *San Diego Union-Tribune,* "Deregulation Timeline."

34. U.S. Congressional Budget Office, "Causes and Lessons of the California Electricity Crisis," p. 4, Box 1.

35. Ibid., p. 4.

36. See PBS, Frontline, "The California Crisis, California Timeline."

37. Pursuant to AB 1890, the utility was required to purchase all power from the PX to meet the needs of its customers. According to PG&E's annual report for 2000, its total cost of power purchases at market prices that year was $9.51 billion. However, PG&E also reported 2000 proceeds from sales into the PX of $2.77 billion, suggesting that the utility's self-generated power accounted for approximately 29 percent of its overall purchases.

38. See EEI Staff Summary on California Energy Crisis.

39. Ibid.

40. October 2000 Short-Term Debt Order, p. 1. Specifically, PG&E requested authority to increase from approximately $1.3 billion to approximately $2.7 billion the amount of short-term debt that PG&E could issue beyond that authorized by Section 823(c) of the California Public Utilities Code. The types of short-term debt for which PG&E sought authority to issue included commercial paper, direct bank borrowings, bank notes, extendible commercial notes, money market notes, and other such debt with a maturity of less than twelve months. Ibid., pp. 1–2. See also Pacific Gas and Electric Company, Application of Pacific Gas and Electric Company for an Expedited Order Modifying Decision no. 87-09-056.

41. See October 2000 Short-Term Debt Order, pp. 1–3. See also Pacific Gas and Electric Company, Application Modifying Decision No. 87-09-056.

42. October 2000 Short-Term Debt Order, p. 9. According to the commission's "conclusions of law" associated with the authorization, PG&E's request for authority to issue additional short-term debt was "reasonable," and immediate action on the application was "necessary . . . in order to avoid the possibility of PG&E being unable to fund its ongoing operations." Ibid., p. 8.

43. Ibid., p. 2. PG&E had also sought authorization to use a portion of the long-term debt authorization for "general corporate purposes" and other purposes authorized under Section 817 of the California Public Utilities Code. See ibid. See also Pacific Gas and Electric Company, Expedited Application of Pacific Gas and Electric Company to Issue, Sell, and Deliver One or More Series of Its First and Refunding Mortgage Bonds.

44. December 2000 Long-Term Debt Order, p. 3.

45. Ibid., p. 30. CPUC also authorized PG&E to use up to $370 million of the additional $2 billion authorized "for the purposes listed in Pub. Util. Code Section 817, but only if PG&E does not need [the] $370 million to finance its TRA undercollection." Ibid., p. 2. In addition, the commission allowed PG&E to accrue interest on the portion of its TRA undercollection financed with long-term debt on more favorable rates (that is, on the lower of [i] the three-month commercial paper rate, or [ii] the actual cost of long-term debt used by PG&E to finance the TRA undercollection), and it allowed PG&E to exclude long-term debt financing of the TRA undercollection from being considered as part of its authorized capital structure. See ibid., pp. 6, 30–31.

46. Ibid., p. 5; that is, there was insufficient headroom, given prices for power four times the frozen retail price in order to allow inclusion of the wholesale power costs in operating expenses.

47. See California Public Utilities Commission, Decision no. 01-05-057 (May 14, 2001), p. 2.

48. See California Public Utilities Commission, January 2001 Gas Accounts Order, p. 3 (private papers of the author).

49. Ibid.

50. Ibid., pp. 3–7.

51. PG&E subsequently petitioned for extensions to the ninety-day authorization, which the commission granted through a number of orders. In February 2001, CPUC granted the utility an additional three months of permission; in doing so, the commission re-

frained from satisfying PG&E's request to receive a full year of approval to pledge customer gas and electric accounts receivable, noting that a total of 180 days "should be adequate for PG&E to procure gas for the remainder of the winter heating season and to replenish much of its core inventory." California Public Utilities Commission, Decision no. 01-02-050 (February 15, 2001), p. 5. Following PG&E's bankruptcy filing, other commission decisions allowed annual extensions to the authorization, with the result that the utility finally had approval to pledge its accounts receivable through May 2004. See California Public Utilities Commission, Decision no. 01-06-074 (June 28, 2001); Decision No. 02-03-025, (March 6, 2002); Decision no. 03-02-061 (February 27, 2003).

52. October 2000 Short-Term Debt Order, p. 8.
53. See Pacific Gas and Electric Company, Emergency Application to Adopt a Rate Stabilization Plan.
54. See Pacific Gas and Electric Company, Application; and Application of PG&E, Southern California Edison, and TURN; Pacific Gas and Electric Company, Emergency Petition to Modify Decision.

CHAPTER 5. THE LONG DISTANCE TELEPHONE NETWORKS AND PARTIAL DEREGULATION

1. Robert W. Crandall and Jerry A. Hausman, "Competition in U.S. Telecommunications Services: Effects of the 1996 Legislation," p. 82.
2. Ibid.
3. Ibid., p. 85.
4. Timothy J. Tardiff, "Pricing Unbundled Network Elements and the FCC's TELRIC Rule: Economic and Modeling Issues," p. 134.
5. Ibid.
6. Tim Sloan, "Creating Better Incentives through Regulation," p. 10.
7. Paul Gottlieb et al., "The Economic Impact of SBC Ameritech's Entry into the Long Distance Market in Ohio," p. 12.
8. See Federal Communications Commission, Second Report and Order in CC Docket no. 96-149 and Third Report and Order in CC Docket no. 96-61, p. 66. When one considers that the geographic extent of a market is defined to be the area within which prices at points of sale tend to equality (after taking account of transportation costs), then it becomes apparent that inter-LATA calls within the United States constitute a market. See Alfred Marshall, *Principles of Economics,* p. 325; Augustin Cournot, *Recherches sur les principes mathematiques de la théories des richesses.*
9. Federal Communications Commission, Second Report and Order in CC Docket no. 96-149 and Third Report and Order in CC Docket no. 96-61, p. 66. Even if there is evidence to suggest that "there is or could be a lack of competition in a particular point-to-point market," the market is still to be considered national in geographic scope if there is also "a showing that geographic rate averaging will sufficiently mitigate the exercise of market power." Ibid.
10. *Communications Act of 1934,* as amended, paragraph 254(g).
11. See WorldCom and MCI Communications, Application of WorldCom, Inc., and MCI Communications Corporation for Transfer and Control of MCI Communications Cor-

poration to WorldCom, Inc., CC Docket no. 97-211. In addition to the domestic markets, the commission also identified three international product markets: (1) mass market, (2) larger business market, and (3) transport capacity market. The geographic markets for the first two products were country-pair routes and for the third product Atlantic, Pacific, and Caribbean/Latin America. See ibid., pp. 79, 84, 123.

12. Wholesale transactions with GTE, Frontier, and WorldCom alone accounted for roughly half of Qwest's network capacity in 1999. See, for example, "Qwest Nipping Heels of IXC Leaders with Partnerships, Expanded Networks"; "BellSouth Begins Long Distance Qwest"; "Qwest Awarded Additional $15 Million Contract from Star Telecommunications" (twenty-year wholesale commitment with Star Telecommunications); "Qwest, Williams Business Models Evolve Beyond Fiber." Qwest announced in December 1998 that it would sell application hosting services as e-commerce systems, Web server hosting, virtual private networks, media streaming services, and managed software services. See "Qwest, Williams Business Models"; "Qwest Communications Speeds Toward Completion of World's First Network Optimized for Internet Communications."

13. The share figures in Table 13 are based on carriers' total toll service revenues, excluding the "local toll" revenues of incumbent local exchange carriers. These were defined as revenues from long distance services within a LATA, a defined area in which the franchise carrier was the local exchange carrier. For example, with the lower peninsula of Michigan divided (by the antitrust court) into two LATAs, a long distance call within one LATA, say from Detroit to Ann Arbor, was a "local toll" call and its revenues accrued to the local exchange carrier. See Federal Communications Commission, "Statistics of Communications Common Carriers," 2003/2004 ed., Table 1.4, and "Statistics of Communications Common Carriers," 2001/2002 ed.

14. For an earlier discussion of the direct intervention of the FCC in market sharing, see Paul W. MacAvoy, *The Failure of Antitrust and Regulation to Establish Competition in Long-Distance Telephone Services,* Chapters 3 and 4.

15. Since the regional and specialized service carrier realized only a portion of national toll service revenues, for whatever of that service they provided the three carriers, they did not account for any increased control of the national market.

16. Paul A. Samuelson and William D. Nordhaus, *Economics,* p. 743.

17. Sources for the MTS price indices include HTL Telemanagement (HTLT), and the Telecommunications Research Action Center (TRAC), a not-for-profit telecommunications industry consumer advocacy group. HTLT makes available for purchase databases of interexchange carrier rate data based on tariffs filed by the firms with the FCC, although data are generally available only for the period before the detariffing of interstate long distance services by the commission in 2001. TRAC makes available for purchase its *TeleTips* publications, which include "Long Distance Comparison Charts" for various residential and small business interexchange plan prices. See, for example, TRAC, "*TeleTips:* Residential Long Distance Comparison Chart."

18. The discount MTS prices shown in Table 15 were calculated as follows: first, using HTLT data, the prices per minute for available discount plans were estimated for the same calling pattern and time-of-day assumptions as for standard plans. For any given period, the

"best available" discount MTS plan—defined to be the one resulting in the lowest price to the consumer given the calling plan assumptions—was selected. For periods after 2000, discount plan data come from the TRAC *TeleTips* publications; again, calling pattern assumptions were held constant and applied where appropriate. For additional information regarding the methodology and assumptions used to construct the discount MTS price series, see Paul W. MacAvoy and Michael A. Williams, *Deregulation of Entry in Long-Distance Telecommunications,* Appendix I.

19. The discount MTS plans for each period were as follows: AT&T discount plans were Reach Out America Block of Time—One-Hour Plan with Day and Evening Option (12/1/88 to 1/15/94), True Reach Savings (1/16/94 to 7/31/96), Simplified Calling Promotion "One Rate" (8/1/96 to 11/10/97), One Rate Plus (11/11/97 to 7/31/99), One Rate 7 Cents Plan (8/1/99 to 7/1/00), One Rate Saver (5/00 to 2/01), 5 Cent Weekends (3/02 to 2/04), and 150 Monthly Minutes (3/04 to present). MCI discount plans were Prime Time (8/1/89 to 5/31/92), AnyTime (6/1/92 to 12/31/96), Basic Calling Plan—Option 1 (1/1/97 to 5/31/97), MCI One (6/1/97 to 5/30/98), Basic Calling Plan—Option 6 (6/1/98 to 10/31/99), Seven Cents Anytime (11/1/99 to 7/1/00), 5 Cent Everyday Plus (5/00 to 2/01), One Net Savings (3/01 to 12/01), Select 200 (1/02 to 5/03), and Nationwide 200 (6/03 to present). Sprint discount plans were Sprint Plus Usage Discounts (5/1/89 to 6/30/94), The Most II (7/1/94 to 10/25/96), Sprint Sense Day (10/26/96 to 5/30/98), Sprint Sense AnyTime (6/1/98 to 7/1/00), Sprint Nickel Nights (5/00 to 2/01), Sprint Nickel Anytime (3/01 to 2/04), and Sprint 7 Cents Anytime (3/04 to 12/04).

20. See MacAvoy, *The Failure of Antitrust and Regulation,* p. 106 n2.

21. See California Public Utilities Commission, "Direct Testimony of John Sumpter on Behalf of AT&T Communications of California, Inc."

22. Assuming toll switch traffic volumes of 5,000, 9,000, 10,000, and 15,000 minutes of use per circuit per month, the study estimated that AT&T's per-minute network costs for switching, transmission, and ancillary network operations across all services were likely to be $0.0129, $0.0072, $0.0065, and $0.0043, respectively. Charles L. Jackson, "A Bottom-Up Estimate of the TELRIC of Long Distance Calling." Additional confirmation comes from AT&T contracts at wholesale that range from $0.01 per minute to $0.02 per minute; on the assumption that AT&T does not give away service at prices below marginal costs, then its marginal operating costs must be less than $0.01 per minute.

23. Wharton Econometric Forecasting Associates, "Economic Impact of Eliminating the Line of Business Restrictions on the Bell Companies," citing Bellcore data, pp. 20–21.

24. These cost studies in effect assume that the incremental network costs of AT&T, MCI, and Sprint are approximately the same. This is not surprising, given that all three firms use the same fiber-optic technology and purchase switches and other equipment from the same suppliers, that is, Ericsson, Lucent, and Nortel.

25. For the purpose of estimating price-cost margins, Wharton Econometric Forecasting Associates' estimate has been used of network operating costs of $0.01 per minute for switched interstate MTS. To the extent that incremental operating costs have declined over time, marginal costs have fallen more rapidly than is estimated here.

26. While the discussion thus far has focused on the standard and discount MTS of the mass market, similar results—steadily rising price-cost margins—are seen when one observes

prices and costs for larger business services. Specifically, I have previously shown that price-cost margins for switched inbound WATS, dedicated inbound WATS, switched outbound WATS and integrated services, and dedicated outbound WATS and integrated services rose substantially over the 1987–2000 period. But the vulnerability of tariff pricing to discounting in the business transactions of the leading carriers is indicated by the increases in market shares of "other" carriers—wholesale and specialized carriers serving large corporate subscribers with contract prices lower than tariff and outside the tariff system. See MacAvoy and Williams, *Deregulation of Entry,* pp. 64–66.

27. See Jim Lande and Kenneth Lynch, "Telecommunications Industry Revenues 2002," Table 9; Federal Communications Commission, "Universal Service Monitoring Report," Table 7.8.

28. As has been discussed elsewhere, ARPM is not an appropriate measure of a transaction price. No consumer has ever picked up the phone, placed a long distance call, and paid ARPM; that is, the probability that the tariff price of a call was equal to ARPM is approximately zero. See MacAvoy and Williams, *Deregulation of Entry,* pp. 43–45.

29. The Lerner index, $(p - mc) / p = $ HHI $(1 + v) / e,$ so that $[v = [((p - mc / p] \cdot e) / $ HHI$] - 1]$ for e equal to market demand elasticity.

30. Total toll service revenues for AT&T, MCI, and Sprint in 2002 were approximately $52.27 billion. In 2002, the toll service revenues of AT&T, MCI, and Sprint were $27.5 billion, $17.7 billion, and $7.1 billion, respectively. See Federal Communications Commission, Industry Analysis and Technology Division, "Trends in Telephone Service," Table 9.6.

31. As in a one-shot Bertrand game, but not a sequential Bertrand game that converged on the price level equal to marginal cost. That this kept the interactive pricing in a single round is shown by the lack of second and third tariff revisions by AT&T after its traditional January and July postings.

32. The other explanation is that this reversal of margins and concentration is a product of decisions made here as to data sources and the numbers themselves. The decision not to include marketing and customer acquisition costs in marginal costs causes the value of v to be overstated, more in later than earlier years. The decision to not try to adjust elasticity estimates each year, even though the widespread movement to cellular probably increased elasticity in later years, causes an underestimate of positive v in later years.

33. Federal Communications Commission, "Detariffing of Long Distance Telephone Industry to Become Effective at the End of the Month."

34. Ibid.

35. The statute reads in part that a "Bell operating company, or any affiliate of that Bell operating company, may provide interLATA services originating in any of its in-region States . . . if the Commission approves the application of such company for such State." Communications Act of 1934, as amended, paragraphs 271(b)(1). See also ibid., paragraphs 271(d)(3).

36. Hawaii and Alaska are the two states for which paragraph 271 approvals have not been sought since neither state had an RBOC as its incumbent local exchange carrier.

37. According to NASDAQ, the North American Telecommunications Index "contains NASDAQ listed companies classified according to the FTSE™ Global Classification as

Television, Radio & Filmed Entertainment, Subscription Entertainment Networks, and Telecommunications Services and Equipment. They include independent radio and television contractors, film production, providers of television, media services and programming facilities including those driven by subscription, operators of wireless and fixed-line telecommunication services, and manufacturers and distributors of digital equipment used in telecommunication." The makeup of the index is relatively fluid; as of November 2004, it was composed of 250 securities. NASDAQ, "Index Descriptions: Indices of the NASDAQ Stock Market."

38. Standard & Poor's 500 index is a capitalization-weighted index of five hundred stocks that represents "the price trend movements of the major common stock of U.S. public companies" and is commonly "used to measure the performance of the entire U.S. domestic stock market." Similarly, the Dow Jones Industrial Average is an index generally "used to measure the performance of the U.S. financial markets." According to the New York Stock Exchange, the Dow "has become the most widely recognized stock market indication in the U.S. and probably in the entire world," reflecting not only "the health of the U.S. economy" but also "providing some insight into the economic well-being of the global economy." New York Stock Exchange, "NYSE Glossary."

39. "Too Many Debts; Too Few Calls—The Telecom Crisis." See also Jessica Hall, "Telecoms Facing a 'Perfect Storm'" (citing FCC Chairman Michael Powell).

40. See, for example, Toby Weber, "Telecom's Broken Backbone"; Simon Romero, "Spectacular Rise, Staggering Fall."

41. See "Too Many Debts; Too Few Calls" (citing Andrew Odlyzko of the University of Minnesota).

42. Jerry Knight, "WorldCom Woes Pop the Region's Telecom Bubble," p. E01.

43. "Too Many Debts; Too Few Calls."

44. Specifically, EBITDA is given as operating income plus depreciation and amortization, which basically equates to net operating revenues less the sum of the following: costs of services and products; selling, general, and administrative expenses; and other expenses categorized as operating expenses (e.g., restructuring and impairment charges). Data were collected from the carriers' 10-K filings with the U.S. Securities and Exchange Commission and represent consolidated results for the companies. Over time, AT&T, MCI, and Sprint have revised and corrected their reported earnings and income figures. The data presented in the figures are the most recent issued by the firms where net income, operating income, and depreciation and amortization are all reported.

45. MCI, which was acquired by WorldCom and then filed for bankruptcy protection, issued a number of substantial restatements to its figures for reported earnings and net income. Data for MCI are reported only back through 1997, as earnings and net income figures reported by the firm before that time appear to be inconsistent with those reported since.

46. Sprint Corporation, Form 10-K for the Fiscal Year Ended December 31, 2002, p. 14.

47. Ibid., p. 22. See also Sprint Corporation, Form 10-K for the Fiscal Year Ended December 31, 2003.

48. See note 3, Chapter 3, above.

49. Data calculated and EVA determined as in note 4, Chapter 3, above.

50. The table also presents EVA for before the merger of MCI and WorldCom. As the table shows, EVA was close to zero for much of the decade and was negative in its last year of existence as a separately tracked company.

51. According to a different estimate by Stern Stewart, AT&T had EVA of *negative* $9.97 billion in 2002; in other words, AT&T saw destruction in net shareholder value of nearly $10 billion that year. Richard A. Brealey and Stewart C. Myers, *Principles of Corporate Finance,* p. 325, citing Stern Stewart data.

52. AT&T, "Universal Service Fund (USF) Revisions—Questions and Answers."

53. See Federal Communications Commission, Report and Order.

54. The market demand curve has to satisfy Marshall's second law, that is, price elasticity is higher for higher prices; there is no information to the contrary for absorption rates of ad valorem taxes in oligopoly. See Sophia Delipalla and Owen O'Donnell, "Estimating Tax Incidence, Market Power and Market Conduct."

55. If the "perfect" cartel were in place, then not only should price-cost margins increase to another level, but the financial performance of those carriers should improve over time and relative to other telecom companies. There was no such improvement. All service revenues declined for the three incumbent carriers during 2000–02 (the years of the greatest control of USF revenues; see Table 25), EBITDA varied from high to negative growth year to year (Table 26), and EVA was negative for all three carriers after 1998 (with the exception of AT&T in 1998–2000; see Table 27).

56. Recall that local exchange and local (intra-LATA) long distance have been subject to franchise grants from state regulatory agencies, with cost-of-service regulation that has become gradually transformed to price-cap ("incentive") regulation. Profit margins in local exchange during the 1990s were in the range of 5 to 15 percent (operating earnings as a percentage of operating revenues), while those in long distance ranged from 10 to more than 60 percent. Such a high margin opportunity was attractive to entry, but it was selective given that as part of the Bertrand story, long distance earnings and EVA in general were low and declining.

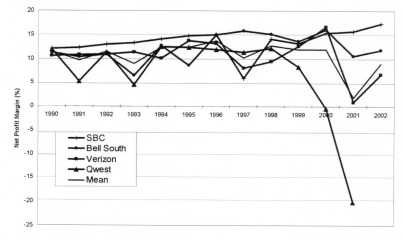

Net profit margins of regional Bell operating companies (*Source:* Company annual reports of operating earnings as a percentage of revenues from local exchange operations.)

57. Jonathan M. Kraushaar, "Fiber Deployment Update End of Year 1998," Table 13, "Fiber and Copper in Subscriber Plant in Relation to Access Lines, 1999."

CHAPTER 6. THE SINGULAR RESULT OF PARTIAL DEREGULATION AND WHAT CAN BE DONE

1. See Jerry Hausman, "Mobile Telephone."
2. Dan Alger, "Open Ownership—Not Common Carriage."
3. Ingo Vogelsang, "Price Regulation for Independent Transmission Companies"; the references on pp. 164–165 provide citations to the previous work.
4. Alger, "Open Ownership," p. 2.
5. Ibid., p. 9.
6. Vogelsang, "Price Regulation," pp. 147, 149.
7. *TR Daily*, March 2, 2006.

Bibliography

Alger, Dan. "Open Ownership—Not Common Carriage." Wellington: New Zealand Institute for the Study of Competition and Regulation, Victoria University, 1999.

Ameritech. Section 271 Application to the Federal Communications Commission.

AT&T. "Universal Service Fund (USF) Revisions—Questions and Answers." ATT-MDL 0005506, June 16, 1998.

"AT&T's New Strategy," Strategy Case Study Series, no. 15. New Haven, CT: Yale School of Management.

"BellSouth Begins Long Distance Qwest." *Fiber Optics News.* April 26, 1999.

Berry, S. Keith. "Generation Search Costs and Ramsey Pricing in a Partially Deregulated Electric Utility Industry." *Journal of Economics and Business* 54, no. 3 (2002): 331–343.

Beynon, Rebecca. "The FCC's Implementation of the 1996 Act: Agency Litigation Strategies and Delay." *Federal Communications Law Journal* 53, no. 1 (2000): 27–47.

Borenstein, Severin, and James Bushnell, "An Empirical Analysis of Market Power in a Deregulated California Electricity Market." *Journal of Industrial Economics* 47 (September 1999): 285–324.

Borenstein, Severin, James Bushnell, and Christopher R. Knittel. "Market Power in Electricity Markets: Beyond Concentration Measures." *Energy Journal* 20, no. 4 (1999): 55–88.

Boskin, Michael. J. "Reflections on the Bush Regulatory Period: The Good, the Bad, and the Ugly." *Regulation: The Cato Review of Business & Government* 16, no. 3 (1993).

Brander, James, and Anming Zhang, "Market Conduct in the Airline Industry: An Empirical Investigation." *Rand Journal of Economics* 21 (1990): 567–583.

Brealey, Richard A., and Stewart C. Myers. *Principles of Corporate Finance.* 7th ed. Boston: Irwin/McGraw-Hill, 2003.

Cabral, Luis. *Introduction to Industrial Organization.* Cambridge, MA: MIT Press, 2000.

California Energy Commission. "Electric Generation Divestiture in California." http://www.energy.ca.gov/electricity/divestiture.html.

California Public Utilities Commission (CPUC). Decision no. 95-12-063. Opinion re: "The Preferred Policy Decision." December 20, 1995.

———. Decision no. 96-01-009. Modifying Order Instituting Rulemaking and Order Instituting Investigation, R.94-04-031/I.94-04-032, April 20, 1994, and Opinion re: "The Preferred Policy Decision," Decision no. 95-12-063 (December 20, 1995). January 10, 1996.

———. Decision no. 99-10-057. Interim Opinion Regarding Application of Pacific Gas and Electric Company for Authority to Establish Post-Transition Period Electric Ratemaking Mechanisms. October 21, 1999.

———. Decision no. 00-10-065. Opinion Regarding Application of Pacific Gas and Electric Company for an Expedited Order Modifying Decision No. 87-09-056. October 19, 2000.

———. Decision 00-12-064. Opinion, Expedited Application of Pacific Gas and Electric Company (U 39 M). December 21, 2000.

———. Decision no. 01-01-018. Interim Opinion Regarding Emergency Requests for Rate Increases. January 2001.

———. Decision no. 01-02-050. Expedited Application of Pacific Gas and Electric Company to Issue, Sell, and Deliver One or More Series of Its First and Refunding Mortgage Bonds. Application no. 00-10-029. February 15, 2001.

———. Decision no 01-05-057. Application of Pacific Gas and Electric Company for Expedited Order Modifying Decision No. 87-09-056. Application no. 00-09-020. May 14, 2001.

———. Decision no. 01-06-074. Expedited Application of Pacific Gas and Electric Company to Issue, Sell and Deliver One or More Series of Its First and Refunding Mortgage Bonds. Application no. 00-10-029. June 28, 2001.

———. Decision no. 02-03-025. Expedited Application of Pacific Gas and Electric Company to Issue, Sell and Deliver One or More Series of Its First and Refunding Mortgage Bonds. Application no. 00-10-029. March 6, 2002.

———. Decision no. 03-02-061. Expedited Application of Pacific Gas and Electric Company to Issue, Sell and Deliver One or More Series of Its First and Refunding Mortgage Bonds. Application no. 00-10-029. February 27, 2003.

———. "Direct Testimony of John Sumpter on Behalf of AT&T Communications of California, Inc." Application of AT&T Communications of California, Inc. (U 5002 C) for Authority to Provide Intrastate AT&T 800 Readyline Service. June 18, 1990.

———. Division of Strategic Planning. "California's Electric Services Industry: Perspectives on the Past, Strategies for the Future." February 3, 1993.

———. "Report on Wholesale Electric Generation Investigation." September 2002.

Carlton, Dennis, and Jeffrey Perloff. *Modern Industrial Organization,* 2nd ed. New York: HarperCollins College Publishers, 1994.

———. *Modern Industrial Organization,* 3rd ed. New York: HarperCollins College Publishers, 2000.

Church, Jeffrey, and Roger Ware. *Industrial Organization: A Strategic Approach.* Boston: Irwin/McGraw-Hill, 2000.

Clark, Roger, and Stephen W. Davies. "Market Structure and Price-Cost Margins." *Economica* 49 (August 1982): 277–287.

Cournot, Augustin. *Recherches sur les principes mathematiques de la theories des richesses.* Paris, 1838.

Cowling, Keith, and Michael Waterson. "Price-Cost Margins and Market Structure." *Economica* 43 (August 1976): 267–274.

Crandall, Robert W., and Jerry A. Hausman. "Competition in U.S. Telecommunications Services: Effects of the 1996 Legislation." In *Deregulation of Network Industries: What's Next?* edited by Sam Peltzman and Clifford Winston. Washington, DC: The Brookings Institution Press, 2000.

Crandall, Robert W., Allan T. Ingraham, and Hal J. Singer. "Do Unbundling Policies Discourage CLEC Facilities-Based Investment?" *Topics in Economic Analysis & Policy* 4, no. 1 (2004).

Dahl, Carol, and Carlos Roman. "Energy Demand Elasticities—Fact or Fiction: A Survey Update." USAEE/IAEE Conference, Washington, DC, July 2004. http://www.mines.edu/academic/courses/econbus/dahl/pw/ch2o.doc.

Delipalla, Sophia, and Owen O'Donnell. "Estimating Tax Incidence, Market Power and Market Conduct." *International Journal of Industrial Organization* 19 (2001): 885–905.

Edison Electric Institute. *Natural Gas Procurement Survey.* Washington, DC: Edison Electric Institute, June 2004.

———. Staff Summary. "California Travails: A Chronology of Events in California's Energy Crisis." January 29, 2001.

Energy and Environmental Analysis. *An Updated Assessment of Pipeline and Storage Infrastructure for the North American Gas Market.* Washington, DC: The INGAA Foundation, 2004.

Energy Information Administration (EIA). "The Changing Structure of the U.S. Electric Power Industry 1970–1991." March 1993. http://tonto.eia.doe.gov/FTPROOT/electricity/0562.pdf.

Federal Communications Commission (FCC). "Detariffing of Long Distance Telephone Industry to Become Effective at the End of the Month." Press release. July 25, 2001.

———. "Federal Communications Commission Authorizes Bell Atlantic to Provide Long Distance Service in New York." Press release. December 22, 1999.

———. Industry Analysis and Technology Division. "Trends in Telephone Service." May 2004.

———. Notice of Inquiry. "Oversight and Recovery Practices for RTOs and ISOs." Docket no. RM04-12-000. September 16, 2004.

———. "Promotion of Competitive Networks in Local Telecommunications Markets." Notice of Proposed Rulemaking and Notice of Inquiry in WT Docket no. 99-217 (1999).

———. Report and Order. Federal-State Joint Board on Universal Service. 17 FCC Rcd24952. April 2003.

———. Second Report and Order in CC Docket no. 96-149 and Third Report and Order in CC Docket no. 96-61. "Regulatory Treatment of LEC Provision of Interexchange Services Originating in the LEC's Local Exchange Area." CC Docket FCC no. 96-149. April 18, 1997.

———. "Statistics of Communications Common Carriers," 2003/2004 edition. Washington, DC.

———. "Statistics of Communications Common Carriers." 2001/2002 edition. Washington, DC.

———. Third Further Notice of Proposed Rulemaking in CC Docket no. 96-98. FCC 99-141 paras. 4, 23, July 7, 1999. (*Competitive Networks Notice*).

———. "Universal Service Monitoring Report." CC Docket no. 98-202. May 2004. Federal Energy Regulatory Commission (FERC). "Market Based Rate List."

———. "Wholesale Power Market Platform: Remedying Undue Discrimination through Open Access Transmission Service and Standard Electricity Market Design." White Paper. Notice of White Paper. Docket no. RM01-12-000. April 23, 2003.

Federal Power Commission. *Annual Report for 1955.* Washington, DC: 1955.

Felder, Frank. Review of Steven Stoft, *Power System Economics: Designing Markets for Electricity* (2002). *IEEE Energy Journal* 23, no. 4 (2002).

Financial Accounting Standards Board (FASB). "Accounting for the Impairment of Long-Lived Assets." Statement of Financial Accounting Standards (SFAS) no. 121, 1995.

Gottlieb, Paul, and others. "The Economic Impact of SBC Ameritech's Entry into the Long Distance Market in Ohio." Center for Regional Economic Issues, Case Western Reserve University. March 2002.

Grant, James L. "Foundations of EVA™ for Investment Managers." *Journal of Portfolio Management* (Fall 1996): 41–48.

Gray, Roger. "The Long-Term Consequences of California's Electricity Deregulation Experiment." November 4, 2004. http://www.energypulse.net.

Guyon, Janet, and Jeanne Saddlers. "The AT&T Breakup—One Year Later." *Wall Street Journal.* December 17, 1984.

Hall, Jessica. "Telecoms Facing a 'Perfect Storm.'" *Ottawa Citizen.* July 31, 2002, p. D2.

Harvey, Scott M., and William W. Hogan. "Market Power and Withholding." December 20, 2001. http://ksghome.harvard.edu/~whogan/Market%20Power%20&%20Withholding%20Harvey-Hogan%2012-20-01.pdf.

Hausman, Jerry. "Mobile Telephone." Chapter 13 in *Handbook of Telecommunications Economics, Vol. 1: Structure, Regulation, and Competition,* edited by Sumit Kumar Majumdar, Ingo Vogelsang, and Martin E. Cave. North Holland, 2002.

Huber, Peter W. "Local Exchange Commission under the 1996 Telecom Act: Red-Lining the Local Residential Customer." November 4, 1997 (privately published).

Hundt, Reed. *You Say You Want a Revolution: A Story of Information Age Politics.* New Haven, CT: Yale University Press, 2000.

Jackson. Charles L. "A Bottom-Up Estimate of the TELRIC of Long Distance Calling." Bethesda, MD: Strategic Policy Research. October 3, 1996.

Jess, Margaret. "Restructuring Energy Industries: Lessons from Natural Gas." *Natural Gas Monthly.* Energy Information Administration. May 1997.

Johnson, Mark S., Marcia Niles, and Stacey Suydam. "Regulatory Changes in the Electric Utility Industry: Investigation of Effects on Shareholder Wealth." *Journal of Accounting and Public Policy* 17 (1998): 1–25.

Joskow, Paul L. "Patterns of Transmission Investment." Draft LV. Cambridge, MA: Department of Economics, March 15, 2005.

Katz, Diane, and Theodore R. Bolema. "Crossed Lines: Regulatory Missteps in Telecom Policy." Midland, MI: Mackinac Center for Public Policy, 2003.

Kiesling, Lynne, and Adrian T. Moore. "Movin' Juice: Making Electricity Transmission More Competitive." Reason Public Policy Institute, Study 314. Los Angeles: The Reason Foundation, September 2003.

Knight, Jerry. "WorldCom Woes Pop the Region's Telecom Bubble." *Washington Post.* July 1, 2002.

Kotlikoff, Laurence J. "Broadband: Breaking the Logjam." *The Milken Institute Review* 1 (2003): 56–64.

Kraushaar, Jonathan M. "Fiber Deployment Update End of Year 1998." Industry Analysis Division, Federal Communications Commission. Washington, DC: 1999.

Lande, Jim, and Kenneth Lynch. "Telecommunications Industry Revenues, 2002." Industry Analysis and Technology Division, Wireline Competition Bureau, Federal Communications Commission. Washington, DC: March 2004.

Landes, William, and Richard Posner. "Market Power in Antitrust Cases." *Harvard Law Review* 95 (August 1982): 1857–1874.

Lerner, Abba. "The Concept of Monopoly and the Measurement of Monopoly Power." *Review of Economics Studies* 1, no. 3 (June 1934): 157–175.

MacAvoy, Paul W. *The Economic Effects of Regulation: The Trunk-Line Railroad Cartels and the Interstate Commerce Commission before 1900.* Cambridge, MA: MIT Press, 1965.

———. *The Failure of Antitrust and Regulation to Establish Competition in Long-Distance Telephone Services.* Cambridge, MA: MIT Press, 1996.

———. *The Natural Gas Market: Sixty Years of Regulation and Deregulation.* New Haven, CT: Yale University Press, 2000.

MacAvoy, Paul W., and Michael A. Williams. *Deregulation of Entry in Long-Distance Telecommunications.* East Lansing: Michigan State University Press, 2002.

Marmer, Vadim, Dmitry Shapiro, and Paul W. MacAvoy. "Bottlenecks in Regional Markets for Natural Gas Transmission Services." Forthcoming in *Energy Economics.*

Marshall, Alfred. *Principles of Economics.* 8th edition. New York: MacMillan, 1953.

Martin, Stephen. *Advanced Industrial Economics.* Cambridge, MA: Blackwell Publishers, 1993.

Melody, William H. "Designing Utility Regulation for 21st Century Markets." In *The Insti-tutionalist Approach to Public Utility Regulation,* edited by Warren J. Samuels and Edythe S. Miller. East Lansing: Michigan State University Press, 2002.

Moody's Investors Service. "Stranded Costs Will Threaten Credit Quality of U.S. Electrics." New York: August 1995.

NASDAQ. "Index Descriptions: Indices of the NASDAQ Stock Market." November 15, 2004. http://quotes.nasdaq.com/reference/IndexDescriptions.stm#IXTC.

New York Stock Exchange. "NYSE Glossary." http://www.nyse.com. November 15, 2004.

Newbery, David M. "Playing the Game." In *Privatization, Restructuring and Regulation of Network Industries.* Cambridge, MA: MIT Press, 2001.

Noll, Roger. *The Slowdown in Regulatory Reform.* Washington, DC: Brookings Institution, 1999.

Pacific Gas and Electric Company (PG&E). Application to California Public Utilities Com-mission of Pacific Gas and Electric Company for an Expedited Order Modifying Deci-sion no. 87-09-056. Application no. 00-09-020. September 8, 2000.

———. Application. September 22, 2000.

———. Application of PG&E, Southern California Edison, and TURN. October 16, 2000.

———. Emergency Application of Pacific Gas and Electric Company to Adopt a Rate Sta-bilization Plan. Application no. 00-11-038. November 22, 2000.

———. Emergency Petition to CPUC to Modify Decision. October 2000.

———. Expedited Application of Pacific Gas and Electric Company to CPUC to Issue, Sell, and Deliver One or More Series of Its First and Refunding Mortgage Bonds, Appli-cation no. 00-10-029. October 18, 2000.

Pacific Gas and Electric Corporation. *1996 Annual Report.* February 1997.

———. *2000 Annual Report.* March 2001.

PBS—Frontline. "The California Crisis, California Timeline." http://www.pbs.org/wgbh/pages/frontline/shows/blackout/california/timeline.html.

Perez, Franklin. "The Case for a Deregulated Free Market Telecommunications Industry." *IEEE Communications Magazine* 34, no. 12 (December 1994): 63–70.

"Qwest Awarded Additional $15 Million Contract from Star Telecommunications." *Business Wire.* March 31, 1999.

"Qwest Communications Speeds toward Completion of World's First Network Optimized for Internet Communications." *Business Wire.* May 10, 1999.

"Qwest Nipping Heels of IXC Leaders with Partnerships, Expanded Networks." *Fiber Op-tics News.* April 12, 1999.

"Qwest, Williams Business Models Evolve Beyond Fiber." *Fiber Optics News.* January 4, 1999.

Reitzes, James D., Robert L. Earle, and Philip Q. Hanser. "Deregulation and Monitoring of Electric Power Markets." *Electricity Journal* 13, no. 8 (October 2000): 11–25.

Romero, Simon. "Spectacular Rise, Staggering Fall." *New York Times.* June 18, 2001, p. C15.

Samuelson, Paul A., and William D. Nordhaus. *Economics.* 14th edition. New York: Mc-Graw-Hill: 1992.

San Diego Union-Tribune. "Deregulation Timeline." 2001. http://www.signonsandiego.com/news/reports/power/timeline.html.

Sloan, Tim. "Creating Better Incentives through Regulation." *Federal Communications Law Journal* 50, no. 2 (March 1998).

Sprint Corporation. Form 10-K: Annual Report Pursuant to Section 13 or 15(d) of the Securities Exchange Act of 1934 for the Fiscal Year Ended December 31, 2002. Washington, DC: Securities and Exchange Commission. March 7, 2003.

———. Form 10-K: Annual Report Pursuant to Section 13 or 15(d) of the Securities Exchange Act of 1934 for the Fiscal Year Ended December 31, 2003. Washington, DC: Securities and Exchange Commission. March 9, 2004.

Stern Stewart. "About EVA." 2004. http://www.sternstewart.com/evaabout/whatis.php.

Sweeney, James L. *The California Electricity Crisis.* Stanford, CA: Hoover Institution Press. 2002.

Tardiff, Timothy J. "Pricing Unbundled Network Elements and the FCC's TELRIC Rule: Economic and Modeling Issues." *Review of Network Economics* 1, no. 2 (September 2002): 132–146.

Telecommunications Research and Action Center (TRAC). "TeleTips: Residential Long Distance Comparison Chart." *TeleTips* 45 (March 2004).

"Too Many Debts; Too Few Calls—The Telecom Crisis." *The Economist.* July 20, 2002.

TR Daily. March 2, 2006.

U.S. Congressional Budget Office. "Causes and Lessons of the California Electricity Crisis." Washington, DC: GPO, September 2001.

U.S. Department of Energy. "National Transmission Grid Study." May 2002. http://www.pi.energy.gov/pdf/library/TransmissionGrid.pdf.

Vogelsang, Ingo. "Network Utilities in the U.S.—Sector Reforms without Privatization." CESifo working paper no. 1142. Munich, Germany: Center for Economic Studies, Ifo Institute, March 2004.

———. "Price Regulation for Independent Transmission Companies." *Journal of Regulatory Economics* 20, no. 2 (2001): 141–165.

Weber, Toby. "Telecom's Broken Backbone." *Telephony.* June 25, 2001.

Wharton Econometric Forecasting Associates. "Economic Impact of Eliminating the Line of Business Restrictions on the Bell Companies." July 1993.

Wolak, Frank A. "Lessons from the California Electricity Crisis." WO 110. Berkeley, CA: UCEI Center for the Study of Energy Markets, University of California. April 2003.

WorldCom and MCI Communications. Application of WorldCom, Inc. and MCI Communications Corporation for Transfer and Control of MCI Communications Corporation to WorldCom, Inc. CC Docket no. 97-211. Federal Communications Commission, Washington, DC, September 14, 1998.

Index

access, open, and process of wheeling, 30, 31

access charges, and interexchange networks, 16, 105–106

access price, and Vogelsang pricing, 140

Adelstein, Jonathan, as FCC commissioner, 22

ADSL (advanced digital subscriber line), 135

Alger, Dan, "Open Ownership—Not Common Carriage," 138

Alger restructuring, 138–140, 141

Algonquin exit node, and gas transmission market, 131

alternative fuels, and PURPA, 29–30

American Telephone and Telegraph (AT&T): antitrust divestiture decree (1984), xvi, 7, 28, 94, 98, 100, 126; downturn in business performance, 117–122, 144; entry of RBOCs in long distance market, 115–117; as incumbent long distance carrier, 7, 95, 98; long distance market share, 1990–2003, 7, 98–102; and phased deregulation, 14–24; and price-cost margins, 103–113, 116–117; and tariff filing with FCC, 114–115; and USF surcharges, 117, 122–125

Ameritech, 21. See also SBC Ameritech

antitrust proceedings, and telecom regulation, 14–24

Arizona (state), and power transmission networks, 6

ARPM (average revenue per minute), and pricing strategies, 107–110, 125

basis differentials: in electricity markets, 1990–2004, 58–65, 67; for gas, at trading hubs, 1986–2003, 41–45; in gas transmission and power distribution, after deregulation, 125–126, 131–132, 143

Bell Atlantic (Verizon), and long distance service, 20, 115

Bell South, and long distance service, 115

Bertrand oligopoly behavior: in electricity market, 65–66, 68; and gas pipeline market, 45–46, 141; and investment process, 125, 139; and price-cost margins, 8–9, 35, 130, 136, 137, 140; and strategic behavior, 8, 9–12; in telecommunications industry, 112, 113, 126, 128, 140, 144; USF charges, 123–124

bilateral contracts, and business subscribers, 130

Boskin, Michael, former chairman, Council of Economic Advisers, xiii

bottlenecks: hub-to-hub, in gas market, 46; and partial deregulation, xiv, 128; and price controls, 35, 130, 140, 144; and pricing of electricity, 66–67; in telecommunications, 16, 126–127, 128

broadband services: and capacity expansion, 140; demands for, and DSL, 135, 136; and Internet access, 128, 143; and local exchange carriers, 145; shortages of, and deregulation, 125–128, 138; on wireline networks, 118

cable television service: growth rates of, 142; and high-speed modem, 128, 135; and telephone service, 144

California (state): electric transmission grid of, 3–6; gas transmission market in, 39, 40, 44–45, 47, 49–50; gas transmission networks in, 6, 42; and partial deregulation, xiii, xiv, 31, 33, 34, 36–37, 54, 55; power crisis in, *2000–2001,* and CAISO response, 69–83; power grid ownership in, and Alger restructuring, 138; and price spikes, *2001–2002,* xii, 32, 33, 57, 58, 85–88, 132, 134

California Energy Commission (CEC), 76–77, 87

California Independent System Operator

(CAISO), 6; and network performance, 58–62, 66, 67–68; and PG&E transmission system, 70, 72, 74; and wholesale electricity market, 75–76, 86, 87–88

California Public Utility Code, Section *817,* 81

California Public Utility Commission (CPUC), 61; debt authorization and, 88–89; and divestiture of PG&E assets, 78–80; and gas distribution, 89–90; and PG&E restructuring, 34, 70–76; and PG&E's utility dividends, 83–85; and power crisis, *2000–2001,* 90–93; "Preferred Policy Decision" and AB *1890,* 72; and rate reduction bonds for PG&E, 82, 85; response of, to PG&E balancing accounts, 80–82

California State Assembly: Bill AB *1890,* 70–74, 78, 82, 91; Bill ABX *118,* 90

Calpine Company, and purchase of PG&E generating assets, 78

capacity expansion, deficiencies in, xii–xiii, 46, 47, 52, 126, 137, 141

capacity utilization, 48

Carthage Hub (Texas), 41, 42

cell phone service, and market structure, 105, 114, 144

Center for Regional Economic Issues (REI), and assessment of TA96, 97–98

Cheyenne Hub (Wyoming), 42

Chicago, Illinois, and gas transportation market, 43, 50, 51

collection, and network technology, 1–3

collective price formation, and FCC regulation, 16

collusion, and price-cost margins, 11–12

Communications Act of *1934,* 99, 115

competition, and oligopoly behavior, 37

congestion: and partial deregulation, 142–143; and prices during bottleneck periods, 66, 67; and Vogelsang pricing, 140

conjectural variation, and oligopoly be-

havior, 10–12; for electric and gas networks, 45–46, 65–66; for long-distance telephone networks, 102–103, 112–113, 124–125. *See also* Bertrand oligopoly behavior
Connecticut (state), and regional electric power prices, 62, 63
consumer surplus, loss of, and deregulation, 131–134, 135, 136
Copps, Michael, as FCC commissioner, 22
cost-of-service levels, and electric networks, 54, 55
cost-of-service pricing: and profit limits, 141; regulation of, 30, 32, 33, 66, 129, 137, 142; and telecom networks, 96–97, 137
cost-of-service reviews, and FERC, 53–54
Cournot oligopoly behavior, 8, 9–12; and Alger and Vogelsang initiatives, 141–142; in electric power markets, 56, 130; and gas pipeline markets, 45, 141; and price levels, 114, 141; and telecom carriers, 112, 126, 141–142, 144
Crandall, Robert, 19, 96

Dahl, Carol, 65
delivery, and network technology, 1–3
demand elasticity, 45, 65, 111
deregulation: effectiveness of, 33; and price reduction, 37; process of, 142–145; roadblocks in, 137–142. *See also* partial deregulation; phased deregulation
detariffing process, and FCC, 115, 116
Diablo Canyon nuclear plants, 78
digital technology and wireless links, 135
discount plans: and incumbent telecom carriers, 104–105, 108, 111, 113, 119; and partial deregulation, 130
divestiture: of electric power plants, 53; and partial deregulation, 130; of PG&E generation assets, 74–75, 78–80

divestiture decree (*1984*), and AT&T, xvi, 7, 28, 94, 98, 100, 126
Dominion Hub (Pennsylvania), 42, 46, 131
DSL (digital subscriber line) service, 128, 135
Duke Energy Power Services, and purchase of PG&E assets, 78

Eastern region: and gas transmission markets, 37–50 *passim;* and plant divestiture, electric power market, 53
EBITDA (earnings before interest, taxes, depreciation, and amortization), and interexchange carriers, 119–120
electric power market, restructuring of, xii–xiii, 52–58, 130
electric transmission networks, 2, 3–6; and oligopoly behavior, 63–68; performance of, *1990–2004,* 58–63; regulation of, 24–26, 29–34
El Paso Natural Gas Transmission, 40, 49–50, 51
Energy and Environmental Analysis, Inc., xii
energy conservation, and PURPA, 29–30
Energy Policy Act of *1992,* 30
ERCOT (Electricity Reliability Council of Texas), and prices of electric power, 58–59, 60, 67–68, 133, 134
EVA (economic value added): and deregulation process, 131, 137; for electric power companies, 67–68; and gas transmission market, 50–51, 52; and interexchange telecom carriers, 120–122; and telephone service markets, 134–135
Excel, as specialized long distance carrier, 100

Federal Communications Commission (FCC): and deregulation process, 143–145; and long distance markets, 98–100, 113, 114–115; and price caps, xvi,

Federal Communications Commission
(FCC) (*continued*)
98–99, 134–144 *passim;* regulatory
practices of, xii, xv, xvi, 14–24, 100,
114–115; and tariffs, 99, 103, 114–115;
and Telecommunications Act (TA96),
xii, 14–24 *passim,* 94, 96, 97, 98, 115;
and USF charges, 122, 124, 125, 140;
and Vogelsang pricing, 140, 141–142
Federal Energy Regulatory Commission
(FERC): and Alger solution, 139; cost-
of-service pricing, 33, 66, 141; FERC
Order *436,* 28; FERC Order *636,* 31, 39,
141; FERC Order *888,* 31, 32; FERC Order *2000,* 31; and ISOs, 34, 53, 54, 56,
141; and partial deregulation, xiii, xv,
33–34, 143; price controls, electric
power, 33–34, 61, 67, 132–134, 141;
price controls, gas transmission, 40,
47–48, 141, 143; regulation by, of
wholesale power markets, 24–34 *passim,* 76, 82; retail regulation by, 32–33,
126, 137; and RTOs, 31, 33–34, 67, 68;
and Vogelsang pricing, 140–141
federal government, and regulation of
electric and gas transmission, 24–34
Federal Power Act, 25, 32
Federal Power Commission (FPC), 24, 25,
26
fiber-optic transmission, 118, 128, 135, 140
fossil fuels: and energy alternatives, 29–
30; and generation assets, PG&E, 78–
79
Frontier, as specialized telecom carrier,
100

gas transmission networks, xii, 2–3, 6;
market structure of, 28–29; performance of, 36–52, 131–132; and PG&E
restructuring, 73, 89–90; and pipeline
capacity, 47–48; profit and price-cost
margins for, 40–41, 46, 47, 130; regulation of, xii, 24–29, 143

generation assets, divestiture of, and
PG&E, 74–75, 78–80, 91
generation divestiture, and network regulation, 31, 33
Geysers Power Company, and purchase of
generating assets, 78
Global Crossing, as telecom carrier, 118
Gray, Roger, xiii
grid networks, expansion of, 61–63
grid separation, 33

Hausman, Jerry, 19, 96
headroom (operating income margins),
68, 72–73, 75, 76, 77
Henry Hub (Louisiana), 41, 42, 46, 131, 138
Herfindahl-Hirschman index (HHI): and
Alger restructuring, 139; and electric
network services, 56; gas transmission
markets, 37–39, 45; and market structure, 9–12; revenue share, long distance
carriers, 101, 102, 103, 111, 113, 140
Humboldt Bay power plant (Eureka, California), 78
hydroelectric facilities, and PG&E, 6, 78,
79, 85, 92
hydroelectric power, 6, 30, 69

incumbent local exchange carriers, 20,
94–98, 144
incumbent long distance carriers, 95; access to UNEs, 18, 96–97, 134–135; Alger restructuring and, 140; and broadband capacity, 125–128, 135–136; and
entry of RBOCs, 94–98, 115–117; and
market conditions, *1998–2000,* 114–115;
price-cost margins of, and FCC tariffs,
103–113; pricing of, and partial deregulation, 98–102, 134–136; pricing of,
and USF charges, 122–125, 140; and
revenue decline, 117–122
incumbent networks, 18, 32, 36, 53
incumbent producers, and network markets, 18, 32, 36, 53

Index   177

independent power marketers: and network markets, 36–37; as public utilities, 32; and retail pricing, 32–33
integrated services, as long distance offering, 99
Internet services: and broadband technologies, 128, 135, 143, 144; as investment opportunity, xvi, 23–24; and telecom carrier performance, 100, 117–119, 128
Interstate Commerce Commission, 25
ISO-NE (Independent System Operator of New England): and electricity prices, 58–59, 62, 63, 67–68
ISOs (independent system operators): and grid management, in Alger restructuring, 139; and network regulation, 31–34, 53–54; performance of, in electricity market, 56–63, 134; and Vogelsang-style adjustments, 141

Katy Hub (Texas), 41, 42
Kingsgate origin hub (Canadian border), 42

Lerner price-cost margin or index, 8–9, 11; and CAISO restructuring, 72; in electric power market, 56; in gas transmission market, 40, 45, 47; in long distance telecommunications, 102–113 *passim,* 124
LMP (locational marginal price), and electric power networks, 57
local exchange carriers, telecom market: and Alger and Vogelsang initiatives, 140, 141–142; and DSL, 135; and long distance service, 20, 126, 143; and pricing, 127–128, 142; and wireless networks, 140, 144. *See also* incumbent local exchange carriers; RBOCs (regional Bell operating companies)
long distance telecom markets: entry of RBOCs in, 115–117; and local exchange

carriers, 143; market conditions, *1998–2000,* 114–115; and partial deregulation, 98–102, 134–137; price-cost margins in, and FCC tariffs, 103–113; and pricing, 98–102, 111; and wireless networks, 144
long distance telephone networks: broadband shortages in, 125–128; interexchange carrier performance, 117–122; interexchange services, 105–106, 108–109; price elasticities in, 111–112; and pricing strategies, 97–98, 103–113; restructuring of, and TA96, 94–97; and USF charges, 122–125

Maine, and regional electric power prices, 62, 63
market structure: and deregulation, xiii–xiv; of gas pipeline networks, 24–29; and network technology, xv, 1–12; and regulatory changes, electricity networks, 24–25, 29–34
Martin, Kevin, as FCC commissioner, 22
Massachusetts: and electric power prices, 62; and gas transmission market, 38
MCI WorldCom: downturn in business performance, 117–122; and long distance market, 7, 16, 20, 95, 98, 100–102; price-cost margins of, and FCC tariffs, 103–116; and USF surcharges, 122–125
message digitalization, and carrier performance, 118
Midwestern region: electricity blackout in, xii, 33; and gas transportation markets, 6, 37–52 *passim,* 131–132; and power costs, 30, 33; and RTOs, 31, 32
modem service, and cable television providers, 128, 135
Modification of Final Judgment (MFJ), and telecom restructuring, 15, 16
monopoly behavior, and pricing coordination, 125

Morro Bay fossil fuel plant (California), 78
Moss Landing fossil fuel plant (California), 78
MTS (message toll service), and discount plans, 99, 103–107, 108

NASDAQ, and telecom stock price index (*1996–2004*), 117–118
Natural Gas Act of *1938,* 25, 26, 27
Natural Gas Pipeline of America (NGPA), 40–41, 49, 51
Natural Gas Policy Act of *1978,* 27
network operations, and market structure, xiv, xv, 1–12, 24–29, 37
network performance: and electric power, 36–37, 52–58; and gas transmission, 37–52; and oligopoly behavior, xiv, xv, 37, 63–68, 102; and RTOs, 31, 32, 58–63, 66–68; and telephone exchange carriers, 94–97, 117–122
network restructuring and regulation, 13–35, 94–98, 129–145
Newbery, David, 35
New England region: electricity price spikes, 134; gas transmission networks, 6; price controls on electricity, 66; and RTOS, 31
New York (state): electricity price spikes, 133–134; and gas pipeline capacity, 38; and price spikes in gas transmission: 50; retail distribution of electric power, 57, 58, 64, 66; and RTOs, 31; Section *271* authorization, 114, 115
node congestion, and partial deregulation, 142
node-link systems, and transmission grids, 31
Noll, Roger, xii
Nordhaus, William, 102
Northeast region: electricity blackouts in, xii; gas transmission networks for, 6, 131; and open entry into power markets, 30

nuclear plants, Diablo Canyon, and PG&E, 78
nuclear power, and retail networks, 6
NYISO (New York Independent System Operator), 59
NYMEX (New York mercantile exchange), and PG&E contract prices, 88

Oakland, California, fossil fuel plant, 78
oligopoly behavior: conditions determining, 63–68; and gas transmission networks, 37, 40, 45; in long distance telecom service, 102; and pricing, xiv, xv, 63–68; theory of, and market behavior, 7–12, 13
Oneok Hub (Texas), 42
Opal Hub (Wyoming), 42, 45, 50
open access, 29, 31
open entry, and wholesale power markets, 30–31
Oregon (state), as source of hydropower, 6

Pacific Gas and Electric Corporation (PG&E), 68; balancing accounts, CPUC response to, 75–76, 80–82; cash management, during power crisis, 75, 80; declaration of utility dividends by, 64, 83–85; divestiture by, of utility assets, 74–75, 78–80, 91; financing of rate reduction bonds, 82; and price controls, xv–xvi; response of, to deregulation, 6, 69–77, 137; and wholesale price spikes, 75, 85–93
partial deregulation: and electric power networks, xii, xiii, 29–34, 36–37, 52–58; and gas transmission markets, xii, 37–52; network performance and, 58–63; and pricing, xv, 12, 35, 129–136, 144; process of, and roadblocks, 137–142; restructuring of, 142–145; results of, 35, 129–142; and telecom networks, xi–xii, 125–128

Pennsylvania (state): and gas pipeline capacity, 38; and RTOs, 31

Pennsylvania Power and Light (PPL), 63, 64

Permian Basin (Texas and New Mexico), 42, 47, 50

phased deregulation, and regulatory agencies, 13–14

pipeline capacity, and gas transmission, 38–40, 47–48

PJM (Pennsylvania–New Jersey–Maryland) RTO, and electricity prices, 59, 63–68 *passim,* 134

Powell, Michael, chairman, FCC, 22, 118

price caps: and Alger restructuring, 138; and California power crisis, 34, 90; in gas transmission and power distribution networks, 27–29, 37, 47, 54, 55, 125; at link bottlenecks, 15, 35, 130, 137; and partial deregulation, xiv–xv, 8, 32, 35, 130, 142–143, 144; in telecommunications industry, 128; and Vogelsang pricing, 140–141

price controls, xv, 26, 27, 126–127, 130, 142–144

price-cost margins: in Alger and Vogelsang models, 140–142; as behavioral indicator, 8–12; in electric power market, 56, 58, 130; in gas transmission market, 45–52 *passim,* 130, 131; and long distance service markets, 102, 103–113, 116–117, 130–131; and partial deregulation, xiv–xv, 130–131, 136; in telecommunications industry, 119, 128, 136, 140

price elasticity, and long distance telecom service, 111

price responsiveness, and oligopoly behavior, xiv, xv, 63–68

price spikes: and Bertrand behavior, 125–126; and California electricity market, *2000–2001,* xv–xvi, 70, 85–93; and consumer surplus, 131–134; and elimi-

nation of price caps, 144; and partial deregulation, 137. *See also* spike periods

pricing: and Alger restructuring, 138; and bottleneck periods, 66–67; economic theory of, and oligopoly, xiv; electricity and gas markets, restructuring of, 36, 37; and long distance communications markets, 98–102, 116–117, 122–125, 126–128; and partial deregulation, xv, 129–130, 137–138; and TELRIC, 19–20, 21, 22, 127, 128; and Vogelsang pricing, 138, 140–142

public utilities: as independent power marketers, 32; and regulatory reform, xi–xv

Public Utility Holding Company Act, 25

PURPA (Public Utility Regulatory Policy Act), 29–30

PX (power exchange), and restructuring of PG&E, 72, 76, 82, 85–86, 88, 93

Qwest, as independent carrier, 100, 101, 115, 118

rate reduction bonds, and PG&E restructuring, 82

RBOCs (regional Bell operating companies): AT&T divestiture of, 15; and Internet service, 23, 128, 135; in long distance market, 16, 20–24, 94–96, 101–102, 114–115, 119

ready-must-run (RMR) plant services, 53

Reagan, Ronald, 16

redundancy, and quality of service, 3

regulation: and complete deregulation, 142–145; improved performance of, 137–142; and network restructuring, 13–35, 94–98; partial deregulation, effects of, 129–137; and price-cost margin levels, 8–12

regulatory agencies: and phased deregulation, 13–14; and price controls, 130; roles of, xiii regulatory reform, and public utilities, xi–xv

renewable fuel sources, and PURPA, 30

restructuring: as initial stage of deregulation, 129; of ownership, and Alger thesis, 138–140; reversal of, in telecom industry, 143–145

retail prices, and partial deregulation, 32–33, 91–93

Rocky Mountains, and gas transmission market, 38, 47, 132

Roman, Carlos, 65

RTOs (regional transmission organizations): and Alger restructuring, 139; performance of, 58–63, 66–68; and transmission grids, 31, 32, 33, 67

Samuelson, Paul, 102

SBC Ameritech, as RBOC, 97, 115

service delivery: and congestion, 142–143; and network technology, 1–3; and partial deregulation, xi, xiv

service providers: and Alger restructuring, 138; and conjectural variation, 10, 45, 65, 112–113; and market share, 7, 129; and oligopoly behavior, xiv, 11–12, 37

Sherman Act, and antitrust proceedings against AT&T, 14, 15

Sloan, Tim, 97

Southern California Edison, 90

Southern Energy (Petrero and Delta), and purchase of PG&E assets, 78

spike periods, and demand elasticity, 65. See also price spikes

Sprint: business performance of, and EVA, 121; and downturn in business performance, 119–120; and long distance market, 7, 16, 20, 95, 98, 100–102; and mass market price-cost margins, 103–113 passim; and tariff filing with FCC, 114–115; and USF surcharges, 122–125

state regulation: of gas and electricity, 24–34 passim, 54–55, 66; in telecommunications, 19–24

stock market value, of interexchange telecom carriers, 117–118, 121

strategic behavior, in Bertrand and Cournot oligopolies, 9–12

Strategic Policy Research, on AT&T's network costs, 106

tariff prices, in long distance market: and FCC, 98–99, 114–115; and price-cost margins, 103–113; and Vogelsang model, 141–142

Telco exit node, and gas transmission market, 131

Telecommunications Act (TA96), xii, 16–24, 94–95, 126; and price-cost margins, 142; and price schedules, 99; Sections 251 and 252, 18, 19, 21, 95–96, 97–98, 126; Section 271, 20–24 passim, 96, 97–98, 114, 115, 126, 128; and tariff posting, 103, 115; and toll service revenues, 101–102; and USF, 122; and wholesale service, 100

telecommunications industry: Alger and Vogelsang initiatives in, 141–142; and independent networks, 6–7; regulation of, and litigation, xii, 14–24; and restructuring reversal, 143–145

telephone networks, long distance, and deregulation, xvi; and broadband capacity shortage, 125–128; changes in carrier performance, 117–122; conduct of firms, 102–103; entry of RBOCs, 115–117; incentives for competition (TA96), 97–98; market conditions, 1998–2000, 114–115; and network restructuring, 94–97; pass through of universal service fund, 122–125; price-cost margins from tariff data, 103–113; pricing in communications markets, 98–102; and technology, 2–3

TELRIC (total element long-run incremental cost): and pricing in telecom market, 98, 127–128, 135, 137, 140; and regulation of telecommunications industry, 19–24

Tennessee Six exit node, and gas transmission market, 131

Texas (state): cost-of-service prices in, 66; and electric power distribution, 57, 58; and gas transmission, 37, 38, 40, 41–42, 49, 132; plant divestiture, electricity market, 53; RTOs and transmission grids in, 31; and SBC authorization, 115

Texas Eastern Entry Hub, 41–42

Transcontinental Gas, and profit margins, 40–41, 51

Transco system, and gas transmission market, 42–43, 49, 131

transition cost, and deregulation, 54

transition cost balancing accounts (TCBA), and PG&E restructuring, 77, 79, 80–82, 85, 86

transition revenue accounts (TRA), and PG&E restructuring, 77, 80–82, 88, 89, 90

transmission grids: and FERC control, xiii; and network technology, 5, 6; and RTOs, 31, 32, 33, 67

UNE (unbundled network elements): and FCC price caps, 135, 142, 144; and incumbent network carriers, 96; and telecom restructuring, 18, 21, 22, 23, 130, 135, 137; and UNE Remand Order, 22

UNE-P (unbundled network elements full platform), 126–127

Universal Service Administrative Company, 123

Universal Service Fund (USF): and long distance carriers, xvi, 122–125; and price-cost margins, 116–117

U.S. Congress: and PURPA, 29; and TA96, 16, 17, 19, 21

U.S. Court of Appeals, Eighth Circuit, *Iowa Utilities Board v. FCC*, 21, 22

U.S. Department of Energy: Energy Information Administration, 30; and FERC, 25

U.S. Supreme Court: and regulation of gas transmission, 26; and TA96 implementation, 22

usage price, and Vogelsang pricing, 140

US West. *See* Qwest

Verizon, and long distance market, 101

Virginia (state), and gas transmission market, 38

Vogelsang, Ingo, 138

Vogelsang pricing, 138, 140–142, 144

Waha Hub (Texas), 42, 44

Washington (state), as source of hydropower, 6

WATS (wide-area telecommunications service), 99, 106

Western region: and gas transmission market, 38, 39, 40, 44–45, 48, 49–50; and plant divestiture, electric power market, 53

Wharton Econometric Forecasting Associates, and network operating expenses, 106

wheeling process, and open access, 30, 31

wholesale power markets: and partial deregulation, 91–93; restructuring of, 33–34, 35

wireless service: and digital technology, 135; and long distance service, 105, 114; and telecom deregulation, 142, 143, 144

wireline network service: capacity of, 118; and digital technology, 135; and price caps, 142; and price-cost margins, 136

Wolak, Frank, chairman, CAISO Market Surveillance Committee, 76

WorldCom: acquisition of MCI, 100; and bankruptcy protection, 118; business performance of, 120–121